The Chinese Communist Army
in Action

The first Chinese Communists captured by the 1st ROK Corps.
They were also the first Chinese to fight UN forces in Korea.

The
Chinese Communist Army
in Action

THE KOREAN WAR AND ITS AFTERMATH

by Alexander L. George

COLUMBIA UNIVERSITY PRESS
NEW YORK AND LONDON : 1967

Alexander L. George is a staff member of The RAND Corporation, and was formerly Head of its Social Science Department, 1961–1963. With his wife, Juliette L. George, Mr. George is the author of Woodrow Wilson and Colonel House (1956). *Mr. George is also the author of* Propaganda Analysis (1959).

For Frank Collbohm

Preface

EVEN in this contemporary era of nuclear and advanced non-nuclear armaments Mao Tse-tung and his followers cling stubbornly to fundamental doctrinal tenets derived from their earlier successes in guerrilla warfare. "Man," they argue, continues to be more important than "weapons." Admittedly, Chinese Communist leaders have no choice for the time being but to make the best of the fact of Chinese inferiority in modern weapons. But their emphasis on "man-over-weapons" cannot be dismissed as mere rationalization or defiant bluster. For it remains true, within important limits to be sure, that superior morale and military skill can compensate for inferior weapons.

Mao, it must be remembered, is by no means the only military thinker to have emphasized the critical importance of the "human element," or morale, in warfare. Indeed, a common core of ideas on how to develop motivation and solidarity among combat soldiers is to be found in the writings of military leaders and theorists who have written about this subject from the vantage point of different backgrounds and experiences.

The Chinese Communist insistence on "man-over-weapons" is not an empty slogan. Behind this slogan lies a military doctrine and a concept of military organization derived from years of experience in fighting better-armed, more modern forces. Both the military doctrine and the concept of military organization have as their main focus precisely the object of enhancing the "human element" in the Chinese Communist Army so that morale can serve as an effective counterpoise under certain well-defined conditions to the military advantages enjoyed by better-equipped foes.

This book examines the ways in which the Chinese Communists attempted to enhance and exploit the "human element" in their army at the time of the Korean War. To this end we shall inquire into the nature and workings of the social organization, the political controls, and the morale system employed within the Chinese army at that time. The strengths and weaknesses of the Chinese Communist military system were exposed during the first eight months of Chinese participation in the Korean War, the period covered in this study. They are revealed through the eyes of the Chinese prisoners that we interviewed.

Fresh from an unexpectedly easy and early victory over the Nationalist armies in the civil war, the Chinese Communists found their national interests engaged in the autumn of 1950 by the turn of events in Korea. The North Korean army's effort to overrun South Korea had boomeranged badly during the summer and its own territory was now being occupied by UN forces. Their warnings of intervention if UN forces tried to occupy North Korea having gone unheeded, the Chinese Communists intervened with large forces. They committed their forces to combat cautiously at first, perhaps in part to assess and safeguard against the possibility of a military overreaction by the United States. However, the Chinese leaders then boldly and confidently committed their "volunteer" armies to the ambitious military objective of defeating the American and allied forces and of evicting them not only from North Korea but from South Korea as well. The Chinese gained impressive victories in the early months of combat, but then encountered increasing difficulties. Not only did they fail in their objective to destroy and evict the UN forces opposing them, but their own forces were severely punished and even placed in serious jeopardy for a brief period in the late spring of 1951.

The limits to which reliance on "man-over-weapons" can be carried against a modern opponent were reached and plainly manifested in Korea. There is no question but that this experience had a traumatic effect on Chinese military leaders. It impressed upon them the importance of modern military technology and organization and the desirability of acquiring it as soon as possible. In the early fifties, even while fighting in Korea dragged on during the prolonged truce discussions, Chinese leaders made determined efforts to modernize and reequip their forces, taking advantage of large-scale Soviet assistance. However, severe strains developed in the Sino-Soviet relationship in the late fifties and, as a result, Chinese leaders were forced or chose to "go it alone" at a slower pace in acquiring a modern military establishment.

The findings reported here about the Chinese Communist Army are, I believe, of more than purely historical interest. The Chinese Communist military model described in this book has been influential in the organization of guerrilla forces and armies in other parts of Southeast Asia and may be imitated elsewhere. The present Chinese Communist Army differs in important respects from the army which fought in Korea. Its social composition changed with the replacement of large numbers of old veterans and former Nationalist soldiers with young conscripts and better-trained new cadres. It is now a better-equipped, more modern force and, generally, a more professional army than fifteen years ago. Yet it is still fundamentally an infantry army and it utilizes the same kind of organizational provisions as it did earlier for enhancing the all-important "human element" and for assuring "politics in command."

In this respect the years since the end of the Korean War have seen almost a full turning of the circle. The revolutionary-egalitarian type of army—without formal ranks, derived from guerrilla warfare days, and operational in Korea—was largely abandoned. In its place the regime attempted to create a modern, more rational military structure cast along the lines of the more professionally oriented military system of the Soviet Union. In the mid-fifties for the first time the Chinese Communists introduced into their armed forces a professional officer corps, drafted conscripts under a selective national service law for a fixed term of service, and established a system of ranks, distinctions, and privileges. Political controls within the armed services were relaxed to allow greater scope for technical experts and military professionalism, but the consequences were so negative from the regime's standpoint that it soon moved to reintroduce the earlier system of tight political controls and to curb military professionalism. In the sixties the regime has returned to many features and practices of the older revolutionary-egalitarian military model. In this respect, the evolution of the Chinese Communist Army reached full circle in 1965 when the system of ranks and distinctions that had been in effect for ten years was abolished.

These developments lend fresh interest to the present study of the nature, organization, and performance of the Chinese forces during the Korean War. Once again, the regime is attempting to enhance the "human element" in its army by recapturing the revolutionary-egalitarian ethos and practices of an earlier day. This is by no means to imply that this book provides an answer to the question of how well the Chinese Communist Army could fight in the future under a variety of different circumstances. Such a query encounters many uncertainties and imponderables, and requires broad professional military judgment which I am not equipped to provide. On the other hand, it seems safe to say that against a strong opponent who can bring to bear superior military firepower, the Chinese will do better in relatively small-scale operations in which its leaders can control the time, place, and duration of actual engagements rather than in protracted, large-scale fighting along fixed lines of battle.

I hope that this book adds new and interesting dimensions to our understanding of the Chinese Communist Army and of the historical events covered. Moreover, in order to convey what is distinctive as well as familiar in the character of the Chinese army, I have found it useful in this study to draw comparisons with other armies. Having gained insight and perspective from the published work of specialists on other military organizations, I hope that this study will contribute in turn to the new field of comparative military sociology.

ALEXANDER L. GEORGE

Santa Monica, California
October, 1966

Acknowledgments

I BEGAN this study in February 1951 as a member of the Social Science Department, The RAND Corporation, as part of its research program for the U.S. Air Force. A report, based largely on information I obtained from Chinese prisoners in Korea during the months of March, April, and May 1951, was submitted to the Air Force in July 1952. In 1965 I had an opportunity to revise and bring up to date the earlier report, taking into account new studies and materials on the performance of the Chinese Communist forces in Korea that had been published in the intervening period. This revision of the original study constitutes the first ten chapters of this book. In June 1966, while on leave from The RAND Corporation, I wrote Chapter 11, summarizing developments in the Chinese Communist Army since the end of the Korean War.

It is a pleasure to record my deep appreciation for the help and encouragement I have received at various stages of research and writing from many persons, not all of whom I am able to mention by name. In Pusan, Korea, Dr. Joseph Lee performed an invaluable service in helping to supervise a group of dedicated interviewers and translators who labored under difficult conditions. My colleagues, Hans Speier, Herbert S. Dinerstein, Herbert Goldhamer, Joseph M. Goldsen, and the late Victor Hunt read and commented on a draft of my initial report in 1952. After this report was updated and revised in 1965, it was given a careful reading by General Samuel B. Griffith, U.S. Marine Corps (Ret.), Morris Janowitz, Professor of Sociology at The University of Chicago, and Lucian W. Pye, Professor of Political Science at the Massachusetts Institute of Technology. From them I received many valuable suggestions and, more, the encouragement needed to proceed with early publication of this study. General Griffith also kindly let me read several chapters from his forthcoming book on the Chinese Communist Army.

I wish to thank General Wallace M. Greene, Jr., Commandant, U.S. Marine Corps, for placing in perspective the intriguing link between the Chinese Communists' "3-by-3 tactic" of organizing combat infantry squads and the U.S. Marine Corps' adoption of the "Fire Team" concept.

My colleagues at RAND have been helpful in many ways. William F. Dorrill and Stephen T. Hosmer read the first ten chapters and offered useful advice. Chapter 11 benefited from suggestions made by Carl W. Chang, Alice Langley Hsieh, David P. Mozingo, Thomas W. Robinson, and William A. Stewart. I am, of course, solely responsible for the views expressed in this book which should not be taken as reflecting those of the people who commented on the manuscript or as the opinion or policy of The RAND Corporation or any of its clients. For help in making arrangements within The RAND Corporation to enable me to publish this book I am indebted particularly to Joseph M. Goldsen, John C. Hogan, and William A. Stewart. Able and timely secretarial help was provided particularly by Juanita Guess, Marcia Teeter, Phyllis Davidson, Lucille Goldsen, and Lynne Lawrence.

It was most generous of the East Asian Research Center of Harvard University, The RAND Corporation, and Stackpole Books to allow me to quote from, respectively, Ellis Joffe, *Party and Army: Professionalism and Political Control in the Chinese Officers Corps, 1949–1964;* Dicks, Shils, and Dinerstein, *Service Conditions and Morale in the Soviet Armed Forces;* and Robert B. Rigg, *Red China's Fighting Hordes.*

My greatest debt is to my wife, Juliette, who always finds a way to help—whether it be as an indispensable coauthor, as on a previous occasion, or as the compassionate bystander who arranged our lives in this case so that I could finish this book.

Contents

Illustrations

CHART

The Chinese Communist Army in Action

1 *The Chinese Intervention in Korea*

You can't fight millions and millions of drugged fanatics, and it's not worth the waste of life to try. What are we here for, anyway? This is supposed to be a police action.

An American officer in Seoul
November 1950

ON SUNDAY, June 25, 1950, the Communist North Korean Army launched a sudden, determined attack against South Korea. The lightly armed South Korean Army was no match for the invasion force of seven divisions that had been armed and trained by the Soviets and was supported by 150 Russian-built tanks. In the next few days the United States, backed by the United Nations, committed itself to the defense of South Korea and began to introduce its own air, land, and sea forces into the conflict. During a summer of difficult, at times desperate fighting, U.S. and Republic of Korea (ROK) forces finally established a defense perimeter around Pusan in the southern part of the peninsula and turned aside repeated assaults by North Korean forces that were aimed at pushing the United Nations forces out of South Korea. Then, in a bold maneuver on September 15, U.S. forces struck deep in the enemy rear, making a successful amphibious landing at Inchon, near Seoul. Shortly thereafter UN forces launched a strong attack from the Pusan beachhead. Caught between the two prongs of the UN counteroffensive and subjected to crippling blows from the air, the North Korean Army was badly mauled; its resistance crumbled and disorganized remnants fled back across the 38th Parallel into North Korea.

The end of the war was now in sight. Disregarding Chinese Communist warnings of intervention, UN forces moved well into North Korea in order to terminate hostilities and to pave the way for unification of North and South Korea under the auspices of the UN General Assembly. On November 24 the U.S. Eighth Army renewed its "home-by-Christmas" offensive to clear and occupy the remainder of

North Korea. The drive was undertaken in the face of evidence that considerable Chinese Communist Forces (CCF*) were present in North Korea, but both the numbers and intentions of the new opponent were underestimated. Two days later on November 26, the commander of the Chinese "volunteers," General Lin Piao, sprang the trap. Counterattacks were launched against the U.S. I and IX Corps while the main body of Chinese troops poured down the central mountain range to drive the ROK II Corps from its anchor position at Tokchon. On November 27, the ROK II Corps collapsed and the communist forces moved southward, in a move to turn the exposed right flank of the Eighth Army, thereby imperiling all noncommunist forces in the area.

The miscalculation of Chinese Communist intentions was now painfully evident. No matter how cautiously Chinese leaders had moved their forces into North Korea since mid-October and how carefully they had tested and evaluated the UN response to their intervention before finally determining the scope of their own objective, it was now evident that the massive counteroffensive of November 26 had the ambitious purpose of defeating the UN forces and driving them out of Korea.[1]

There followed in the next two months the longest retreat in United States military history. The possibility was seriously considered that UN forces might have to be evacuated from South Korea altogether. "At the front throughout December the moral collapse of the Eighth Army was complete, as bug-out fever raged everywhere, and even GHQ succumbed to what the naval historian M. C. Cagle calls 'panic and inertia.' "[2]

On the battlefield the extremes of heroism and demoralization were displayed. The shock of defeat and the enemy's novel tactics quickly produced, as always, inflated images of the opponent. The Chinese People's Liberation Army (PLA) was pictured as being composed of "drug-crazed fanatics" who attacked in "hordes," relying upon "human wave" tactics to overrun opposing forces without regard to casualties. In time a better-founded, more realistic appreciation emerged of the strengths and weaknesses of the Chinese Communist Army and of the individual soldiers comprising it. An account of this

* The elements of the People's Liberation Army which entered Korea were referred to by official U.S. sources as Chinese Communist Forces.

more realistic appraisal of the fighting qualities and tactics of the Chinese soldier will provide a useful backdrop for our study. For this purpose we quote from the official U.S. Marine Corps history of the Korean War:

Although the Chinese Reds were represented by a peasant army, it was also a first-rate army when judged by its own tactical and strategic standards. Military poverty might be blamed for some of its deficiencies in arms and equipment, but its semiguerrilla tactics were based on a mobility which could not be burdened with heavy weapons and transport. The Chinese coolie in the padded cotton uniform could do one thing better than any other soldier on earth; he could infiltrate around an enemy position in the darkness with unbelievable stealth. Only Americans who have had such an experience can realize what a shock it is to be surprised at midnight with the grenades and submachine gun slugs of gnomelike attackers who seem to rise out of the very earth.

Press correspondents were fond of referring to "the human sea tactics of the Asiatic hordes." Nothing could be further from the truth. In reality the Chinese seldom attacked in units larger than a regiment. Even these efforts were usually reduced to a seemingly endless succession of platoon infiltrations. It was not mass but deception and surprise which made the Chinese Red formidable.[3]

. . . .

A generation of warfare against material odds had established a pattern of attack which proved effective against armies possessing an advantage in arms and equipment. One Marine officer has aptly defined a Chinese attack as "assembly on the objective." The coolie in the CCF [PLA] ranks had no superior in the world at making long approach marches by night and hiding by day, with as many as fifty men sharing a hut or cave and subsisting on a few handfuls of rice apiece. Night attacks were so much the rule that any exception came as a surprise. The advancing columns took such natural routes as draws or stream beds, deploying as soon as they met resistance. Combat groups then peeled off from the tactical columns, one at a time, and closed with rifles, submachine guns, and grenades.

Once engaged and under fire, the attackers hit the ground. Rising at any lull, they came on until engaged again; but when fully committed, they did not relinquish the attack even when riddled with casualties. Other Chinese came forward to take their places, and the build-up continued until a penetration was made, usually on the front of one or two platoons. After consolidating the ground, the combat troops then crept or wriggled forward against the open flank of the next platoon position. Each step of the assault was executed with practiced stealth and boldness, and the results of several such penetrations on a battalion front could be devastating.

The pattern of attack was varied somewhat to suit different occasions. . . .[4]

. . . .

CCF attacking forces ranged as a rule from a platoon to a company in size, being continually built up as casualties thinned the ranks. Reports by newspaper correspondents of "hordes" and "human sea" assaults were so unrealistic as to inspire a derisive Marine comment: "How many hordes are there in a Chinese platoon?"

After giving CCF tactics due credit for their merits, some serious weaknesses were also apparent. The primitive logistical system put such restrictions on ammunition supplies, particularly artillery and mortar shells, that a Chinese battalion sometimes had to be pulled back to wait for replenishments if the first night's attack failed. At best the infantry received little help from supporting arms.

POW interrogations revealed that in many instances each soldier was issued 80 rounds of small arms ammunition upon crossing the Yalu. This was his total supply. The artillery and mortars were so limited that they must reserve their fire for the front line while passing up lucrative targets in the rear areas. Some attempts were made to bring reserve stocks up to forward supply dumps about 30 miles behind the front, but not much could be accomplished with animal and human transport.

A primitive communications system also accounted for CCF shortcomings. The radio net extended only down to the regimental level, and telephones only to battalions or occasionally companies. Below the battalion, communication depended on runners or such signaling devices as bugles, whistles, flares, and flashlights.

The consequence was a tactical rigidity which at times was fatal. Apparently CCF commanding officers had little or no option below the battalion level. A battalion once committed to the attack often kept on as long as its ammunition lasted, even if events indicated that it was beating out its brains against the strongest part of the opposing line. The result in many such instances was tactical suicide.

After these defects are taken into full account, however, the Chinese soldier and the Korean terrain made a formidable combination. Ironically, Americans fighting the first war of the new Atomic Age were encountering conditions reminiscent of the border warfare waged by their pioneer forefathers against the Indians. . . .[5]

This picture of PLA tactics provides in sharper focus than does the image of "drug-crazed fanatics" the considerable demands which leaders of the PLA placed on their men. While the Chinese soldiers did not attack in "hordes" on a wide front, nonetheless on a smaller scale with platoons and companies rather than whole divisions and armies, the PLA commanders did indeed employ "human wave" tactics. They did so, disregarding casualties, in order to overrun an often well-chosen tactical position in a bid to make a critical penetration. This is amply confirmed by accounts of many specific attacks against the U.S. 1st Marine Division.[6]

The ability of PLA authorities to create the level of morale, discipline, and control needed to extract this kind of military performance from their combat forces remained an important question, therefore, even after the image of "drug-crazed fanatics" was abandoned. That the Chinese Communists traditionally had relied upon intensive political indoctrination of their forces and employed a political "commissar" system was well known. The defeats suffered by United States forces in December and January at the hands of the technically inferior Chinese armies made it a matter of some importance to arrive at a better understanding of how the Chinese Communist military system created high morale and combat motivation of the type displayed time and again by many relatively small combat units operating under extremely severe conditions. It is to this question that the present study, initiated in February 1951, was directed. We shall defer to Chapter 2 a description of how the study was organized. We shall present in the remaining pages of Chapter 1 a brief history of the first eight months of the Chinese intervention in the Korean War which provides the context for an appraisal of the performance of the PLA.

The Korean War, coming closely upon the heels of the Chinese civil war, had caught the PLA in the midst of a transitional period. What this meant, more concretely, was that the composition, training, indoctrination, military efficiency, morale, and political reliability of different units varied considerably throughout the PLA. Of particular importance to our study is the fact that the leadership structure of different units (companies) was not always fully manned by cadres who were well-indoctrinated and reliable Party soldiers, as called for in the PLA organizational model.

Chinese Communist leaders selected the best units in the entire PLA, drawn from the crack 4th Field Army and the 3d Field Army, to intervene in Korea. In putting together an initial intervention force of 30 divisions, numbering some 300,000 soldiers, they took into account the political strength and reliability of different units as well as the quality of military weapons, training, and experience.

Our interviews with eighteen "hard core" cadre members confirmed in detail that there were, from a political standpoint, significant qualitative differences between and within the PLA Field Armies. There was general agreement among our respondents as to which were the best PLA Armies and, also, the factors which accounted for their high quality. The 4th Field Army, under Lin Piao, was generally credited with being the best of the five field armies.[7] The 38th, 39th, and 40th Armies (of the 13th Army Group), and the 42d Army (of the 14th Army Group)—all four of which were selected to be a part of the initial intervention force—were said by our respondents to have been especially strong. These armies held the honorary title of "Iron" troops. They had fought successfully in the civil war against better equipped Chinese Nationalist armies (CNA) and had subsequently strengthened themselves by incorporating Nationalist prisoners who possessed military skills needed in the PLA. They had had generally a longer period of time than other Chinese Communist armies in which to indoctrinate and assimilate these former Nationalist soldiers. And, finally, these armies contained a relatively low percentage of new recruits. An important exception in some of these respects was the 50th Army, another component of the 4th Field Army sent to Korea as part of the initial intervention force. The 50th Army was formerly the Nationalist 60th Army, which defected to the Chinese Communists during the civil war and was taken over virtually intact and renamed the 50th Army after taking on communist cadre.

While the 3d Field Army as a whole was not rated by our respondents as particularly strong, several of them said that its 26th Army—also part of the initial intervention force—was a crack unit. (In addition to the 26th Army, the 20th and 27th Armies of the 3d Field Army were also part of the initial intervention force.) The initial intervention force included no elements of the 2d Field Army and only the 66th Army from the 1st Field Army. According to some of our respondents, the 66th Army was well regarded because of its reputation for political trustworthiness. It was "somewhat similar to the bodyguard unit of Mao Tse-tung which had been stationed in the Peiping area." [8]

There are indications that Chinese Communist leaders expected a quick and relatively easy victory. They launched their major offensives of late November and New Year's Day, 1951, with confidence that the superior military doctrine, tactics, and morale of their best armies could defeat the better-equipped foe.

This initial force failed to accomplish the ambitious objective assigned to it of destroying and evicting UN forces from South Korea. Following the collapse of the Chinese "Third Phase" offensive in January 1951, their armies fell back to stronger defensive positions close to the 38th Parallel to rest and prepare for renewed ground operations. At about this time, too, Lin Piao was replaced by General P'eng Teh-huai as commander of the Chinese armies in Korea, and the Peking government decided to send in fresh armies from China. Once again the entire PLA was combed for units considered suitable for the task. A sizeable new force, this time drawn largely from the 1st and 2d Field Armies, was selected and sent into Korea.

One of the best units in the 2d Field Army, the 18th Army, had already been sent to Tibet in 1950; accordingly, the 12th, 15th, and 60th Armies were selected from the 2d Field Army for duty in Korea. From the 1st Field Army, the 63d, 64th, and 65th Armies were chosen. These three armies, comprising the 19th Army Group, were reported by our respondents to be the strongest within the 1st Field Army; they had been successful in the civil war and enjoyed a reputation for political trustworthiness. Apart from the 19th Army Group, the 1st Field Army was said to be one of the weakest in the PLA. The second wave of forces sent to Korea also included the 47th Army of the 4th Field Army, which was evidently not considered one of the crack armies of this field army. [9]

These armies entered Korea in late February, March, and early April in time to participate, together with the remainder of the original intervention force, in the Chinese spring offensives. As a result of this major reinforcement, the build-up of the Chinese forces in Korea had reached a level of about nineteen armies by mid-April (approximately 57 divisions), of which 36 divisions were estimated by EUSAK intelligence to be on the line at the time of the start of the first Chinese spring offensive. [10]

Altogether the combined strength of Chinese and North Korean forces was now estimated to be on the order of 70 divisions, numbering about 700,000 troops. Against them was arrayed a total UN force of about 420,000 ground troops with a frontline strength of about 230,000. Eighteen air groups of the Far East Air Forces (FEAF) were in action, and each of the United States divisions had been brought up to full strength of 18,000 men, including at least four battalions of artillery.[11]

The long-awaited spring offensive was launched in bright moonlight on the night of April 22. Radio Pyongyang confidently predicted it would destroy the UN Command. The Reds attacked everywhere across the western front with the major objective of enveloping the U.S. I and IX Corps, thereby isolating and capturing Seoul and cutting off these forces from their communication lines. It was estimated that some 337,000 Red troops took part in what was the single greatest effort hurled by Red forces against the defenders in the entire Korean War. Although fighting valiantly and inflicting heavy casualties, the Eighth Army troops were ordered to fall back in a fighting retreat after the collapse of an ROK division created the threat of envelopment. The "First Step" of their "Fifth Phase" offensive, as the Chinese called the opening of their massive spring offensive, ended on April 29, with their armies halted short of Seoul and north of the Han River.

Preparations for a resumption of the offensive were evident almost immediately. Despite hindering attacks by UN ground and air units, Chinese preparations and concentration of forces were completed and the offensive was resumed on May 16, this time on the eastern front. An estimated twelve PLA divisions supported by North Korean units struck southward toward Hongchon in a major attempt to press into South Korea and outflank the Eighth Army. ROK soldiers again broke under the attack, exposing the flank of the U.S. 2d Infantry Division. Red troops pressed forward in the face of United States ground reinforcements, and punishing artillery and air attacks, and almost reached Hongchon before the "Second Step" of their "Fifth Phase" collapsed on May 20.

The critical turning point of the war was now at hand as the UN forces immediately seized the initiative:

Always before, when their offensives spent themselves, the Reds had withdrawn beyond artillery range to reorganize and resupply. In May, however, United Nations ground forces recoiled only slightly, and by the fifth day of the Red attack . . . General Van Fleet launched the Eighth Army forward in a vicious counteroffensive, forcing the Reds into an exodus from South Korea which soon became a precipitous flight.

According to General Van Fleet's order, the American I, IX, and X Corps launched a coordinated counteroffensive on 23 May designed to cut the enemy's main supply routes and destroy him.[12]

What followed is succinctly described in the official U.S. Marine Corps history:

Only from the air could the effects of the UN counterstroke of May and June 1951 be fully appreciated. It was more than a CCF withdrawal; it was a flight of beaten troops under very little control in some instances. They were scourged with bullets, rockets, and napalm as planes swooped down upon them like hawks scattering chickens. And where it had been rare for a single Chinese soldier to surrender voluntarily, remnants of platoons, companies, and even battalions were now giving up after throwing down their arms.

There had been nothing like it before, and its like would never be seen in Korea again. The enemy was on the run! [13]

The pursuit phase of UN ground operations ended on June 2. Communist casualties sustained from May 15–31 were estimated by the Eighth Army at 105,000. This figure included 17,000 known dead and the unprecedented total of 11,526 prisoners, most of them Chinese taken during the last week of May amid frantic efforts to escape.

Thus ended Chinese Communist hopes of reunifying Korea on their terms. Negotiations and partition of Korea were now inevitable, since Washington's strategy by this time had become firmly anchored to limited objectives: "to establish the authority of the Republic of Korea over all of Korea south of a northern boundary line suitable for defense and administration and not substantially below the 38th Parallel. . . ." [14] In accord with this policy decision, limits had been imposed on the advance of the Eighth Army beyond the 38th Parallel.

By the beginning of June the whole of South Korea except for a small portion on the extreme western flank had been cleared of Red forces. Fortification of the "Kansas" line in the vicinity of the 38th

Parallel began in early June. Additional local advances were authorized to clear the small portion south of the 38th Parallel and to secure better ground north of it. A limited offensive northwards was undertaken to occupy Chorwon and Kumhwa, two of the anchor points of the Red "Iron Triangle," the strongly fortified area which had been the enemy's main assembly zone for concentrating troops and supplies for his spring offensives. These towns were occupied on June 11, virtually without opposition. Two days later task forces of American tanks entered Pyongyang, the other anchor point of the "Iron Triangle," but were shortly withdrawn lest they be "mouse-trapped" by Chinese troops in the area.[15]

Could the Eighth Army have converted the disorganized retreat of Red forces into a complete rout? Was the possibility of a far-reaching military victory in early June negated by the political decisions referred to above? [16] This question lies beyond the scope of our study except insofar as it raises the question of the impact which these military defeats had upon the strength and functioning of the political organization within the PLA.

Even before the events of late May and early June, as we shall indicate in this study, prolonged and severe combat had weakened the political hard core cadres in numbers and morale in company-level combat units throughout much of the Chinese army. Given the importance of the political hard core in the PLA system, they were always potentially a critical vulnerability in the Chinese Communist military system. It is likely that this problem became acute when the collapse of the Chinese spring offensives was followed immediately by the heavy counterblows of the Eighth Army and supporting air forces. Evidence of the disintegration of an increasing number of frontline Chinese combat units, expressed in uncontrolled retreat and "desertion to the rear" and group surrenders of the remnants of larger units, to which reference has already been made, must have been extremely worrisome to the Chinese Communist High Command. Certainly the Chinese commanders urgently needed time to reestablish control over their badly mauled forces. Precisely what role this problem played in the communist decision to seek a cease-fire or in the timing of the request—made on June 23 with studied casualness by Jacob Malik,

Soviet Ambassador to the UN—is an intriguing question which cannot be answered here.

It is important, however, to take note of a related question. The political outcome of the Korean War, finally agreed upon in July 1953 after two years of armistice negotiations, was in overall terms a standoff. Both sides, after a prolonged and costly struggle, accepted a territorial division of North and South Korea based upon the existing battle line which, in turn, closely approximated the territorial *status quo ante*. They accepted this outcome after each, in turn, had attempted unsuccessfully to achieve a military victory and thereby to unify Korea on their own terms.

From this political outcome of the war, some observers have drawn the conclusion that the Chinese Communist armies fought UN forces to a military stalemate. This proposition requires closer examination. It is true that the Chinese Communist forces, intervening in the autumn of 1950 after the defeat of the North Korean forces, prevented UN forces from achieving their military-political objective of occupying and pacifying North Korea, preparatory to reunifying the country as a whole. It is also true that during the two years of frustrating truce negotiations, beginning in July 1951, a military stalemate within the set of existing political-military constraints emerged between opposing forces of comparable strength, a military stalemate that was demonstrated by the difficult, costly, and inconclusive series of limited engagements fought over a period of two years. These were substantial military achievements by the PLA, and carried with them important political consequences.

But the fact remains that a military stalemate and a relative balance of military forces between the two sides did *not* exist on the battlefield *at the time the truce talks began*. It was achieved by the feverish military preparations the communist side made *after* the truce talks were agreed upon. The communist forces seized the opportunity given them by their opponent's self-imposed constraints. In his recent study of the Korean War, David Rees rightly distinguishes the question whether the UN forces could have inflicted a decisive defeat on the badly mauled Red forces in June 1950, had they not been constrained by political directives, from the question whether continuation of the momentum built up in May and June might have succeeded in securing an armistice agreement more quickly, thereby avoiding the costly positional warfare of the next two years in which United States casualties alone ran to about 60,000. Agreeing with earlier assessments that it was a mistake to curtail military pressure once truce discussions began, Rees concludes:

There can be no doubt that there was an excellent chance that a truce might have been forced from the Communists by the end of 1951 if the pressure had been kept up, not by using the MacArthur or Van Fleet plans, but by fighting a different kind of limited war to that which the Administration found itself committed once the truce talks started.[17]

Chinese Communist prisoners rest following their capture by US forces.

2 *The Interviews*

> Although these interviews may not meet the exacting standards
> of scientific sampling, they constitute a body of relevant data that
> can suggest a whole range of hypotheses in spheres which can
> only be crudely approached by more conventional historical and
> institutional methods of study, methods which are usually based
> on admittedly incomplete data.
>
> *Lucian Pye, Guerrilla Communism in Malaya*

WHAT motivated the Chinese soldiers and enabled them to
fight so well in Korea? This question remained a perplexing and
nagging one during the winter of 1950–1951 as the shock of the
initial Chinese successes slowly abated. In search of better answers to
this question the author organized special interviews with approximately three hundred prisoners during the months of March, April,
and May 1951.

Early in the study it became evident that most activities affecting
service conditions, morale, combat motivation, and performance were
the responsibility of the political organization within the PLA. The
political apparatus in this army was all-pervasive, more so than in
the Soviet Army. It paralleled and straddled the military command
structure from top to bottom. The familiar communist organizational
device of dual political and military authority was employed down to
and including company level. In addition, Chinese authorities had attempted to "politicize" the entire military cadre structure of their
army by installing Party soldiers insofar as possible in all leadership
positions, including those at platoon and squad level. Moreover, each
combat squad was further subdivided into several "groups of three,"
each of which was led whenever possible by a person considered to be
reliable by the Party apparatus. It was immediately evident, therefore, that to deal incisively with the question of motivation and combat morale in the Chinese forces the investigator would have to
clarify the role, activities, and performance of the *political organization* within the PLA.

The decision to look closely at the PLA's organizational framework was influenced also by available research findings on military morale in other armies during and since World War II. These earlier studies had underscored the importance of the small combat groups to which individual soldiers belonged, and called attention to organizational and environmental factors that shaped these small groups and affected their linkage to the larger military structure of authority. It was found that the comradely ties that developed among soldiers in small combat units under certain conditions were of particular importance for good morale. Sociologists enriched the interpretation of these findings by relating them to the concept of "primary groups," which refers to small social groupings in which social behavior is governed by intimate face-to-face relations.

The sociological perspective on morale has broadened further in the past twenty years. Mature reflection on the accumulated research experience in this area has led to the conclusion that the concept of "morale" is too limited and needs to be replaced by a more inclusive theory of organizational behavior. In his recent comprehensive review of research trends in this field, Morris Janowitz adds that morale can no longer be regarded as "a vague dimension of organizational behavior grounded in personal attitudes. Even in the smallest unit there is an 'iron framework' of organization which serves as a basis of social control." [1]

In these respects modern sociological research has rediscovered the wisdom of military leaders who have reflected thoughtfully on these problems in the past. Thus, by 1880 Colonel Ardant du Picq, a French combat officer and military theorist, had already subjected the problem of combat morale and discipline in modern warfare to a penetrating analysis. In his *Battle Studies*, long since a classic, du Picq noted the special social and organizational requirements needed to sustain the individual soldier under the changed conditions of modern warfare:

But to order discipline is not enough. . . . Discipline itself depends on moral pressure which actuates men to advance from sentiments of fear or pride. But it depends also on surveillance, the mutual supervision of groups of men who know each other well.
A wise organization insures that the personnel of combat groups changes as little as possible, so that comrades in peace time maneuvres

shall be comrades in war. From living together, and obeying the same chiefs, from commanding the same men, from sharing fatigue and rest, from cooperation among men who quickly understand each other in the execution of warlike movements, may be bred brotherhood, professional knowledge, sentiment, above all unity. The duty of obedience, the right of imposing discipline and the impossibility of escaping from it, would naturally follow.*

The design of the present study, therefore, was influenced by the theory of morale that had emerged from earlier research on several different armies, and by the many indications available to the author in early 1951 that the political organization played a central role in the PLA's morale-building system. Accordingly, the interviews with Chinese prisoners were designed to clarify three major questions:

The first task was to obtain a detailed description of *the kind of military organization,* or model, that Chinese Communist leaders had developed earlier in their guerrilla forces and had continued to apply in converting these older units into a larger, more modern army. For reasons already indicated, our description of this military model focuses on the kind of social organization and small comradely groups of a politicized (Communist) character that PLA authorities attempted to create within their armed forces. We also obtained an account of the major policies and practices employed by PLA authorities in efforts to mold and shape the human material available to them at that time into the kinds of soldiers, cadres, and social groups that were desired. To highlight what was distinctive about the Chinese military model in these respects, we have compared it in the pages which follow with the Soviet Army, the U.S. Armed Forces, and the German Wehrmacht of World War II.

A second objective of the study was to determine *the extent to which PLA authorities had managed to develop their army along the requirements of their military model.* The Korean conflict caught the PLA in the midst of an important transition. The civil war had seen a vast expansion of the PLA, achieved in good part by incorporation of Nationalist army defectors and prisoners. The collapse of the Chinese Nationalist armies had occurred much sooner than expected. Shortly thereafter, the Korean War broke out at a time when Chinese Com-

---

* Colonel Ardant du Picq, *Battle Studies: Ancient and Modern Battle,* translated from the eighth edition in French by Colonel John N. Greely and Major Robert C. Cotton (Harrisburg, Pa.: the Military Service Publishing Co., 1958).

munist leaders were still engaged in converting their revolutionary army, hardly grown out of its guerrilla origins, into a national Communist army of the type their military model called for. In addition, they had only begun to reequip with more modern weapons. In many respects, as Colonel Rigg has aptly observed, the Chinese Communist Forces were still a nineteenth-century army attempting to fight a twentieth-century war in Korea.

How well did this army achieve the organizational model or blueprint that its leaders had laid down? What pragmatic compromises in this respect had been introduced and accepted? To what extent was the military cadre structure "politicized," as the blueprint called for, by having reliable, well-indoctrinated Party soldiers in all cadre positions? To what extent were rank-and-file soldiers genuinely assimilated into the kind of comradely life which the political organization within each unit sponsored? To what extent were the motivation and compliance patterns desired by PLA authorities actually achieved? Were the major policies and practices employed to achieve these objectives operating successfully? Wherein were they failing?

The third set of questions concerned the *performance* of the PLA armies committed to Korea. Here the focus of the interviews was on the ability of the political apparatus to perform its many interrelated responsibilities for creating cohesive, strongly motivated combat groups, and for maintaining morale and assuring combat performance under adverse conditions. How well did the combat units sent to Korea, the best in the PLA as we have already noted in Chapter 1, function under the stress of increasingly severe, prolonged combat against a modernly equipped foe?

In his recent review of theory and empirical research on military morale, Morris Janowitz argues that the dynamics of small comradely combat groups can best be studied when the organization is under pressure. But this kind of research is not easily arranged. Wherever possible the investigator must take advantage of stressful experiences which the military organization encounters in real life—experiences which then constitute "natural experiments," as it were, for the researcher; or else morale has to be studied during large-scale field exercises or simulations. From this standpoint, the first eight months of the Chinese Communist intervention that are covered in this study provide an extremely good "test-bed" for assessing the workings of the Chinese military morale system since a pronounced shift in the military fortunes of the PLA took place during this period.

Ideally, the most advantageous way to study the workings of the Chinese Communist morale system would have been for a team of investigators to have observed many PLA combat groups directly, as "participant observers," over a period of time and in a variety of situations and circumstances.* Since this vantage point was not possible, the investigator adopted a less satisfactory expedient of utilizing Chinese prisoners as informants on these matters. It is important to note, however, that the prisoners we interviewed were not utilized as individual members of what hopefully might constitute a representative sample of some kind. Rather, each prisoner was regarded as an *informant* on matters affecting the development of small group ties and the status of morale in the unit to which he had belonged. We shall comment further on this in discussing the method of analysis employed in this study.

As was to be expected, the prisoners varied in their usefulness as informants. Some had been keener observers of the ramifications of the morale system than others. And some were more articulate than others in recalling what life in the PLA had been like. Unwillingness to provide accurate information was far less a limitation than the fact that, at best, each respondent was a potential source of information only on those parts of the organization and its performance in which he had personally participated or learned about. Each respondent was in the first instance an informant on the nature and development of his own attitudes and behavior. But in addition —since the interviews attempted to place prisoners in the role of participant observers—each respondent also provided useful information about others in his unit.

The nature and workings of the Chinese military system can be studied not only through interviews with prisoners, of course, but also

---

* One of the few examples of the utilization of this preferred research approach is the study by Roger W. Little, currently with the Office of Military Psychology and Leadership, United States Military Academy, who from November 1952 through February 1953 directly observed a single U.S. army combat unit in Korea. The results of his study, which later comprised a Ph.D. dissertation, were summarized in an article, "Buddy Relations and Combat Performance," in M. Janowitz (ed.), *The New Military,* pp. 195–223.

by utilizing documentary materials of the kind traditionally available to the scholar—newspapers and journals, the firsthand reports of journalists and travelers, etc. The analysis of our interviews was supplemented by selective use of such materials. But interviews with prisoners constituted a unique source of information on the kinds of problems addressed in this study; more so than Chinese military publications these interviews provided direct access to personal and psychological dimensions, and to the internal social processes of the Chinese military organization.

The interviews with Chinese prisoners were all conducted in what was known as Prisoner-of-War (POW) Camp No. 5 in the Pusan area. At that time prisoners captured at all points on the front filtered back to Camp No. 5 for processing. Most prisoners arrived at Camp No. 5 approximately a week to ten days after capture, except for those hospitalized at Camp No. 1 who passed through the Processing Center sometime later. The interviewing unit employed in this study was stationed at the Processing Center and, within certain limits, had access to all of the prisoners who came through. Prisoners remained in the Processing Center for several days before being assigned to more permanent enclosures in the Camp.

Much of the data on which this study is based were obtained from 84 interviews. The questionnaire used for this purpose was developed by the author after reviewing available information on the Chinese army and after making approximately 25 exploratory interviews with knowledgeable Chinese prisoners. (This basic questionnaire is reproduced in the Research Note.) Sixty-one of these interviews were with Chinese privates (most of these were former Nationalist soldiers); 23 were with cadre members, most of whom held positions of company commanders, platoon, or squad leaders. Most of these 84 prisoners had been captured during late March and April, and in a few cases in early May 1951. The interviews took place in April and early May.[2]

While a larger number of interviews would have been quite desirable, these 84 are adequate for the purpose of the study and the method of analysis employed. Moreover, it was possible to identify and partly correct some of the inadequacies and ambiguities of the information obtained from these interviews. Thus, a quick preliminary analysis was made of respondents' replies to this basic questionnaire and, as a result, additional questions were formulated on which information would be desirable. A second questionnaire of a more specialized nature was then prepared for interviews with 18 prisoners who had been members of the Party hard core cadre over a period of time. From these particularly knowledgeable informants a more detailed account was obtained about the impact of severe prolonged combat in Korea on the attitudes, morale, and numerical strength of the hard core cadres in different combat units.

The study also draws on materials contained in interviews with two other questionnaires drawn up by the author. Ninety-eight interviews were made on various aspects of the military experiences of the PLA in Korea and 80 interviews on psychological reactions to combat. Some of the same questions were asked in these interviews that had been employed in the basic questionnaire. Hence, for parts of the analysis reported in this study, data was available for more than the 84 respondents to the basic questionnaire. Altogether, data from approximately 300 special interviews arranged by the author have been used in this study. Most of these soldiers had become prisoners as a result of being captured; relatively few had defected.

In a study of this kind the task and methods of analysis differ substantially from those of a Gallup Poll type of sample survey of opinions, even though both make use of a questionnaire and are concerned with the respondents' information and attitudes. In the present study, the interviews are analyzed by evaluating specific items of information provided by each prisoner on the basis of his particular background and experience in the small unit to which he had belonged. From this standpoint, each prisoner (even though not always an ideal informant) can be regarded as a "sample" of a very small universe. Our effort to characterize the PLA as a whole, as much as was possible, had to be satisfied by interviewing a sufficient number and variety of prisoners who, collectively, could throw light on the three major research problems referred to above. The individual respondents and the items of information they provided are treated for purposes of analysis as pieces of the larger mosaic (or "universe") that was the PLA as a whole. The task of analysis is to reconstruct insofar as possible those aspects of the organization and functioning of the PLA in which we are interested on the basis of the useful but incomplete material provided by the informants.

US Army Photograph

A captured Chinese Communist soldier is interrogated by US troops, March 7, 1951.

US Army Photograph

This technique of analysis is not in itself novel; some variant of it is applied in studies of many different kinds of problems. This method inevitably rests heavily on judgment, interpretation, and skill in inferring and generalizing from limited circumstantial evidence. Some parts of the mosaic can be reconstructed and filled in with greater confidence than others. The results of the overall analysis represent at best a judicious mixture of what is known with considerable confidence, what is probably or likely to be true, and what is merely suggested by the available data. An effort is made throughout the report to differentiate what is presented in these terms.

While the findings of the study are necessarily of this character, it goes beyond an impressionistic analysis of the problem. The interview materials were collected systematically and in a focused manner. They were designed to obtain relevant data bearing on the problems of interest. Accordingly, the analysis is not forced to rely on fragmentary data on political organization and morale that happened to be available as a result of prisoner interviews having primarily another purpose. The disadvantages of an exploratory, "fishing expedition" type of study were avoided in the present case; both the questions asked and the analysis of replies obtained benefited from available theory and knowledge about morale in small military units, gained from earlier studies of World War II experience. Moreover, our questionnaires were constructed after a preliminary assessment of what was already known about the role and functioning of the political organization in the PLA. Finally, this study differs from an impressionistic account in that its findings are not the result of a casual inspection or single reading of the interviews but, rather, from a detailed and painstaking analysis of them.

There are, of course, substantial difficulties in trying to find out what soldiers thought about life in their units by interviewing them after they have become prisoners. We tried to anticipate and minimize some of these difficulties—which might lead the respondent to play down or forget his previous attachment to his unit—by establishing a sympathetic interview atmosphere, by interviewing sufficiently after the time of capture so that fear of reprisals for "wrong" (i.e., pro-PLA) answers was reduced, and by avoiding insofar as possible direct requests to the respondent to give his own attitude. The fact that Korean civilians rather than U.S. Army personnel were used as interviewers may have encouraged respondents to give franker statements.

In the period immediately preceding capture most of the prisoners interviewed had experienced severe hardship and anxiety due to uncertain food supplies, extreme physical danger, and enforced combat imposed by leaders. A soldier's positive ties to leadership and to his small combat group would tend to be weakened as a result of such experiences. The problem in the interview, therefore, was to get the soldier to try to recall his earlier attitudes and, in any case, to infer what these had been from the replies he made to various indirect questions asked him. How well did we succeed in this respect?

We believe that the characterizations of soldiers' attitudes to service conditions in the PLA are not unduly distorted by immediate precapture or postcapture experiences, but reflect the soldiers' adjustments to their units and leaders while still in China and during earlier phases of Korean combat. We feel confident of this for several reasons. In the interviews prisoners frequently referred to estimates of their political officers which they had held for some time as well as to more recent changes in these estimates. In many instances when a private conveyed a negative attitude to the PLA system, his remarks indicated that important elements of it were long-standing. Thus, it appeared unjustified to discount the striking frequency and severity of negative attitudes conveyed by the respondents by hypothesizing that a radical shift from positive to negative orientation took place immediately prior to capture or thereafter. Rather the severe and cumulative hardships of the Korean campaign pushed attitudes steadily in a negative direction. Materials in our interviews strongly suggested that many privates viewed at least certain aspects of PLA group life negatively prior to their entry into Korea.

In this connection, it is probably correct to assume that in the PLA, as in other military organizations, attitudes toward leaders are often ambivalent or of a mixed quality. While the soldier is still a member of the military group, he is dependent upon the skill and goodwill of his leaders. There is usually a basis for at least some positive attitude toward leaders in the care, protection, and direction which they provide. And the authoritarian nature of the relationship, backed as it is by the ultimate threat of sanctions, encourages some soldiers to repress or suppress negative components of an ambivalent attitude to their leaders while still intimately dependent upon them. However, once detached from his unit and a prisoner, the soldier is no longer dependent on former leaders and need no longer repress expression of negative attitudes.

There is considerable evidence in our materials that ambivalent, mixed attitudes had been widely held by privates in PLA units. We note, for example, that the predominant form of adjustment by the sixty-one privates interviewed to the PLA system was one of conscious dissimulation. While positive morale was widely simulated and signs of negative morale were suppressed by these privates, many of them did not lack *some* genuinely positive estimates of the company political officer or favorable evaluations of certain aspects of the PLA system.

In sum, we readily acknowledge that questions of the validity, representative nature, and precise meaning of the findings reported here regarding the adjustments made by soldiers within their units cannot be answered conclusively. Nonetheless, the materials obtained from these prisoners do give us a unique basis for assessing the nature of the Chinese Communist Army's organization and morale system, its impact on many soldiers, and its performance when put to a severe test in Korea.

3 The Chinese Communist Military Model

A revolutionary army must have discipline that is established on a limited democratic basis. In all armies, obedience of the subordinates to their superiors must be exacted. This is true in the case of guerrilla discipline, but the basis for guerrilla discipline must be the individual conscience. With guerrillas, a discipline of compulsion is ineffective. . . . [It] must be self-imposed, because only when it is, is the soldier able to understand completely why he fights and how he must obey. This type of discipline becomes a tower of strength within the army, and it is the only type that can truly harmonize the relationship that exists between officers and soldiers.

Mao Tse-tung

SOLDIERS can be made to follow the hardships and dangerous risks of army life in two ways. They may come to believe that it is necessary to endure them, a feeling created when military service is accepted as legitimate and its requirements are internalized; or they may anticipate even worse deprivations if they seek to avoid these demands. As the quotation from Mao Tse-tung indicates, the Chinese Communists learned from their rich experience in guerrilla warfare that an army fights best when discipline and the performance of military duties rest at least in part on genuinely voluntaristic motives and are not extracted solely through fear of punishment for disobedience. Chinese Communist leaders, of course, are not alone in recognizing the desirability of blending coercion with persuasion. In other armies, too, efforts are made to induce soldiers to accept and to internalize the basic demands of the organization by subjecting them to indoctrination, by resocializing them and assimilating them into the social organization of the army, and by bringing to bear material induce-ments as well as symbolic rewards and deprivations.

While not unique in these respects, the military model that grew out of Chinese Communist guerrilla experience contained distinctive elements. Perhaps foremost among these was the conscious effort made to create within the armed guerrilla formations a type of social organization consonant with the revolutionary aspirations of Chinese Communist leaders. Induction of new soldiers into this army involved more than temporarily removing them from civilian life; they were not merely indoctrinated and trained for military duty but were resocialized for participation in a new way of life afterwards as well. Moreover, as we shall see, the Chinese Communists developed an organizational doctrine and structure that was well suited for securing compliance either through inculcation of voluntaristic motivations or, failing that, through coercion in various forms. The PLA offered new soldiers many opportunities to "commit" themselves to the ideals and demands of the organization, at first primarily through reliance on methods of persuasion and patient instruction but, if and when necessary, through more explicit reliance on methods of "struggle" and coercive controls.

THE IDEAL OF COMRADELY RELATIONS

The informal comradely ties that often develop among soldiers in small military groups can contribute greatly to morale and performance of combat duties. This is particularly true in revolutionary guerrilla warfare which requires highly motivated, closely knit small groups. Drawing upon their own rich experience in this respect, Chinese Communist leaders made explicit provision for creating and maintaining small social groups of this kind as their revolutionary army increased in size and complexity. Moreover, in encouraging the development of comradely relations within their army, Chinese leaders were continuing a characteristic feature of Chinese society in which kinship and personal ties are important aspects of bureaucratic organization.

What is novel and intriguing about the PLA is not this feature but, rather, the fact that its leaders insisted that comradely ties among the men should have an explicit political-ethical content. It was not enough, as in other modern armies, that morale and loyalty should rest upon informal comradely ties of a nonpolitical character. Rather, small groups within PLA units were supposed to be closely knit in a special way. A communist pattern of thought and way of life was cultivated within these groups in the expectation that it would generate political loyalties that would strengthen the military cohesiveness of the army. The Chinese Communist military model was imbued with an ethical and missionary flavor that was appreciably stronger than that typical in the history of the Soviet Army. As a result, the type of small group life the PLA tried to establish recalls in some ways the closely knit military-religious orders of the past.[1]

The kind of group life sought within the PLA will be characterized in some detail in later chapters. Here we shall present only the more striking and unusual features of the pattern of social organization within the army to which Chinese Communist leaders aspired. These are highlighted by contrasting the PLA with other modern armies— the U.S. Armed Forces, the Soviet Army, and the German Wehrmacht of World War II—on which similar information is available.

In the U.S. Armed Forces the development of comradely ties among members of small units is largely a consequence of the men's recognition that they are working together on a common job, that each is dependent on the other, and that teamwork is to everyone's advantage.[2] Good morale takes the form of loyalty to the unit and pride in one's outfit. Teamwork and good morale are aided by the emergence of spontaneous informal relationships within the military structure, which supplement and coexist with formal military discipline. It is expected that most soldiers have the capacity, derived from earlier experiences in civilian society, to develop comradely ties within their units that will reinforce the workings of formal organization and authority.

Informal group life within the U.S. Army has an autonomous character. It lacks an overt political or ideological character. There is, to be sure, widespread tacit acceptance by soldiers of the worth of the American political system and of the legitimacy of its demand for military service, and these beliefs undoubtedly facilitate the formation of informal groups within the military structure. But American military authorities place little, if any, reliance upon ideological symbols and political rituals in their efforts to promote cohesive groups and positive morale. Rather, it is tacitly understood that more immediate considerations of self-respect, professionalism, and human factors connected with the daily life and work of the unit are more powerful factors than political "heroics" in knitting individuals into a group and in developing a high level of teamwork. Indeed, it is at least implicitly understood that political heroics utilized for this purpose might well damage attitudes toward leadership by provoking the men's resentment or mirth.[3] Thus, for example, when General Matthew Ridgway assumed command of the U.S. Eighth Army in Korea in December 1950 after its long retreat occasioned by the Chinese Communist intervention, he found that attempts were being made to restore morale in some units by giving political peptalks. Instead, Ridgway insisted on the restoration of strict barrack-room discipline wherever possible. From that time the Eighth Army started to become a professional army, fighting not for the United Nations or against communism but fighting because it was ordered to. A regimental commander told *Time* magazine at the end of February 1951, "The boys aren't up there fighting for democracy now. They're fighting because the platoon leader is leading them, and the platoon leader is fighting because of the command, and so on up right to the top." *

The United States military system does not operate—as did the PLA—on the assumption that only political motives which are self-consciously held, articulated, and closely related to day-to-day tasks provide a sound basis for good morale and combat motivation. Rather, the informal ties that cement small groups within the U.S. Army are extraordinarily spontaneous, overtly apolitical, and largely unregulated by higher authorities. Higher leadership in the U.S. Army does not feel its control threatened by the autonomous comradely ties which develop between the men. In fact, it encourages such relationships. It regards the personal loyalties felt by the men toward one another not as inimical to, but as contributing to good military discipline and combat effectiveness. Thus, it builds upon small group loyalties to create larger loyalties; it accepts the informal ties that bind men to each other and to their immediate leaders as a means of reinforcing the formal authority structure. Nor do United States military

---

* David Rees, *Korea: The Limited War* (New York: St. Martins Press, 1964), p. 190. At the same time, however, it should be noted that General Ridgway did not neglect to answer the question: "Why are we here? What are we fighting for?" After completing his first tour of the combat area he sat down and wrote a personal declaration of faith, answering this question, which was sent to all troops of the Eighth Army. Matthew B. Ridgway, U.S.A. Ret., *Soldier* (New York: Harper & Bros., 1956), pp. 207–8.

authorities fear that group solidarity based on informal, apolitical ties increases vulnerability to subversion by political or psychological warfare.*

In contrast, the political organization within the PLA took an active and controlling interest in the development of small group ties. It did not permit these ties to have an autonomous basis, for it felt threatened by informal group ties and loyalties that were essentially apolitical in character. Interpersonal relations within combat units that were cemented by human considerations and to which the men gave priority over political values would be regarded as potentially threatening by the PLA political organization. Not only was it believed that political motives provided a stronger, more reliable basis for morale, but it was feared that ties based solely on human considerations were more vulnerable to political subversion and might transform themselves into oppositional activity.

A comparison of PLA and Soviet Army models for small group life also indicates important differences. From an early stage in the history of the Soviet Union there were major disagreements among the leaders of the Communist Party over whether the Soviet Army should be modeled on revolutionary, egalitarian precepts or follow the more traditional practices of a professional military establishment.[4] While the history of the Soviet Army is marked by many changes and reversals in the role of the Party within the military organization, its leaders recognized the importance of military professionalism from the beginning and there has been over the years a trend toward greater professionalism. Many of the strikingly egalitarian features of the revolutionary model still visible in the PLA at the time of the Korean War were either altogether lacking in Soviet experience, were present only in its early history, or have survived only in a much attenuated form. The greater emphasis on professionalism

---

* This is not to overlook the fact that under conditions of prolonged stress group ties within combat units in the U.S. Armed Forces can lead to resistance to the norms and demands of the organization, as transmitted by the orders of leaders higher up in the chain of command. On this point, see the discussion by Morris Janowitz and Roger W. Little, in Janowitz (ed.), *The New Military*, pp. 192, 213. For a more general discussion of whether peer group cohesion at the lower levels of an organization necessarily contributes to its effectiveness, see Janowitz and Little, *Sociology and the Military Establishment*, p. 78, and Amitai Etzioni, *A Comparative Analysis of Complex Organizations*, Chapter VIII, "Compliance and Cohesion" (New York: Free Press, 1961).

in the modern Soviet Army is evident in many respects: for example, in the attempt authorities make under garrison and training conditions to keep relations between officers and men on a formal, hierarchical basis. In contrast, the PLA system actively encouraged the development of friendly, comradely relations between leaders and men in periods of indoctrination and training, and under garrison conditions.

The PLA differed from the Soviet Army also in that the system of ranks and distinctions was formally abolished. In practice, too, there was greater equality between leaders and ordinary soldiers in the PLA than in the Soviet Army, and less emphasis upon extreme forms of discipline. The company political officer in the PLA attempted to play the role of a "good guy," and encouraged platoon and squad leaders to model themselves along the same lines in developing group solidarity in their subunits.

In the Soviet Army, though officially discouraged in peacetime, comradely ties between officers and men did develop spontaneously in combat during World War II.[5] These comradely ties were often grounded in or associated with patriotism; but what the Russian soldier typically expressed thereby was a nationalism that was largely divorced from communist ideology. Soviet leaders realized early in the war that there existed a large reserve of patriotism in the Russian masses that could be utilized for purposes of military as well as civilian morale. They were the more willing, therefore, to soft-pedal communist themes in morale-building propaganda and to avoid a doctrinaire insistence on the part of the political apparatus within the Soviet Army that combat morale must be grounded in communist convictions.

In contrast, the PLA system we have seen prior to and during the Korean conflict had very little tolerance for the development of comradely ties that were not cemented by mutually shared communist conviction or orientation. It is not certain whether this attitude on the part of Chinese Communist leaders can be attributed solely to an underlying dogmatism or reflected certain pragmatic calculations as well. Perhaps PLA leaders would have been more flexible in this respect if they had felt that patriotism and national feeling among Chinese soldiers were strong enough to dispense with the communist *motif*. While Chinese nationalism had been increasing in recent decades, it is problematical whether it had become strong enough among soldiers in the PLA at the time of the Korean War to permit reliance upon it as a means of building and reinforcing small group ties and military loyalty. Probably more important, PLA leaders may have thought that it would be difficult in any case to mobilize existing patriotic motives among their soldiers on behalf of intervention in a conflict beyond Chinese borders, admittedly before China itself was invaded.

POLICIES AND PRACTICES FOR ACHIEVING THE MODEL

We turn now to a description of the measures employed by Chinese leaders in order to mold the human material available to them into the kinds of soldiers, cadres, and social groups that were desired. The policies and practices employed to this end, it must be remembered, took place in a very special organizational context; the PLA's organizational doctrine and structure were well designed to facilitate the objectives and techniques of indoctrination. This will become fully evident later in this chapter when we have described the PLA organizational model in detail.

Many of the policies and techniques the Party applied to produce the kind of soldiers and small groups it desired were, indeed, in the older Chinese tradition: for example, persuasion in lieu of coercion; precombat exhortations and oaths; the obligation of the State to reward meritorious deeds and to care for the families of soldiers who had "established merit." Other measures employed by the PLA, on the other hand, were not in the Chinese tradition; at least they had not been utilized within the Nationalist Army in recent times. The PLA's indoctrination practices and its policies for dealing with conditions of service have been described in general terms, of course, in Chinese Communist writings.[6] The following account of them is based largely on information supplied by the prisoners we interviewed, and supplemented by several accounts of earlier observers of the Chinese Communist Army.[7]

Political Conversion

The purpose of basic training and indoctrination in the PLA was not simply to produce "good soldiers." Rather, Chinese Communist leaders were engaged in an ambitious pedagogical enterprise which, if successful, would alter important aspects of the individual's personality, attitudes, and behavior in order to make a "good *communist* soldier" out of him. Assimilation of soldiers into the peculiar political-military group life officially sponsored in the PLA was possible only if a rather thorough transformation of the individual's personality took place.

In order to bring about such a transformation, several tasks were involved. It was necessary to inculcate in the individual the basic moral and ethical standards of Chinese Communism: anti-individualism, dedication of self to the interests of the "people," acceptance of leadership of the Party. This was part of the effort to create a new communist "conscience" in the individual, which would make him deeply dissatisfied with things as they are, cause him to maintain a constant alertness and watchfulness against the appearance of "evil" in himself or in others around him, and impel him to be an "activist" on behalf of political and social reform and in the performance of his military duties. To the extent that this kind of basic political indoctrination was successful, the individual would be left with a strong positive inner motivation that facilitated his acceptance and implementation of day-to-day tasks. Such goals and expectations were explicit in Chinese Communist doctrine and practice; they help explain why poor performance of day-to-day tasks within the army was invariably taken by PLA leaders as an indication that a man's political ideology was weak.

All new soldiers were typically subjected to an initial period of intensive political indoctrination that might last from several weeks to several months and vary accordingly in its thoroughness. Initial indoctrination does not appear to have resulted in full-fledged conversions to communism, nor was this usually its goal. Rather, in most cases it seems to have had more limited objectives. It gave communist instructors an opportunity to assess the individual's political personality and his background and to rate his potential for conversion to communism. It was also hoped that the initial indoctrination would predispose the individual to cooperate with subsequent efforts to transform him into a good communist soldier.

Political indoctrination was a continuous process in the PLA. To become a trusted, reliable communist required, in most cases, a lengthy period of indoctrination and surveillance. Understanding of and adherence to communism had to be demonstrated in everyday life under a variety of conditions which "tested" the individual. The initial period of indoctrination was of considerable importance, nonetheless, and might include what has been referred to as "brainwashing" or "thought reform" by American commentators.[8] The present study does not delve into this aspect of PLA indoctrination. However, the materials obtained from our interviews do throw light on various aspects of the broader pedagogical program of the PLA, especially as this was pursued after the initial phase of indoctrination ended and the individual was assigned to a regular unit.

Much of the subsequent political indoctrination took place in small groups. This enabled PLA leaders to utilize and manipulate group pressures for pedagogical purposes, and to tie in theoretical and ideological instruction with practical guidance in group life. Also noteworthy is that, in contrast to Western armies which often separate efforts to indoctrinate new soldiers from later efforts to assimilate them into regular units, the PLA combined these two tasks. Indoctrination was not viewed narrowly as a matter of changing an individual's attitudes, important though that might be. Rather, the individual soldier received much of his indoctrination in a group context as part of the procedure for assimilating him into a small group whose structure and character was predetermined. Group meetings provided opportunities for uncommitted individuals to strengthen their sense of commitment by entering into group situations. Once again, in this respect as in others, the PLA is a microcosm of the larger macrocosm of Chinese Communist organizational theory and practice that can be seen in other sectors of life as well. As H. F. Schurmann puts it:

The Chinese Communists never permit participation in group activity to be simply verbal. In most instances "study groups" and "work groups" are one, so that an individual subjected to verbal pressures in one group context will find himself being tested by his concrete work in the same group context. . . . Both work and talk are forms of participation, and coming together they compound the pressures, to involve an individual in the "cause" or organization in question.[9]

In approaching the task of indoctrination the PLA also rejected the assumption, prevalent in Western countries, that to change an individual's attitudes and behavior is fundamentally a question of transforming his intellectual judgments by means of rational arguments. In contrast, the pedagogy employed by the PLA emphasized the technique of isolating the individual soldier socially and psychologically, virtually denying him the possibility of close, informal relations with others or participation in a small group *except* within the prescribed political framework. A number of organizational devices, described later in the study, were used for this purpose.

If an individual soldier did not fit himself into the inner life of the authorized small group, he was left isolated and lonely, for the PLA system ruled out any other safe possibility of close human relationships. It was also very difficult if the individual soldier *preferred* to lead a lonely existence "outside" the authorized group. For, as a soldier, he could not easily lead a retiring, private life. Moreover, he was likely to be quickly impressed by the fact that his own physical welfare and survival demanded cooperation with fellow unit members. The PLA system also made it unpleasant and dangerous for him not to participate actively in the prescribed ways of the group. Any effort to limit himself to a purely formal, minimal relationship with the group aroused suspicion and the danger of being stigmatized as a political "reactionary." He found himself watched more closely; the slightest "error" on his part could be reported and might make him the subject for criticism or disciplinary action.

The political organization within the PLA did not usually allow individual soldiers to assume a neutral or detached view toward its teachings. The revolutionary fervor of the older Chinese Communists lent a missionary flavor to their indoctrination efforts. They applied themselves assiduously to the "conversion" and spiritual transformation of noncommunist soldiers. In this respect, too, the political organization in the PLA differed from its counterpart in the Soviet Army. Chinese Communist leaders have placed greater emphasis on securing the psychological transformation of individuals than did Soviet leaders, who have never developed systematic methods of "thought reform." [10] Indoctrination in the PLA was more vital and dynamic than seems generally to have been the case in the Soviet Army of recent years. Indoctrination activities in small groups were seldom pursued in the mechanical fashion attributed to many political leaders in the Soviet Army simply in order to fulfill formal requirements. Consequently the pressure on the men in the PLA to transform themselves was considerable.

One of the broader aims of Chinese Communist leaders was to teach the masses to give political expression of the desired kind to their aspirations and discontent. To this end people were encouraged to give up private philosophies and politically passive or antithetical religions. This objective was reflected within the army in the political organization's insistent demand that the men interpret everything of interest to them in political terms. Political leaders encouraged and taught them to do so by providing them with a few simple political slogans and doctrines that not only explained any difficulty encountered but also ostensibly provided the guidepost to action in any contingency. To get along well within his unit, the individual soldier had to learn and correctly utilize the special political language with which all problems—even those which did not seem to be political in character—were discussed.

Among the chief devices employed for indoctrination and assimilation were the "mutual criticism" and "self-criticism" meetings held frequently within squads, platoons, and companies. These institutions have of course a long and established tradition in the history of Bolshevism.[11] More intriguing is the fact that a closely analogous practice of *"schuld capitel"* (joint confession) was employed by Augustinian monks in the fifteenth century as a means of indoctrinating new members.[12] Our materials suggest that criticism meetings had a vitality and impact in the PLA apparently lacking in much of the experience of the Soviet Army, and that they contributed to indoctrination in a number of ways.

Essential to the operation of criticism meetings was the pervasive system of surveillance of the men's behavior and attitudes. Criticism meetings would indeed lose much of their effectiveness if the men felt that they could get away with infractions without being observed. The anxiety caused by the possibility of later being criticized in a group meeting and thereby getting into trouble exercised a profound influence over the men's behavior.

Other devices were also employed for shaping the character of small group relations and raising morale and performance. Wide use was made of the practice of written group oaths and individual oaths. Before an important combat operation, for example, the members of each squad bound themselves by signing a joint oath to fight bravely in the forthcoming action. The purpose of this device was ostensibly to promote mutual identification within the small combat group and to commit an individual soldier, before his fellow soldiers, to fight bravely with them in the coming engagement. Various techniques were utilized to develop pride within the unit and to stimulate competition between different units.

Egalitarianism and Voluntarism

PLA authorities discarded many traditional military practices in an effort to create a "modern" army, one in which naked coercion would be minimized in favor of voluntary participation and cooperation of a type consonant with Chinese Communist ideology and teachings. The egalitarian spirit of Chinese revolutionary communism expressed itself in many different ways. Its leaders attempted to eliminate illiteracy and to equalize living conditions between cadres and ordinary soldiers. Leadership cadres were recruited from the ranks, and the features of an officer caste system were actively discouraged. Instead, efforts were made to "democratize" respect and comradely relations between cadres and ordinary soldiers. Chinese authorities translated the communist concept of "democratic centralism" into practice by arranging a form of popular participation in group decision-making and in the administration of the affairs of small military units. More generally, PLA leaders encouraged and at times insisted upon mass participation in official ideology and rituals, and they attempted to develop widespread understanding of PLA war aims.

Much has been written in the past about provisions in the PLA for the participation of rank-and-file soldiers in the discussion, solution, and administration of various problems connected with everyday life. While some accounts are naive in implying that the PLA strove for, or achieved democratic perfection in this respect, other accounts perhaps unduly minimize the advantages that PLA leaders derived from these egalitarian practices. Thus it is a general practice of Chinese Communists to involve the masses in decision-making and decision-implementing processes in order to expedite their control over them.[13] While the full impact of these practices on soldiers cannot be easily evaluated, nonetheless it is obvious from the recollections of the prisoners interviewed that these practices powerfully attracted many new soldiers. They were encouraged as a result to identify with, and participate in, the type of group life offered them.

It was a new and gratifying experience for many Chinese soldiers that a political regime should value their "spiritual" participation in political and national life. Not surprisingly, many new soldiers in the PLA had felt flattered and attracted by the persistent efforts to obtain their participation in the ideology, rituals, and programs of the new regime. Chinese communism provided—indeed it insisted upon—the same secular religion for the masses as for the elite; in this sense, it did seem genuinely to democratize political and spiritual values.

The abolition of ranks in favor of calling officers by their job titles (for example, "company commander," "platoon leader") did not do away entirely with a system of privileges associated with status differences, but it did help to soften the hierarchical stratification of relationships within units. Working to the same end was the establishment of a common uniform,* the practice of addressing the men in polite language, the abolition of extreme forms of discipline and military courtesy, the encouragement of comradely relations between leaders and men, and the avoidance of gross disparities in food according to rank or status.

Finally, career opportunities were plentiful for those who qualified. While political acceptability was a prerequisite for advancement in the army, the recruitment of both Party members and military cadres took place on a large scale within the rank and file. The internal social structure within the PLA, therefore, was not frozen but was characterized by ample opportunities for advancement.

The Disciplinary System. In its disciplinary practices the PLA made a concerted effort to eliminate arbitrary, discriminatory, and sadistic features in favor of a more rationally conceived system. Punishment was utilized for broader pedagogical ends. Beatings and abuse were officially forbidden, and a serious effort was made by the political officers to force military cadres to conform to the desired model of leader-men relations in this respect. More than one prisoner among those who had seen service earlier in the Nationalist Army said that what he liked best about the PLA was that beatings were abolished. An effective channel for hearing the men's complaints against cadres existed in practically all of the many units sampled in this study.

---

* In Korea certain minor differences in uniform were noted which served to distinguish soldiers of different grades, but insignia of rank were not worn. As a matter of fact, according to prisoners interviewed, one could not definitely know a higher leader's rank except by memorizing it.

Especially under garrison conditions was a mild official attitude shown toward most infractions. The preference for correcting and persuading, and the willingness either to "forgive" initial offenses or to be satisfied with issuing reprimands and warnings was also a noteworthy contrast to the severity of the Soviet system. "Public shaming" of offenders at group criticism meetings—not merely of ordinary soldiers but also of Party members—played an important role in the PLA disciplinary and pedagogical system, again seemingly to a somewhat greater extent than in the Soviet system.

The determination of punishments was carefully controlled by the political organization. There is evidence of standardization and differentiation of penalties, hierarchical review of determinations, and bureaucratic cautions against imposing unwarranted and mistaken punishments.

As in the Soviet Army the surveillance and disciplinary system was, if anything, more severe upon cadres and Party members than on rank-and-file soldiers. Reduction in rank and temporary loss of Party membership appeared to be a frequent penalty. But it is noteworthy that offenders subjected to such penalties were permitted to "work their passage back" and to resume progress in their careers.

The Awards System. The awards system was designed and administered with some ingenuity with a view of increasing group solidarity and motivation. Egalitarian principles and practices of status differentiation were, in fact, rather effectively combined. The underlying purpose seemed to be to permit a very wide distribution of decorations while retaining, in the complex hierarchy of the awards, a basis for competition and status differentiation.

The awards system combined appeals to honor with material rewards. It tied the soldier's performance with the welfare and social position of his family back home.

There was a single awards system and awards procedure for cadres and men, for Party and non-Party soldiers. While this minimized the possibility that discrimination would be felt, it did not prevent the awards system from having its greatest motivational impact upon the hard core political-military cadres who play such an important role in the PLA system of leadership and control.

Social Prestige of the Soldierly Profession. "You do not make good iron into a nail; you do not make a good man into a soldier." This

Chinese saying conveys the traditional disrepute in which soldiering was held. The negative attitude toward military service in pre-Communist China was reflected by the extent to which conscription practices were dominated by graft, bribery, and influence as well as outright coercion. To win peasants to the revolutionary army, Chinese Communist leaders have attempted since the earliest days of their army to place relations between armed forces and the civilian population on a new basis and to raise the prestige of the soldierly profession. Forcible conscription was replaced, though not entirely, by a system of obtaining "volunteers" which relied upon a combination of persuasion, propaganda, and organized social pressure. (On the other hand, our interviews with soldiers recently conscripted into the army suggested that after intervening in Korea PLA authorities relied more on coercion than persuasion to obtain recruits.) Preferential economic treatment was given to families who provided recruits. In addition, efforts were made to make it appear an honor to join the army. The "volunteer" was often given a feast by his whole village, decorated with a banner, and given a colorful farewell parade. Quotas were set for each local district and it was left to the local leaders to encourage "volunteering." When not under the stress of a military campaign, the political authorities were quite patient in recruiting and might invest several weeks in propaganda and in manipulating social pressure in order to encourage the required number to "volunteer."

Even though he was frequently tricked or cajoled in one way or another into the army, the recruit was officially regarded as a volunteer and treated as such by the army. The reception he received in arriving at military camp was calculated to demonstrate the prestige of the service and the friendliness that awaited him in the army.

As guerrilla forces the Chinese Communists were dependent upon the positive cooperation and support of the civilian population. The need to place troop relationships with civilians on a correct, friendly basis was, therefore, obvious from the first. "Unity of the Army and the People" was a watchword. PLA authorities tried in many different ways to change the traditionally negative image of the soldier into that of a "friend of the people." Soldiers were ordered to be helpful and correct in dealings with the population. Their contacts with civilians were closely regulated and controlled; a special subsection in the political organization was charged with carrying out all necessary dealings between the army and the civil populace and with promoting good relations.

The importance to the PLA of placing soldier-civilian relationships upon a positive basis cannot be overemphasized. Our interviews indicate that this was one of the major tasks of indoctrination—and one of the leading disciplinary problems within their units.

By raising the prestige of the soldierly profession the PLA hoped to enhance the self-respect of the soldier, thereby providing an additional basis for group formation and positive morale.

Ethnically Homogeneous Units. The task of developing cohesive ties within small units was complicated by the many dialects of the Chinese language and by the variety of subcultures and regional differences within the broad expanse of the country. To meet this problem the PLA, as well as the Chinese Nationalist Army, attempted to create units with a homogeneous ethnic composition insofar as possible.

The traditional procedure of the Chinese Communist Army has been to organize men recruited from one village into a single company, several companies from a community into a battalion, battalions into regiments, and so on, until the web of composition within a large PLA formation can be said to center upon the villages of China, with its threads entwining the higher regional governments until finally a major geographical area of China has been encompassed.[14]

Efforts have also been made to employ PLA formations as integral units in military operations. During the earlier campaigns in China it was PLA policy to withdraw entire divisions from combat when their strength was depleted and to replace them with fresh units. Whenever possible, the entire unit was returned to its home province for replacement and recuitment, thus maintaining its ethnic homogeneity. This system of replacement was preferred over the more conventional method of an army-wide replacement and training command. Under the PLA plan, the manpower potential of any one province was ticketed for the army initially formed within its boundaries.

While this system reduced flexibility of organization and operation to some extent, it had the advantage of maintaining units of homogeneous ethnic composition. It was probably true that the individual Chinese soldier fought better when serving with men from his native area.

The extent to which developments in the final phase of the Chinese civil war and the Korean campaign forced PLA leaders to modify this policy could not be determined in the present investigation. In our interviews we did not attempt to question respondents directly on this point and only several of our respondents volunteered information on the matter. The solidarity of relations within combat units evidently suffered when ethnic elements were mixed within any given unit. According to one private whom we interviewed, the recruits added to his unit shortly before it was sent to Korea in early spring, 1951, were Manchurians; they could not understand the company political officer who came from South China and spoke with an unfamiliar pronunciation. This acted as a severe barrier to the development of close comradely relations. This private reported that whereas the veterans and Party men in his unit (presumably all from South China) liked the political officer and conversed with him intimately, the new recruits from Manchuria developed a dislike of him.

Provision for Material Needs. PLA authorities attached considerable importance to assuring the individual soldier his basic living needs as a means of getting him to accept their system and its demands. PLA leaders had learned from the failure of Chinese Nationalist military leaders in this respect. Chinese Communist troops were paid not in money, which inflationary pressures made relatively worthless, but in an adequate daily living standard supplemented by occasional goods which added something to creature comforts. Also, the "squeeze" which had been prevalent in the CNA, and the habit of stealing from farmers were discouraged. From an early period in their revolutionary warfare Chinese Communist leaders had learned that manpower and logistics must be kept in balance, that more men should not be kept under arms than can be reasonably well-fed and clothed. In periods of inaction or need, they put their soldiers to work raising their own food. More than one Chinese captive we interviewed remarked that what he liked most about the PLA was that he could fill his belly full.

Authoritative Interpretations. It is evident from our interviews that political officers at the company level had the responsibility for coping with the negative impact of adverse events and conditions upon unit morale. They did this by structuring and guiding the interpretations which the men placed upon experiences of this kind by offering them authoritative explanations and forecasts. Typically, a political officer offered his own interpretation of events as a model for the men to accept and make their own. Other Party members in the unit could be relied upon to accept his interpretation, to elaborate and reinforce it so that it quickly took on the character of a shared group interpretation. The interpretations sponsored by the political officer were designed, of course, to preserve group morale under the impact of adverse conditions. The object of his analyses of the situation and his forecasts was to structure the expectations and demands of the men under him in ways that would continue to bind them to the group and make them willing to endure sacrifices and carry out additional tasks imposed upon them.

Members of a hard-pressed combat group in any army need authoritative interpretations and reassurances from their leaders to enable them to adjust more readily to difficulties and to maintain an adequate level of performance. In the PLA it was the task of the company political officer to provide the men with authoritative, morale-maintaining communications of different kinds. They were assured that the difficulties the unit was encountering were known to higher authorities, and that their leaders were doing everything possible to improve matters. When the unit was under severe pressure that threatened to undermine its cohesion, the political officer tried to prevent panic and tendencies toward disintegration by seeing to it that they were given clear and relevant tasks. If necessary, he made it clear that members of the unit, including its leaders at any level, would be ruthlessly disciplined if through selfish action or incompetence they endangered the safety and welfare of the rest of the group. He offered them hope that things would change for the better, and assurances that the prospects for military success and ultimate victory remained good.

PLA combat propaganda and information to the troops about war developments relied largely on oral, informal, face-to-face communication. Although ostensibly directed to all soldiers, the real objective of combat propaganda was often that of maintaining the morale of the political "hard core" in each unit whose job it was to direct and control demoralized rank-and-file soldiers. In adverse circumstances combat propaganda often had a modest function; it provided versions of reality and rationalizations that would hopefully enable the men to accept the demands imposed upon them more willingly.

To the extent that it was successful in these respects, combat propaganda reduced the necessity for combat enforcement by direct means.

We have seen now the norms and standards PLA authorities applied in attempting to mold the men into the kinds of soldiers and small groups the Chinese Communist military model called for. And we have reviewed quickly the policies and practices employed to this end. It remains now to sketch the organizational doctrine and structure within which these activities took place.

ORGANIZATIONAL STRUCTURE AND DOCTRINE

The prototype of communist military organization emerged in the early years of the Bolshevik revolution. This has been a dynamic model, for on numerous occasions since 1917 Soviet leaders have changed some features of the political organization within their armed forces in response to shifting circumstances and pressures, and in an effort to learn from earlier experience. The history of the Soviet Army in this respect, therefore, has provided a rich body of experience; several variants of the political commissar system have been available for leaders of communist movements in other countries to choose from in developing an organization model for their own armed forces.[15]

It is an irony of history that the Soviet political commissar system was introduced into China not by the Chinese Communists but rather by Chiang Kai-shek, who had become familiar with it while in Moscow in the early twenties. In January 1923 Sun Yat-sen and the Soviet Union came to an agreement regarding the principles and conditions under which Russia and the Communist International were to aid the Chinese revolutionary effort to achieve national unification. A number of Soviet political and military advisers were then sent to China. The Kuomintang (KMT) was reorganized and membership in it was extended to individual Chinese Communists who were willing to accept its principles and discipline. The KMT established the Whampoa Military Academy, and General Chiang Kai-shek was made its director. (Chou En-lai was at one time the chief political commissar of the Academy.) Soviet methods were utilized in officer training, with the help of Russian advisers. In 1926, Kuomintang "party representatives" were attached to units of the KMT National Revolutionary Army participating in the "Northern Expedition," under Chiang Kai-shek's command, to destroy the power of the warlords in the North. As Chalmers Johnson has noted, the Chinese Communists themselves claimed (during the united front period of World War II) that their political commissars dated from this early KMT practice.[16]

From an early stage, the Chinese Communist version of the political commissar system differed somewhat in concept, functions, and perhaps effectiveness from the Soviet model. Part of the explanation for this undoubtedly may be traced to the fact that the historical-revolutionary setting differed in Russia and in China. In organizing revolutionary armies, therefore, the leaders of the communist movements in these two countries were confronted with different problems and had available to them different resources for this purpose. We shall return to this interesting comparison in Chapter 6.

At the time of the Korean War there was superimposed on the hierarchical military organization of the PLA, and in fact intertwined with it, a complex political apparatus comprised of five semiautonomous but interrelated agencies. Within the divisional military staff organization there were *Political Departments* (or offices) at each echelon down to and including regimental level. Each of these Political Departments was subdivided into five sections: Organization, Education and Propaganda, Political Defense or Surveillance, Youth Instruction, and Popular Movement. The hierarchy of Political Departments culminated at PLA General Headquarters in the Political Office of the General Political Bureau.[17] (In Political Departments at echelons above divisional level, a Liaison and Labor section was added.)

The *Political Defense* sections of the Political Departments, entrusted with special surveillance and security functions, should probably be singled out as one of the semiautonomous components of the political apparatus. While Political Departments were not established lower than regimental level, personnel of the regimental Political Defense sections operated at battalion and company levels. For this reason, as well as because of the nature of their work, it is reasonable to regard the Political Defense sections as one of the agencies having a semiautonomous character.

At each echelon of command, down to and including company level, there was a *political co-commander* (or commissar), whose formal job title was variously phrased. He shared joint responsibility for the unit at every level with its military commander. Since these political commissars had their own channel of command and communication, there was in effect established within the PLA a dual system of authority.* (We shall examine the nature and workings of this dual command system in some detail in Chapter 6.)

In addition to the Political Departments within the regular military staff organization and the political co-commanders at every echelon, separate *Party Committees* were established "outside" but parallel to the organizational structure of the Army.†

Finally, *Communist Youth Association Branches* were organized by the head of each Political Department at division and regimental levels, and by the political commissars at battalion and company levels. These Youth Association Branches included those soldiers in the eighteen to twenty-four year age bracket who were considered to be qualified as candidates for membership in the Communist Party. They were indoctrinated by the staff of the Political Departments and were considered auxiliaries of the Party.

There was some overlapping of membership in these five agencies. The political commander (or commissar) of each military formation was usually also the secretary (head) of the Party Committee at that echelon. The assistant political commander of a formation was usually also the head of the staff Political Department (or Office) at that echelon. This intricate meshing of the different components of the overall political organization is conveyed in Chart 1: "The Political Organization of a PLA Division," which was reconstructed from our interviews with cadres.

---

* In this respect the PLA reflected the dual command practice followed in the Soviet Army at an earlier period in its history rather than in recent times, during which unit political officers were technically subordinate to the military commander and had the title, "deputy commander for political affairs." See Dicks, Shils, and Dinerstein, *Service Conditions and Morale,* p. 285; Brzezinski, "Party Controls in the Soviet Army," pp. 565–68, 572.

† The existence of a Party organization separate from but parallel with the organizational lines of management was not confined to the PLA but characterized Chinese Communist organizational practice as a whole. (See, for example, H. F. Schurmann, "Organizational Principles of the Chinese Communists," pp. 53–54.) And, moreover, this is not a distinctively Chinese Communist practice but has been utilized by Soviet and other communists as well.

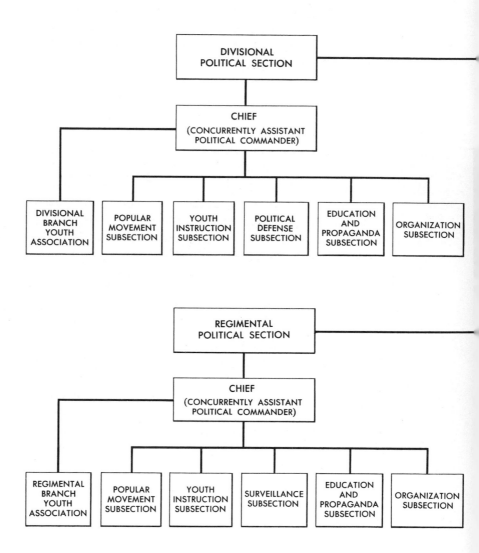

CHART 1

The Political Organization of a PLA Division

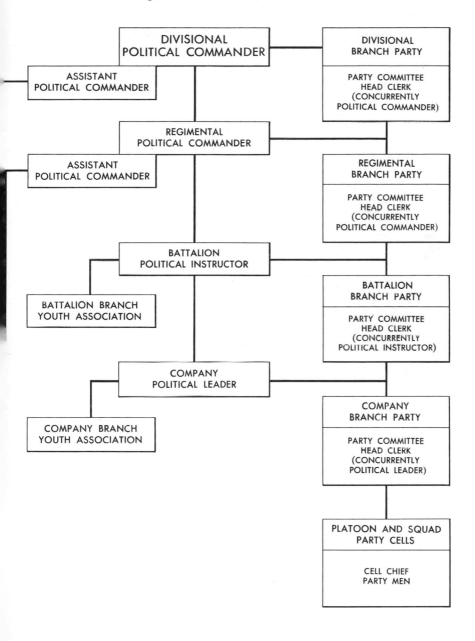

DIVISIONAL
POLITICAL COMMANDER

ASSISTANT
POLITICAL COMMANDER

DIVISIONAL
BRANCH PARTY

PARTY COMMITTEE
HEAD CLERK
(CONCURRENTLY
POLITICAL COMMANDER)

REGIMENTAL
POLITICAL COMMANDER

ASSISTANT
POLITICAL COMMANDER

REGIMENTAL
BRANCH PARTY

PARTY COMMITTEE
HEAD CLERK
(CONCURRENTLY
POLITICAL COMMANDER)

BATTALION
POLITICAL INSTRUCTOR

BATTALION BRANCH
YOUTH ASSOCIATION

BATTALION
BRANCH PARTY

PARTY COMMITTEE
HEAD CLERK
(CONCURRENTLY
POLITICAL INSTRUCTOR)

COMPANY
POLITICAL LEADER

COMPANY BRANCH
YOUTH ASSOCIATION

COMPANY
BRANCH PARTY

PARTY COMMITTEE
HEAD CLERK
(CONCURRENTLY
POLITICAL LEADER)

PLATOON AND SQUAD
PARTY CELLS

CELL CHIEF
PARTY MEN

It will be instructive to look more closely at the functions and intricate interrelationships of the different components of this political apparatus. A special word on the functions and organization of the Political Defense sections is desirable. Their general task was to ferret out "ideological reaction" and to guard against conspiracy, desertion, subversion, and sabotage. Since there was no Political Department at battalion and company levels, the Regimental Political Defense section designated special personnel to exercise its functions at battalion and company level.[18] These special political defense personnel apparently were not responsible for their special work to the battalion and company political officers; rather, they represented and evidently reported directly to the higher regimental echelon. In this fashion political defense work at battalion and company levels was given a certain autonomy. As a result, the dual relationship between the military commander and the political commissar tended to become a triangular relationship in some respects at battalion and company levels.

The presence and especially the identity of political defense personnel within the company were not publicized. Many of the privates interviewed seemed to be unaware of political defense activity within their unit; perhaps they could not distinguish it from other surveillance activities to which they were subjected. Even junior cadres did not have a clear or consistent picture of the scope of political defense surveillance within the company, which extended to Party personnel as well as non-Party leaders within their unit. Several respondents, including a battalion political officer, spoke of the "triangular" relationship and the mutual fear that existed between the military commander, the political officer, and the political defense agent. (This respondent added, however, that the authority of the unit Party Committee was nonetheless supreme.)

From corps (army) level downward there was, in addition to the Political Departments, a Party Committee at each echelon. The five to nine Party members who held leadership positions in the political and military apparatus at that level constituted the membership of the Party Committee. The company was the lowest echelon at which Party Committees were organized; at platoon and squad levels small Party cells were maintained under the aegis of the Company Party Committee.

A peculiar aspect of Party Committees was that, as distinct from the individuals comprising them and unlike the Political Departments, they were evidently not part of the formal organization of the PLA. Rather, they appeared to serve as auxiliary bodies with their own channel of communication. The Party Committee system was evidently intended to strengthen PLA military organization and to ensure that military action was taken in accord with Party policies. Party Committees not only reinforced the influence of political officers upon military commanders and mediated conflicts between them, these Committees also provided an additional channel of control and surveillance which operated on political officers and all political personnel as well as on military leaders. The Party Committee system appears to have had the more general function of ensuring that during the course of military service Party soldiers would not gradually weaken in their identification with the Party and in their support of its goals and demands. The existence of the Party Committee at each military echelon was a constant reminder to all Party soldiers serving in positions of political and military leadership that the Party remained supreme, and that its demands must be the yardstick by means of which the complex of military activities was ultimately to be guided and evaluated. The Party Committee system, therefore, was intended to guard against the development of any autonomous set of apolitical or counterrevolutionary military values and considerations, or of a professional military caste or doctrine.

Each Party Committee served as a deliberative agency for promoting solidarity and unity within the controlling group at that echelon. Secret meetings of the Committee provided an opportunity for ironing out differences, making necessary compromises, and reaching decisions on action to be taken. For example, if the unit military commander and the unit political officer disagreed over the implementation of an order from a higher echelon, a meeting of the Party Committee was held at which the matter was discussed and a decision rendered. If unable to reach agreement or if one party was dissatisfied with the decision, the matter could be referred to the superior authority.

The Party Committee also served as an organ through which the unit political officer, who usually headed the committee, directed the activities of Party men within that unit. After the political officer and the unit military commander agreed on an order, the former assembled leading Party men and assigned them specific tasks for helping to implement the order. Through the Committee meetings, then, the Party men who comprised the hard core cadre structure of the unit were readied to organize and lead rank-and-file soldiers in the accomplishment of the order.

The Party Committee also had the task of evaluating and disciplining Party personnel. At Regimental and higher levels, the appropriate Political Department would take part in this process. But at battalion and company levels where there was no Political Department, the Party Committee held frequent meetings of Party soldiers, giving them an opportunity for self-scrutiny, mutual criticism, and grading of each other's performance. Such meetings could also be used to counter lowering of standards and increased toleration of deficiencies. Finally, mention should be made of the fact that Party Committees were also used to conduct surveillance of military cadres, particularly when the latter were not Party members or when they had only recently entered the Party.

Thus far, we have discussed one important aspect of the PLA's organizational concept: a complex political apparatus comprised of five semiautonomous but interrelated components that were superimposed upon, and intertwined with the successive echelons of the standard military organization of the army. We turn now to another important feature of the organizational model that PLA authorities utilized at the time of the Korean War: the effort to create a military cadre structure within the entire PLA that would be politicized from the top to the bottom. More specifically, PLA authorities hoped to fill each position in the military cadre structure of the army with a well-indoctrinated, reliable member of the Party or Communist Youth Association. The goal was that every person occupying a position of leadership in the military command hierarchy down to and including the subsquad level, at which "groups" of three were organized, should be a Party member or have received at least some political indoctrination to which he had responded favorably. In this fashion the PLA goal of a unified political-military leadership was to be achieved at all levels, even down to squad and subsquad organizational levels.

In this respect the PLA model differed significantly from that of the Soviet Army. If the respective tables of organization of the Soviet Army and the PLA at the time are compared, the similarities between their political organizations might easily obscure the fact that a more thorough application of the political cadre principle was called for in the PLA. The tentacles of the political apparatus reached further down into its military units than was the case in the Soviet Army.

For a number of years the lowest echelon at which the Soviets stationed a political commissar was the battalion; in 1950, it was reported, the commissar system was extended to company level which was the same as in the PLA.[19] While both Soviet and Chinese political commissars utilized military cadres in their subunits (platoon and squad leaders) as part-time assistants for carrying out certain political duties, this practice was more thoroughly and systematically organized in the PLA. Thus, only in the PLA, as already noted, were all cadres, including the subsquad group leaders, supposed to be Party members or aspirants to Party membership. In contrast, while there was some politization of military leadership in the Soviet Army, it apparently fell far short of the goal and achievement of the PLA in this respect.[20]

Many of the prisoners we interviewed mentioned that the squads in their units were organized into three or four groups, each of which was composed of three or four men. One of these men was designated as the "group leader." The assistant squad leader usually led one of the groups. The other two group leaders were typically privates who, ideally, already had had some combat experience. The leader had relatively free command over the others in his group, though he himself was under the orders of the squad leader.

Curiously, few accounts of the military organization and performance of the Chinese Communist Army published in the West have taken note of the "3-by-3" organization of squads or recognized its full significance. An exception is the account published in 1953 by General James Van Fleet, who had assumed command in Korea of the Eighth Army in April 1951. Van Fleet noted that while most of the soldiers in the PLA were not Communists at all, yet even they were "great soldiers." This he attributed to the influence of the 3-by-3 organizational device:

The Red Chinese Army is divided at the very bottom into units of three men, with each assigned to watch the others and aware that they in turn are watching him. Even when one of them goes to the latrine, the other two follow. No soldier dares fail to obey orders or even complain. . . . The little teams of three, each man warily watching the others, begin the advance. . . . Yet—although terribly alone in the fight despite the two men at his side, made even more lonely by the doubt whether the two are there to help him or to spy on him—the Red soldier moves ever forward. . . .[21]

While this account oversimplifies the nature and workings of the groups of three within PLA squads, nonetheless it remains one of the few published accounts in the West calling attention to the importance of this organizational device within the PLA.

The origins of the Chinese Communist basic infantry squad organization of groups of three are obscure. In an article in *People's Daily,* October 28, 1960, General Liu Ya-lou credited Lin Piao with having propounded the 3-by-3 organizational device during the Liberation War. General Samuel B. Griffith, USMC (Ret.), has recalled that this method of organizing combat infantry squads was in effect in the Chinese Communist Army as early as 1937, when it came to the attention of Colonel (then Major) Evans Carlson, USMC, during the course of a six months' sojourn in North China with the Communists.[22] Whatever the precise circumstances of the origin of the 3-by-3 tactic and whether it represents a purely indigenous development or reflects borrowing from Western experience, this method of organizing the squads must have appealed to Chinese Communist leaders on several grounds. As General Liu Ya-lou noted, the 3-by-3 tactic facilitated command and control by the squad leader, and was also useful for employing small groups in quick actions with provision for mutual cover.

More generally, Chinese Communist basic infantry squad organization was without doubt also influenced by a desire to solve a long-standing problem of warfare that modern weapons have only exacerbated, namely the problem of getting everyone in combat units to fight. As early as the nineteenth century, Colonel Ardant du Picq of the French Army noted that the problem of troop morale had worsened with the increase in the destructive power of weapons, resulting in the courage to face these new weapons becoming more rare. Du Picq thought that the solution lay in mutual aid, in strengthening the organization of combat units:

Four brave men who do not know each other will not dare to attack a lion. Four less brave men, but knowing each other well, sure of their reliability and consequently of mutual aid, will attack resolutely. There is the science of the organization of armies in a nutshell.[23]

Major Carlson was so impressed with the efficacy of the 3-by-3 device that, according to Griffith, in 1942 he organized squads in his Second Raider Battalion this way, with a tenth man as squad leader. In the spring of 1943, Griffith reorganized the First Raider Battalion squads in the same way, adding a fourth man to each group. These subsquad groups in the Raider Battalions were called "Fire Teams." Members of the Fire Team worked, slept, and ate together; this structure developed an unusually strong group cohesion. The men sensed this and saw how effectively the system worked in combat.[24]

Many features of the revolutionary-egalitarian military model described in this chapter, including the practice of organizing combat squads into groups of 3, were taken over by Vo Nguyen Giap in organizing the Viet Minh People's Army which fought and finally defeated the French Army in Indochina.[25] The Viet Cong in South Vietnam are also using the 3-by-3 method of organizing combat squads.[26]

Noncommunist armies have also employed some variant of a political hard core system. It may be useful to contrast the PLA in this respect with the German Wehrmacht during the Nazi regime. The PLA made greater use of this concept of organization than did the German Nazis. Hitler inherited a small, but highly competent professional army, and attempted by various means to ensure loyalty as well as efficiency in using it as a nucleus for building a larger army. It has been estimated that the Nazi hard core in the German Wehrmacht as a whole during World War II "approximated about ten to fifteen percent of the total of enlisted men; the percentage was higher for noncommissioned officers and was very much higher among the junior officers." [27] While the Nazi hard core was numerically large, it was quite unevenly distributed within different kinds of units. In this respect there is a sharp contrast between the Nazi and PLA models. Nazi leaders evidently did not attempt to make systematic or exclusive use of the political hard core organizational device in the German Wehrmacht. Some units such as the elite Waffen SS divisions and paratroop divisions were given a larger Nazi hard core component than regular divisions of the Wehrmacht, so large in fact as to embrace at times almost the entire membership of these elite units. At the other extreme, in certain *Volksgrenadier* divisions, a Nazi hard core was almost entirely lacking. As in the PLA, the cohesion and military effectiveness of different types of units in the Wehrmacht was generally dependent upon the size of the hard core therein.

The Nazi military model differed from that of the PLA in other respects as well. Junior officers of the Wehrmacht were carefully selected, but their selection was on the basis of criteria other than Nazi Party membership and, moreover, it was not considered necessary to bring junior officers subsequently into the Party. Also, again in contrast with the PLA model, the Nazi leaders tolerated and relied upon an apolitical cadre. The all-important senior NCO's, who provided firm, competent leadership and "were everywhere appreciated as the most solid asset of the Wehrmacht," were mostly older veterans of the pre-Nazi German Army; they were mostly non-Nazi and apolitical, being tough military professionals in outlook and training.[28]

We have emphasized the fact that the PLA organizational model called for merging the entire military cadre structure, even down to squad level, into the Party and hence the political organization of the army. This fact is of central importance, as we shall see, for understanding the social organization and the morale-building system in its combat units, and for explaining the strengths and latent weaknesses of the PLA in Korea.

The use of communist personnel, insofar as possible, as leaders of platoons, squads, and subsquad groups was particularly useful for shaping group life along desired lines. The division of each PLA squad into three or four smaller groups ensured a greater tightness of control and surveillance over interpersonal relations. By extending political control and direction down to the group level, PLA authorities tried to ensure that comradeliness would take on a communist hue. Since every two or three ordinary soldiers were placed under the direction of a group leader who was, insofar as possible, either a Party adherent or in some stage of being recruited or indoctrinated for Party membership, there remained little opportunity for the development of autonomous comradely ties. And since recruitment of military cadres was closely paralleled by recruitment of the same soldiers into the Party, the PLA attempted to ensure that all soldiers exhibiting capacity for military leadership would eventually become well-indoctrinated adherents of the Party.

4 *The Role and Performance of Company Political Officers*

Experience has proved that the system of Party representatives must not be abolished. As the Party branch is organized on the company basis, the Party representative at the company level is particularly important. . . . Facts have proved that the better the company Party representative is, the better is the company. . . .

Mao Tse-tung

AN OVERVIEW

We have completed our description of the Chinese Communist military model and turn in the rest of this study to an examination of how well the official programmatic goals had in fact been achieved within the armies sent to Korea, and how well the morale system in these armies—the best in the entire PLA—performed under the stress of severe, prolonged combat in a foreign country. The attempt to provide answers to these questions requires us to depart from descriptive analysis and to venture into explanations of complex human behavior within the organizational system of the PLA. The answers we seek can be glimpsed and reconstructed only through the eyes and memories of soldiers who had become prisoners.

It is appropriate to begin our evaluation by focusing on the role and performance of company political officers. For, to the men in the unit, the company political officer was the symbol as well as the chief architect for achieving the military model we have described. It was his task to mold the unit and its members according to the officially prescribed model. He was given broad control over the means by which the character of the unit and its members could be shaped. Thus, he was directly or indirectly responsible for securing results in the following spheres: material welfare, medical care, assistance to soldiers' families; indoctrination and education, information and propaganda; promotion of comradeliness, cohesion, and positive morale; counseling on soldiers' service problems; processing of leave, furlough, and marriage applications; allocation of praise and blame, rewards and punishments; surveillance of the behavior of military leaders toward the men and of their conduct in military affairs; regulation of relations between unit members and civilian populations; protection of the unit from subversive influences, etc.

The enumeration of his responsibilities makes it obvious that the job of a company political officer was exceedingly demanding. He was asked to play a complex role in the life of the unit, one which combined a number of functions that could not be easily harmonized in practice.

Our materials suggest that the performance of company political officers in the PLA varied considerably from unit to unit. While the higher political organization defined requirements for indoctrination and standards for assimilation of new personnel, it did not at the same time provide the company political officer with a detailed blueprint of how to do his job in such a way as to ensure good results with the men. Indeed, the nature of the task was such that only general guidelines could be furnished the company political officer.

It was not surprising, therefore, to learn that company political officers differed widely in their popularity and success. Most of our respondents attributed difference in performance of company political officers to variations in their personal character. While this explanation undoubtedly has a certain validity, it is at best a half-truth; for few of the prisoners we interviewed were sufficiently detached and analytically minded to grasp the inherent difficulty of performing the many complex duties of a company political officer.

Nonetheless, it is useful to note the personal characteristics (as reconstructed from our interviews) that evidently did help a company political officer to win the allegiance of the men to the PLA system:

a mild manner in dealing with the men's shortcomings and in disciplining them; patience, gentleness, lenience, restraint, no cursing or physical abuse of men;
intelligence, education, wisdom;
fluency and eloquence as a speaker;
good-natured, friendly, affectionate manner;
an understanding, sympathetic, helpful attitude;

sincerity and earnestness;
honesty, reliability, correspondence between his words and deeds;
willingness to exert himself and sacrifice to help the men;
modesty.

Thirty-five of our sixty-one privates offered a favorable or mixed estimate of their company political officer's personal character. Twenty-four gave him a negative rating. (Two gave no information.) Success or failure as a political officer did not depend, of course, solely upon his personal qualities. The role a company political officer was supposed to play in his relations with soldiers in the unit was complex in its requirements. Higher authorities expected political officers to impose strict requirements upon the men but at the same time to enforce these demands in a patient, kindly manner. Not all political officers were able to adhere consistently to the method of patient persuasion that the PLA system of instruction called for. They often resorted to harsher methods of dealing with the men's shortcomings.

The method of criticizing their defects was perhaps the leading factor alienating many soldiers from their company political officer and dissipating the goodwill that other aspects of his performance were able to create. Thus, while our sixty-one privates conceded almost unanimously that their company political officers had been ready to praise them when they did their tasks well, their satisfaction on this score was counterbalanced in most cases by the political officer's persistent and nagging criticism of their inadequacies. This factor also evidently outweighed the widespread appreciation felt for other aspects of his performance. Thus, as Table 1 indicates, the men drew sharp distinctions in assessing the political officers' performance of different tasks. It should be kept in mind that in this table, as in others presented later, quantitative tabulations are offered merely to provide a context for discussion and analysis; in and of themselves these numerical characterizations do not purport to be "representative" of the PLA as a whole or in part.

The necessity to criticize the men for their shortcomings easily conflicted in practice with the political officer's responsibility for cultivating comradely relations with them. There were other conflicting elements in the complex role which the company political officer was

TABLE 1

SUMMARY OF SIXTY-ONE PLA PRIVATES' RATINGS OF
COMPANY POLITICAL OFFICER (C.P.O.)

	Favor-able	Mixed	Negative	No answer
C.P.O.'s praise and rewards for men's good deeds	}59 a{		2	
C.P.O.'s handling of men's complaints against military officers	48	5	6	2
Adequacy of material care provided by C.P.O.	33	11	13	4
C.P.O.'s handling of welfare problems and consultation	7	35	19	
C.P.O.'s personal character	}35{		24	2
Overall orientation to C.P.O. and unit group life	19	7	35	

ᵃ On two ratings of the company political officer's performance our materials did not enable us to distinguish reliably between "favorable" and "mixed" ratings; hence, we have combined the two different kinds of responses.

enjoined to play. In his person, he was supposed to provide the men with a channel for consultation on service problems and a source for consolation with respect to deprivations inherent in military service. In practice political officers often gave a lower priority to their responsibility for consoling the men than to their pedagogical task. When the men in his unit came to talk over service problems with him, the political officer often succumbed to the temptation to seize the opportunity to lecture them and to encourage them to repress unsatisfied needs. As a result the channel for consultation and consolation on service problems which the political officer was supposed to provide tended to fall into disuse.

Circumstances of military life beyond his control hampered the political officer's effort to achieve good results with the men. He was seriously embarrassed, for example, by being linked in the men's eyes with official policies on matters of leave, marriage, detachment from the service, etc., which in many cases did not satisfy minimum human needs. Similarly, on many occasions the company political officer had little choice but to impose unreasonable demands on the men and to enforce them. In situations of prolonged hardship, moreover, he often succumbed to the temptation to utilize deceptive propaganda and other shortsighted practices to encourage the men and to secure their compliance, thereby risking loss of their confidence and friendship.

In order to better mold the men to fit the PLA model the company political officer should have been able to identify to some extent with them, to keep their confidences when they brought service problems to him for consultation and, finally, to exercise a type of leadership which was to some degree autonomous of the demands of higher authorities. But the PLA system tended to deny him these possibilities by insisting that he identify completely with the organization and its goals.

Nonetheless, as long as the organizational demands of higher PLA authorities were not too severe and conditions of life and combat not too unfavorable, the fact that the company political officer was essentially the faithful and inexorable instrument of the organization was not plainly evident to the men. They could still believe, with a belief fortified by hope, that the political officer was indeed benevolent, as in fact he often was or at least pretended to be. They could still count upon his human sympathies to work on their behalf independently to some extent of the demands of the organization. A positive relationship to the company political officer often did exist even under difficult conditions, if he were skillful in playing his role. The men expressed their gratitude to him for the various indulgences he provided by obeying orders willingly and by cooperating in the tasks of the unit. Moreover, when deprivations had to be endured, they tended to respond more readily to his exhortations to put up with the difficulties and to carry on.

ORIENTATION OF PRIVATES

In the PLA a soldier's attitude toward his company political officer was generally a reliable indicator of the degree of his assimilation into the unit. It was also a reflection of the soldier's overall orientation to the kind of group life that was officially sponsored. This was necessarily so because company political officers played a central role in defining, implementing, and enforcing the officially prescribed PLA model of small group life.

What, then, had been the overall orientation of privates toward their company political officer and to the kind of group life he attempted to superimpose on their unit? We are not concerned here with the question of whether the orientation and adjustment of the sixty-one privates interviewed on this score was broadly representative of the situation in the PLA as a whole. Rather, we wish to compare their overall adjustments with their reactions to specific features of the PLA system and to different aspects of the political officer's behavior toward them.

The entire interview with each private was taken into account in arriving at an impressionistic judgment of what his overall attitude had been toward his company political officer and the group life of the unit. In doing so we attempted to penetrate beyond the most recent attitudes a soldier had held in order to assess his adjustment to the PLA system at an earlier period before he encountered the worst hardships of Korean combat. It is particularly important in this connection to keep in mind that the PLA attempted to assimilate soldiers into the officially prescribed group life *before* a unit was subjected to the stress of combat. In this respect PLA practice differed from that of Soviet and American armies, in both of which group solidarity is achieved within units more typically *as a result* of exposure to combat.[1]

The full range of possible orientations toward the political officer, from very favorable to very negative, was encountered among the sixty-one privates interviewed. As noted in Table 1, thirty-five of these privates held a negative attitude in this respect; seven were of mixed orientation while the remaining nineteen could be said to have a positive overall orientation toward the political officer and to group life within the unit. This diversity of orientations among our sixty-one privates is useful in reconstructing the different ways in which soldiers with different backgrounds reacted to the performance of their company political officers.

PERSONAL CHARACTER

Company political officers generally made a favorable initial impression upon most new soldiers. This was neither surprising nor fortuitous since the political officers made a special effort at the beginning to establish a positive relationship with new soldiers. The men were attracted particularly by the friendliness and mildness which the political officer affected, and by the knowledge and verbal fluency he demonstrated.

In time, however, as the men came to know their political officer better, their initially favorable impression often wore thin. The "other side" of his character was demonstrated to the men when, sooner or later, circumstances repeatedly obliged him to implement less pleasant official duties. The manner in which a company political officer dealt with the men's shortcomings was often the most important factor in shaping deeper, more enduring judgments of his character. Initially positive impressions of him were revised frequently also because the men caught the political officer in flagrant or repeated inconsistencies, lies, and deceptions.

Despite the disillusionment that frequently set in, most privates interviewed on this point (thirty-five of sixty-one) had retained a favorable or mixed estimate of their political officer's personal character. In most instances a soldier's estimate of his political officer's character was consistent with the overall orientation which that soldier developed to the group life of the unit. However, it is noteworthy that thirteen soldiers retained a favorable or mixed judgment regarding the political officer's personal character despite the fact that they came to evaluate his overall performance negatively and to form a relatively poor adjustment to group life within the unit. In these instances at least, the "failure" of the political officer to win these soldiers to the PLA system cannot be attributed to flaws in his personal character; rather it appears to have stemmed primarily from the difficult circumstances under which he had to carry out his many tasks.

The comments of the respondents suggest that they had formed their judgment of the political officer's character largely with reference to three traits: whether he was kind, well-educated, and friendly. By far most frequently mentioned in a positive sense (twenty-six privates) was the political officer's knowledge, education, and fluency.* The trait depicted negatively most often (twenty privates) was the political officer's bad temper, abuse, and the severity of his criticism.

In view of the importance to the political officer of being able to benefit from the men's respect for learning, we will look more closely at their respective educational levels. There was apparently considerable variation in the amount of formal education received by political officers in the PLA. Almost all political officers at lower echelons possessed at least some formal education and were literate. Some had only a few years of elementary school; some had completed elementary school. Others had attended middle school and, in some cases, completed it.† It seems reasonable to assume that in addition to whatever formal education they had received most political officers had also spent considerable time in self-study and in indoctrination courses that had enhanced their "knowledge" and ability to speak fluently, at least on subjects covered in communist readings and lectures.

In contrast, the level of literacy and education among PLA privates was appreciably lower. Of the sixty-one privates interviewed, forty-two were either illiterate or had only a few years of elementary school. It is almost exclusively within this group of illiterate and semiliterate privates that we find those who volunteered favorable comment on the "knowledge and eloquence" of their company political officers. (Of the forty-two illiterate or semiliterate privates, twenty-six made such statements; whereas only four of the nineteen literate privates did so.)

COMRADELY RELATIONS

Through the institution and person of the company political officer, the PLA system attempted to provide for, and to utilize, the time-

* In his study of Malayan Communists, Lucian Pye also noted remnants of the traditional Chinese respect for the educated person. Better educated Malayan Communists (mostly of Chinese extraction) noted that their less well-educated associates readily turned to them for advice and informal leadership. And they assumed that because of their better education they were deserving of leadership. Pye, *Guerrilla Communism in Malaya* (Princeton: Princeton University Press, 1956), p. 154.

† Statements on educational levels of political officers are based on estimates volunteered not only by some of the sixty-one privates, but also by approximately twenty cadres, and two political officers.

honored Chinese respect for sentiments of male comradeship. The company political officer sponsored a type of group life within the unit that offered the men an opportunity for warm, comradely relations with respected, relatively well-educated persons. Being at the same time a person of great influence with a command of resources and access to the channels of the organization, the company political officer drew the men to his person, encouraging them to act on the view, basic to traditional Chinese culture, that "personal connections" are the primary force in human affairs.[2]

Within the company the political officer had major responsibility for achieving the PLA ideal of comradely interpersonal relations. Moreover, it was important that he should manage to establish a friendly relationship with the men for purposes of dealing with them successfully in other respects. It was often difficult to determine from our interviews whether a soldier had actually participated in the intimate, comradely relations sponsored within his unit by the company political officer. The ability to recall earlier experiences of this kind was sometimes clouded by traumatic experiences associated with prolonged combat and capture. We were able to formulate a reasonably firm judgment on this point for only about half of the sixty-one privates interviewed. Seventeen of the privates had evidently enjoyed very friendly relations with their company political officer; fourteen had felt pronounced unfriendliness toward him which, however, they usually had not openly manifested.[3]

The fact that a soldier had experienced comradely relations with his political officer evidently helped develop a favorable orientation to the officially sponsored group life of the unit. Not surprisingly, if a company political officer succeeded in establishing and maintaining informal, friendly relations with the men, he was more likely to obtain their cooperation and willing obedience. Several of our respondents may be quoted on this point:

The political officers had been promoted from the ranks and had a good understanding of the hardships of the men. They always chatted with ordinary men in the unit without any discrimination of rank and position, and shared the joys and sorrows of the men. So we became attached to them and obeyed their orders unconditionally.

[*private, former Nationalist*] *

* The references in brackets at the end of quotes to "former Nationalist," "former Nationalist master sergeant," etc., are, of course, to the Chinese Nationalist Army.

The political officer was a man of amiable character to some extent and was kind to the men. Getting along well with the men, he was never haughty; he was really a good guy. . . . As the political officer loved the men, they liked him, naturally. . . . The men in the unit respected and obeyed him as a natural result. [*private, former Nationalist*]

The majority of the men liked the political officers, listened to their indoctrination lectures, and observed their orders obediently—and in so doing, expressed their affection toward them.

[*private, former Nationalist master sergeant*]

We liked the chief political officer. He was an active lad. When he was not busy we talked and laughed with him all the time, but he never made a wry face. Furthermore, he used to visit every squad and came into contact with the privates. . . . [*private, former Nationalist*]

Some political officers, however, were apparently incapable of warm relations with the men or did not make a real effort to establish friendly contacts with them. They tended to impress the men as being "haughty" and "cold":

The political officer was skillful in lecturing. He made us accept his ideology naturally by his fluent speech. But I don't think he was a great man because, though he was somewhat skillful in oratory, he was a very cold man at other times.

[*private, former Nationalist assistant squad leader*]

Although many political officers were initially successful in establishing comradely ties with the men, they often destroyed this relationship eventually as a result of disciplining and imposing heavy burdens upon them. The most serious challenge to comradely ties arose from the men's resentment over the way in which the political officer exercised his criticism function. In all twenty-four cases in which a cross-comparison was possible, a direct correspondence was found between a private's satisfaction (or dissatisfaction) with the manner in which his political officer corrected shortcomings and the existence (or nonexistence) of comradely relations between them.

MATERIAL NEEDS

The maxim that an army fights on its stomach is universally applicable. Care for the material needs of the soldier is a standard obligation of the military leader. In the PLA this responsibility, too, fell under the purview of the political organization.*

* The PLA logistics system lies outside the scope of this report.

The task of providing for the daily necessities of a soldier's life was affected by special difficulties and considerations in China. The economic organization of the country, primitive to begin with, had been severely disrupted by prolonged international and civil war. Moreover, Chinese Communist leaders had laid down a political strategy that required military personnel to forego methods of requisitioning that would alienate the Chinese civilian population. At the same time, a rapidly expanding army had to be fed, clothed, and sheltered. PLA authorities had undertaken a formidable task in attempting to reorient the ideology and loyalties of large numbers of former Nationalist soldiers and new recruits, and to assimilate them into a revolutionary army. PLA leaders realized that achievement of this goal would be possible only if they could provide a sound material basis of existence within the armed forces. That they were reasonably successful in this regard in China is well known. Even after special difficulties encountered in Korea, thirty-three of our sixty-one privates interviewed on one of our questionnaires expressed satisfaction with the material care generally provided in their unit. Dissatisfaction was expressed by thirteen privates; the other eleven men stressed that the material care provided varied widely from time to time, or that it had shifted from good to bad after their unit came to Korea. (Four privates did not answer.)

Chiefly responsible for morale in the unit, the company political officer was necessarily interested in the material well-being of the troops. In this sphere his duties were less operational than supervisory. His main role was to verify that the men's daily needs were being met, to supervise and cooperate with those directly charged with meeting such needs, and to control all requisitioning from civilian populations. The political officer's ability to take an informal and sympathetic approach to the men's material needs and his tight supervision of supply channels is noteworthy:

The political personnel were interested in what we ate. They often asked the opinions of the men and gave instructions to the platoon or squad leaders concerning the preparation of food.   [*private*]

The political officer dealt with food matters for the men's welfare; for example, if the quantity of a meal was too small or the side-dish were too salty, the political officer gave a solution to it, often hearing the men's opinion. . . .   [*private, former Nationalist*]

In peacetime the political officer goes the round every day and comes in contact with the men, and asks them if there is any personal or family difficulty. And when it is possible for him to solve such problems he either does so himself or makes a request to high quarters for their disposition.

[private, former Nationalist platoon leader]

I worked in the section of provisions and supply, and I transacted [my affairs] according to the instructions of political officers, rather than the battalion commander. . . . I received searching inquiries [from the political officer] frequently; so he was a source of constant anxiety to me.

[private, veteran, clerk in supply section]

When a political officer took a solicitous attitude in matters concerning the men's daily needs it was likely to make a strong impression even upon disgruntled former Nationalist officers who had been demoted to private when incorporated into the PLA:

The political officer always looked after the comfort of the men. During a march if anyone became weak, the political officer himself carried the man's pack for him. *[private, former Nationalist corporal]*

If during some task the political officer knew that one of the men had to do something beyond his strength, he would at once help the soldier. If necessary, he made the Youth League or Party members help the men.

[private, former Nationalist platoon leader]

The political officer . . . sometimes consoled us morally. For instance, when a political officer saw a man in the unit shivering from the cold, he approached him and asked, "Are you cold, friend?" When he answered he was very cold, the political officer said he was cold too, and consoled him saying that if all of them overcame the difficulties they could live peacefully in the future.

[private, former Nationalist corporal]

The political officers always took care of the unit members. When the members feel ill, they ardently contrived to send them to a hospital or to bring some medicine to them. *[private, former Nationalist sergeant]*

By appearing as vigilant and solicitous champions of the men's welfare, company political officers of course hoped to create favorable predispositions toward themselves. Organizational devices were provided for channeling the expression of the men's gratitude:

The political officers were careful about the food problem lest soldiers should complain. When soldiers knew that their living condition was improved owing to our effort, they greeted and saluted us when they saw us on the road. The newly nominated political officer and the military staff member were very much interested in taking care of the soldiers so that they would say and think we were very good men. I was very happy when I heard of it [the men talking like this].

[veteran, assistant company commander]

The political and military officers strove in everything [in doing their best in matters of welfare] not to lose prestige with the men. . . . The veterans of the PLA and Party men expressed their gratitude for the staff's work at the examination or self-criticism forum.

[cultural instructor]

In such a case [when the political officers solved some of the men's problems], some of the Party men proposed to the men that we express our gratitude to the political officers for their kindness. The gratitude was delivered to the political officers through the squad leader or platoon leader. . . .   *[corporal, former Nationalist lieutenant]*

Whether a soldier credited or blamed the political officer was not simply a matter of whether he had received adequate food, clothing, and other amenities. Some political officers, while seeing to it that the men were provided for, failed to display a more personal concern for the men's needs. Accordingly, many soldiers gave the political officers no special credit, regarding the efforts they made as part of their job. Other political officers apparently were clumsy in attempting to capitalize upon their role as providers of daily necessities with the result that the men were repelled. This was true particularly in the case of some of the more sophisticated former Nationalist soldiers:

The political officer did his best. The PLA veterans and the ignorant among the recruits appreciated it. . . . But the educated among the former Chinese Nationalist soldiers and among the recruits didn't appreciate what he did. For the purpose of his exertion was not truly the well-being of the men but the attempt to attain his objectives by winning the men's friendship, taking advantage of their innocence in order at the same time to indoctrinate them in communist thought.

[captain, former Nationalist captain]

No one was grateful to the political officers because they did not make special efforts themselves but merely issued commands to a person in charge of cooking with regard to the preparation of meals . . . their efforts were only in words, telling us to conquer all difficulties.

[private, former Nationalist master sergeant]

The political officer pretended to take care of the men and he always exaggerated his efforts. In fact, he did nothing for them. Sometimes he gave them cigarettes but, except for this, he did nothing for the men.

[platoon leader, former Nationalist 2d lieutenant]

The political officers made considerable efforts [to improve the daily living condition of the men]. But the men did not feel grateful because those fellows also moved just as their superiors had ordered, and because the goods which they got for us were the commodities of the army for which they did not pay a cent from their own pockets.

[*private, former Nationalist sergeant*]

Only the older men in service and the communists were thankful for the political officers' efforts. Whenever they met the political officers they bowed politely and showed their respect.

[*private, former Nationalist*]

Scrutiny of supply and distribution channels by members of the political organization evidently succeeded in keeping illegal practices of a flagrant and noticeable kind to a minimum. In no case did the captured soldiers we interviewed report any such activity or criticize the political officers for favoring themselves. In fact, many former Nationalist soldiers contrasted lack of corruption in the PLA favorably with the "squeeze" that had been widely prevalent in the CNA. Differentials in food and clothing allowances undoubtedly existed, but were generally unnoticed by privates in combat units. There were such complaints, as we note below, with regard to other aspects of welfare. But, judging from our interviews, complaints about discriminatory treatment in matters of food, clothing, and medical care were at most only very minor irritants to morale.

On the other hand, several respondents reported that their political officer lost the trust of the men as a result of making false promises of improvement in the food situation:

As the political officer used to lie, the men did not trust him. . . . When the men were starving owing to lack of food, he deceived us saying that food would be supplied tomorrow. [*private*]

Our unit members did not believe the political officers at all because they calmly told lies that were disclosed a few days later. For example, when provisions were used up they said we would get much more from the rear in a few days and should bear with the shortage for the meantime. But we didn't receive them frequently even after a week. [*private*]

The willingness with which orders were accepted by many of the ordinary soldiers often seemed highly dependent upon whether they were well fed:

The political officers made efforts to improve our food condition. We thanked them for their affectionate efforts. Being fed with good and sufficient food, we were all satisfied. We endeavored to perform what they ordered.   [*private, former Nationalist assistant company commander*]

The political officer exerted himself to improve these problems [i. e., of daily life]. The company members welcomed his effort, were fond of him and paid homage to him. . . . Enlisted men, especially privates and privates first class, obeyed absolutely their superior's order, content to have a belly full of food and warm clothing, not thinking of personal problems.
[*private, former Nationalist corporal*]

In some cases, a political officer who already enjoyed a positive relation with the men was able to keep their favor despite temporary food shortages by demonstrating that he had done his best:

Political officers did their best to improve the daily life of the men. The men in the unit were grateful to them. They expressed their gratitude by executing strictly what the political officers ordered and didn't complain about anything. For instance, when the men felt hungry for want of food, they thought that, despite the efforts of the political officer, food could not be supplied sufficiently and they did not complain. Even though there were some who grumbled about it, other members soothed them saying that it was not good to be discontented, having no consideration of the efforts of the political officers.
[*private, a former Nationalist private who reported a very favorable attitude toward the political officer in his unit*]

But even a highly respected political officer could lose the allegiance of the men if food shortages continued too long:

The political officer made efforts to solve these problems [material care]. We thanked him for his efforts. His effort, however, did not take effect. Food was always lacking. The men appealed their hunger to him. When they filled their stomach with food they obeyed his order; when they felt hungry, they did not obey his order.   [*private, conscript*]

The importance of food as a means of raising the men's performance is seen also in its direct use in combat motivation. During the civil war, whenever circumstances permitted, the men were specially well fed just before an important combat. In Korea this practice was apparently restricted by shortages; most of the respondents stated that there had been no special treatment prior to an offensive or an important combat:

They didn't do anything special for us before our unit started an offensive [in Korea]. . . . However, when we were in China we were enter-

tained with plenty of good food and drink before we went into combat.
[*private*]

For two or three days before starting an offensive, we could eat meat and other good food. [*platoon leader*]

In sum, the political officers were generally effective in seeing to it that the men's principal material needs were met. When difficulties were encountered, the men's disappointment was generally tempered by the realization that the political officer was trying to solve the problem.

WELFARE PROBLEMS AND CONSULTATION

PLA leaders had to deal with a variety of personal and family concerns of soldiers. Cases of family hardship, apparently numerous, could have been easily disposed of if existing provisions for state aid were implemented promptly and uniformly. However, while these provisions were publicized and promises of aid were given to the men, our materials indicate that many PLA soldiers did not have the feeling that their families and dependents always received the assistance promised them.

Service conditions having to do with the possibility of furloughs, passes, marriage applications, and detachment from the service also offered PLA authorities considerable difficulty. For a variety of reasons they found it necessary to adopt rather severe policies on such matters. Prerequisites for more generous policies were often lacking: for example, transportation facilities, which would cut down the time a soldier on furlough was absent from the unit. In addition, PLA leaders seemed to feel that morale and efficiency required that many military personnel be isolated from existing family ties and discouraged from forming any new ties with civilians. Several privates commented on this:

The soldiers were aware that the political officers were afraid that if leaves were granted the men would come to hate army life when they met their parents and family. And in the case of impoverished homes, their parents and family would not let the soldier return to the army because they had no hands for farming. Thus, home leave would not only change the mental state of the person in question, but would undermine all the men of his unit. [*private, former Nationalist*]

The political officers worried that if members were given leave they would dislike the army more upon returning to it, having had a glimpse of society. Also, they worried that men given furloughs would not want to return to the restrained army life having tasted the freedom of home life. They feared that the spirit of the army would be weakened by families who harbored resentment against sending their young boy to the army again. So they hardly granted such requests. . . .

[*private, former Nationalist sergeant*]

Related to this was the concern that a more liberal leave policy would facilitate and increase desertion. Even under garrison conditions in China, desertion was apparently frequent enough to make granting of furloughs a risky matter and apparently many Nationalist soldiers taken prisoner during the civil war were inducted directly into the PLA and had not been permitted to return home since then.

Another major sore point was the absence of a specific, limited term of service. There were, moreover, few reasons for which a soldier might be discharged except for severe physical disability or old age. A man "volunteered" or was conscripted for the "duration." The Chinese civil war was not officially regarded as concluded when the decision to intervene with "volunteer" forces in Korea was made. Many of our respondents alluded to this problem in ways that suggested that the lack of a definite term of service was in many cases an important factor in low morale.[4]

The basic handicap of the company political officer in dealing with the men's welfare problems was that he had to work with policies which, except perhaps for aid to needy families, did not take into account minimum human needs. The severity of PLA welfare policies created disappointments and frustrations in the men that encouraged disaffection. It was difficult for the company political officer to prevent demoralization over such issues, since it was his job to process, and in most cases turn down, applications for leave, compassionate furloughs, permission to marry, retirement from the service, etc. As a result, he was directly implicated in the eyes of the men with the severe policies of the PLA on welfare matters.

Moreover, in processing their requests the company political officer obtained information on the men's desires for leave, marriage, etc., which he was tempted to utilize in exercising another of his functions, that of remolding the men's personalities. To the extent that he succumbed to this temptation, of course, his function as a consultant and spiritual adviser to the men was thereby seriously prejudiced. It did not take the men long to find out that the political officer utilized their requests as a means of informing himself on questions of morale and loyalty, and thereafter criticizing and disciplining them.

As a result, the service channel provided by the PLA for consultation and consolation on welfare problems of this kind quickly dried up. The men in the unit avoided bringing requests and welfare problems of this kind to the political officer's attention because they knew that it was both useless and dangerous to do so.* When a soldier did consult with his political officer on such a matter, he was likely to be subjected to detailed questioning and to be chided instead of being treated sympathetically. At worst, he might even become subject to increased surveillance and public criticism.

Our interviews impressively document the extent to which the channel for consultation on welfare matters fell into disuse for these reasons. Statements by a few of our respondents will suffice to illustrate what appears to have been an almost universal attitude:

When we consulted with the political officer on personal or family problems . . . he asked many questions and gave no facilities. And we were apt to be watched more strictly. So we did not take any problems to him.   [*cultural instructor*]

We never consulted with them, regardless of the problem, because even if we consulted with them no problem was solved sufficiently, and because if we did so we would be watched specially.
                                                    [*private, former Nationalist corporal*]

Because it was not only useless to take such problems to the political officer but this was apt to attract his attention, the men did not feel free to do so.   [*private, former Nationalist corporal*]

There were many problems that we did not feel free to take to the political officer. For example, the problem of marriage or vacation. During the term of service we could never be permitted to marry. They never granted leave of absence for fear of evasion of service. And they also criticized and blamed us; for these reasons we hesitated to consult them.
                                                                 [*private, former Nationalist*]

Only seven of sixty-one privates gave a positive rating to their political officer's performance of his welfare and consultation functions.

---

* However, the consultation channel frequently remained open for many privates with regard to problems of daily life within the unit—food, clothing, etc. —if not for welfare problems.

Men of the Chinese People's Militia attend a political training class.

Nineteen privates expressed a distinctly negative attitude, and the remaining thirty-five gave a mixed reaction on this point.

Exposed again is a major weakness inherent in PLA machinery for developing group cohesion and protecting morale. Political officers were assigned competing, contradictory tasks that were difficult to reconcile in practice. To deal sympathetically with the men's disappointments in these matters the political officer would have had to be a somewhat detached, confidential intermediary between the bureaucratic apparatus that dealt severely with welfare problems and the men who suffered thereby. But, as it was, the political officer was part of the apparatus which dealt severely with the men's welfare needs.

The political officer has been likened by some observers to the chaplain in the U.S. Armed Forces. But in this crucial respect, the parallel breaks down. There was no true counterpart in the PLA to a chaplain or Red Cross worker; nor was there the newspaper correspondent who writes about the men's hardships and publicizes their grievances. In the PLA there was no "outside" authority or channel to which the soldier might turn; there was only the organization.

Given the immutable severity of welfare policies, any sympathy displayed by the political officer tended to take the form of an effort to get the men to repress their desires and adopt a stoic attitude. Since this was the way in which his own welfare needs were generally handled by the political apparatus, the company political officer probably found it difficult to pamper the men or to concede that *non-Party* soldiers were entitled to more sympathetic treatment. Nor could he permit the implication that the PLA system was at fault in any way for not satisfying the individual's needs. In these circumstances the situation was likely to be defined by the political officer as offering him a useful pedagogical opportunity. Accordingly, he tended to identify persistent desires for leave, marriage, vacations, etc., as "private" matters which, if advanced too strongly or frequently by the men, indicated that they were still afflicted with "individualist" notions.[5] To change the personalities of soldiers in this respect was a major goal of political indoctrination. This required inculcation of new moral standards of an anti-individualistic character which required subordination of "private" claims.

The soldier who permitted himself to become homesick, to worry too much about his family, to entertain desires for marriage, to wish leave from his unit, etc., had indeed bad morale from the standpoint of the PLA and was, ultimately, a political risk. Conversely, the mark of good morale and political loyalty inevitably included a willingness to accept any deprivations implicit in the PLA's welfare policies. If the army could not satisfy personal needs of the individual, it was incumbent upon him to repress such needs. The following statements illustrate this pedagogical approach to the handling of welfare problems:

When the men took such problems [marriage, leave] to the political officer, they were severely reprimanded with these words: "You are not firm in ideology yet; you have not a strong will yet. In military life you must dismiss all worldly thoughts and devote yourself solely to military duties. You are worrying about your family because you are weak in military spirit, etc." Therefore the men were reluctant to take such problems to him.   [*private, former Nationalist*]

It was possible for the men to take their problems to the political officer, but they were not granted. Because the soldiers were supposed to have abandoned all worries and be faithful to military duty. If anyone took such problems often to the political officer, he was criticized without fail as having a "corrupt spirit," or "reactionary thoughts," etc. and no favor was granted.   [*private, former Nationalist*]

There were many problems of a personal character that the men did not feel free to take to the political officers; for example, asking leave of absence, marriage, going out, etc. They said: "If one would join in military service as a military man, one ought to give up all the worldly thoughts, and devote oneself to military service in order to become a good soldier. Nevertheless you are talking about your family situation, or you are going to marry. Thus, you are already rotten and have degenerated spiritually. Eventually you will be one who is ideologically depraved and destroys military discipline and regulations." So the men hesitated to take these problems to the political officer lest they should be blamed and attacked.   [*private, former Nationalist*]

If someone consulted with the political officer about worries concerning home, he would only have been scolded on the charge of counterrevolutionary thoughts.
[*private, former Nationalist sergeant who claimed his parents had been killed by the communists on the charge of being propertied persons*]

In a word, the practice of the PLA was to deny the legitimacy of personal needs which it could not satisfy, and to attempt to force the men to repress such needs.

COMPLAINTS AGAINST MILITARY LEADERS

The PLA placed considerable emphasis upon creating positive relations between military leaders and their men. In order to eliminate abusive practices associated with certain older military traditions and to obtain the type of leadership desired, explicit provision was made for hearing complaints against leaders. Political officers usually did not hesitate to warn or reprimand cadres within the company when the charges against them were justified. As a result the PLA code of conduct was impressed upon the cadres and the prestige of the company political officer was strengthened in the eyes of the men.

Our materials indicate that there was widespread satisfaction among ordinary privates with this aspect of the PLA system. Most of the privates (forty-eight of sixty-one) interviewed on this point gave their political officers positive ratings for keeping open the channel for receiving complaints and for demonstrating a real interest in protecting the men from the abuse of military leaders. However, while relations between military leaders and men were undoubtedly improved, this did not generally suffice to counterbalance other major dissatisfactions with the political officer and the PLA system.

The most frequent type of complaint made by the men against their military leaders appeared to be one of physical or strong verbal abuse.[6] In order to receive a sympathetic hearing from the political officer, the complaint could not be "trivial" or of a purely individual character not affecting the unit as a whole. Similarly, the complaint had to be based upon "authentic evidence." There is no evidence in our materials that the men deliberately abused the privilege of complaining against their military leaders. It may be taken for granted that the political officer was alert to such a possibility and tried to ensure against it. As one private observed: "We had first to present the complaint at the squad meeting and discuss it with caution before offering it to the higher officers." Another reason for a preliminary screening of complaints may have been the desire to place the burden for adjusting minor conflicts between leaders and men on the smaller unit and hopefully, thereby, to contribute to group cohesion at those levels. Several privates indicated that complaints against their platoon and squad leaders were always solved before they reached the company political officer. Another private indicated that the possibility of going to the political officer was used as a weapon over the head of a stubborn subunit leader:

When the words and deeds of a squad leader or a platoon leader were deficient, one of the members of the group gave him his advice. If the leader was obstinate, insisting that he was right, the man accused the leader to the political officer and made him judge the case. But if the leader recognized his own faults, and reformed his conduct, the man did not accuse him to the political officer.   [*private, former Nationalist*]

The channel provided for airing complaints, however, was apparently flexible enough to permit the company political officer to adjust to circumstances. For example, sometimes a complaint was taken directly to the political officer by a representative of the platoon or squad. The latter procedure, more confidential in nature, was favored in some units when an attempt was made to spare the accused military leader the shame of a public accusation.

Some of our respondents reported that the channel tended to be blocked when the subject of complaint was a higher cadre. More generally, our interviewees stated in a number of cases that it was "useless" to complain against the cadres, that the men seldom took advantage of the privilege, that only Party men and veterans could safely do so, and that the political officer might threaten a complainant and bring him under closer surveillance.

Most of the respondents were satisfied that complaints were not heard simply to enable the men to let off steam but were actually used by political officers to discipline military leaders and to improve conditions. Almost no one we interviewed held that public rebukes were administered to cadres by the political officers in a perfunctory manner simply for propaganda effect.

If he regarded the complaint as justified, the political officer might begin by admonishing the accused cadre member calmly, advising him to love his subordinates and to reform his behavior toward them. Thereupon the guilty cadre might publicly "apologize" at a group meeting. In cases of repeated misconduct, the political officer might decide to publicly rebuke the military leader or to report him to the battalion or regimental political officer. At this level it would be decided whether to give the accused leader an official reprimand, place him under disciplinary confinement, or, in extreme cases, to reduce him in position and dismiss him from his post.

TREATMENT OF INADEQUACIES

Chinese Communist authorities appreciated very much the fact that a way had to be found for correcting mistakes and inadequacies without alienating the men. This consideration undoubtedly motivated them to forbid military leaders to engage in the traditional practice of physically abusing and cursing the men. Our interviews furnish many indications that the PLA policy of "patient persuasion" had played an important role in winning over numerous rank-and-file soldiers. Many (seventeen) of the privates interviewed volunteered the information that they had been quite favorably impressed by the practice of no physical abuse or insults. The context of their remarks made it clear, too, that this had helped shape their overall orientation and adjustment to the PLA system:

Most of the men respected the political officers. They did not beat or curse at the men for any slight mistake but quietly explained things to them. So the men tried to execute any command from the political officers quickly. [*private, former Nationalist corporal*]

The political officers never struck the men or insulted them. . . . All men paid respect to the political officers of the company. They were so kind that the men obeyed them absolutely. . . . A majority of the men in the company preferred the political officer to the military commander of the company. The military commander often became angry and cursed them. Therefore all the men followed the political officer, excluding company commander from their warm relationship. [*private*]

That the policy of nonabuse was not more successful in winning over the soldiers was in large part due, as has already been suggested, to the fact that the preferred method of "patient persuasion" often degenerated into a form of criticism which alienated the men. For many of the privates, the experience of being repeatedly criticized by the political officer and publicly shamed in group meetings came in time to dominate their feelings toward the company political officer and to the group life within the unit. Initially favorable impressions of the political officer as a kindly, warm person were dissipated and often replaced by the strongly negative image of him as a "two-faced" person. While disenchantment with company political officers was widespread among the privates interviewed, it often took on a special flavor with former Nationalist soldiers, who professed to regard the practice of criticism in the PLA as worse than the physical abuse they had suffered in the CNA:

> The political officers said that no one would be beaten or cursed in the PLA but would be taught kindly. In practice, however, one was punished through self-criticism meetings which were many times more horrible than beatings and cursing. . . .
>
> [*private, former Nationalist master sergeant*]

> Though they did not beat nor insult the men . . . they always tortured us by political means. . . .   [*private, former Nationalist corporal*]

Discontent with the political officer's method of criticizing was expressed in various ways. Some soldiers described him as having an overly strict attitude that led him to criticize every trivial mistake. The severity of his criticism was felt to be out of proportion to the importance of the mistake. Some privates reacted most adversely to the harshness and frequency of his censure; they felt he had a fondness for faultfinding that bordered on the perverse. In this type of situation, the men "saw through" the egalitarian and fraternal pretensions of the political officer and began to adopt the practice of dissimulation as a means of adjusting to the system:

> The political officers always pretended to be kind, calling us "Comrade Chang" or "Comrade Lee". . . . They always motivated the men with honeyed words and criticized them even when the men made little mistakes. . . . As they always observed our conduct, we also pretended to be on good terms with them.   [*private, former Nationalist*]

> The political officer was very kind to all unit members in appearance, but he was like the man who is called "womanminded in appearance, demonminded at heart." So if some cases concerning ideological shortcomings occurred, he scolded, pursued, and attacked the offenders dreadfully. So I could not take him as a good man.
>
> [*private, former Nationalist captain*]

> They were very kind to privates outwardly but they were wolves inwardly.   [*private, former Nationalist lieutenant*]

> The majority of the men disliked them . . . when they wanted to make use of the men, they pretended kindness and talked pleasantly: "Did you take a meal satisfactorily?" and the like in order to please the men vainly. When political officers talked in such a manner, the men disliked them realizing that something was afoot. . . .
>
> [*private, former Nationalist master sergeant*]

If for one reason or another a political officer was unable to enter into comradely relations with some men in the unit, his criticism of their shortcomings was likely to be made ungraciously as well as received with resentment. In any case, it was evidently difficult for a political officer to cultivate for any length of time a comradely relationship with men who did not make quick progress in identifying with the goals and demands of the PLA. The political officer could not overlook their shortcomings indefinitely. Coupled with this was the highly annoying factor that the men's shortcomings could not be accepted as merely *human* limitations, since Party leaders within the PLA tended to interpret defects in performance as stemming from *ideological and political* deficiencies.

DEVELOPMENT OF "OUT-GROUP" CONSCIOUSNESS

Despite the best efforts of the company political officer to unify the men, the unit often divided into an "in-group" and an "out-group," particularly when he was unskillful in performing his complex role. This development evidently was widespread, having taken place in most of the PLA units we glimpsed through the eyes of our respondents. With this development the process of gradual assimilation of soldiers into the PLA system tended to slow up or halt. When the division of the unit into an in-group and an out-group became pronounced, it was often tacitly accepted by the political officer and other Party soldiers. The goal of indoctrinating soldiers into positive adherents of the PLA was then replaced by the more modest objective of fostering conformity and extracting at least a minimum performance of duties.

The in-group, of course, refers to those soldiers who identified with and participated actively in the officially prescribed pattern of group life within the unit. The out-group was in most cases only a nascent or potential group. It comprised those individual soldiers who remained poorly assimilated, and were more or less alienated from the ongoing, officially sanctioned group life of the unit. It was clear that of the sixty-one privates in our sample, forty-six had come to regard themselves as "outsiders" in their unit at some point well before their capture. Fourteen other privates had evidently remained identified with the officially sponsored in-group until the last.[7]

Except under unusual circumstances when the surveillance and control system within the unit weakened, discontented soldiers did not have elaborate or intimate relations with one another independent of the prescribed system of social behavior. To the extent that outsiders in a PLA unit communicated their private thoughts to one another, they had to do so covertly and with caution. The political hard core soldiers in a unit actively discouraged the development of any form of autonomous group life.

Under garrison conditions in China and during much of the eight month period of Korean operations under survey the PLA system of control and surveillance largely succeeded in preventing individuals who were outsiders within a unit from forming a group or clique of their own. But in most of the units about which we gained information the control system had not been able to prevent disaffected soldiers from at least recognizing each other as outsiders. Occasionally, however, surveillance mechanisms succeeded so well in forcing these men to simulate good morale that it had been difficult for one outsider to recognize another, that is, to realize that his own true thoughts and feelings were shared by other men in the unit.

When the PLA system of surveillance operated at this high a level of efficiency, as we suspect it did more frequently in training and under garrison conditions than in Korea, individual soldiers were permitted few opportunities on or off duty to arrive at a correct insight into each other's true feelings about the PLA.

In this fashion, at its best, the internal surveillance and control system achieved a virtual "atomization" of the discontented individual and forced him to conceal his existence. Even among our sample of sixty-one privates, whose units had been subjected to severe hardship in Korea, there were several who had not been aware that others in the unit had also shared their discontent:

> There was no way of knowing the true mind of the men; on the surface they seemed to like the political officers. . . . As we had always been under the watch of Communist Party men, we couldn't do everything as we liked; even between very intimate friends we couldn't criticize the Party or the political officers. As a result, we couldn't but believe what the political officers told us. And as we couldn't know what every man's true idea was, others appeared to be believing what the political officers said. But I didn't think the political officers were honest, for their speech and conduct often didn't jibe.   [*private, former Nationalist corporal*]

> The political officers watched our actions and words using the Party members for this purpose. Not knowing who was a Party member, we could not talk freely.   [*private, former Nationalist lieutenant*]

So far-reaching a degree of control was difficult to maintain when conditions affecting a unit deteriorated beyond a certain point, and, particularly, when the hard core cadre structure within the unit weakened in numbers and quality. Under these circumstances, discontented soldiers were no longer forced to dissimulate as effectively as before. This stage had been reached in most of the units to which the sixty-one privates interviewed belonged. Prior to their capture, therefore, these men had gained a clearer picture of the extent to which their own negative feelings were shared by other members of the unit. They had become aware that many if not the majority of men in their unit were simulating correct attitudes and good morale only when in danger of being observed. And in some cases disgruntled soldiers had exchanged confidences behind the backs of Party members:

Most of the men whispered that the political leaders were just like publicity men. . . . [private, former Nationalist]

Ordinary soldiers disliked the political officers. Though they obeyed their instructions superficially, they spoke ill of them when no communists were around. [private, former Nationalist assistant squad leader]

Usually when they met the political officer they greeted him politely. But though they pretended to like him, after he passed they thrust out their tongues, showing signs of cursing.
[private, former Nationalist assistant squad leader]

The presence of a large percentage of former Nationalist soldiers in most, if not all, of the units to which the sixty-one privates in our sample belonged provided a basis for the eventual emergence of outgroup consciousness. In units comprising the initial intervention force sent to Korea in late 1950 the percentage of former CNA soldiers per unit was estimated to range as high as 50 to 70 percent.[8] (In the PLA as a whole, numbering some 2,500,000 men on the eve of the Korean War, approximately half were former Nationalist troops.) Units entering Korea in early 1951 frequently included a somewhat lower proportion of former CNA soldiers. In many cases these units had taken in a rather large number of new recruits shortly before entering Korea, which correspondingly reduced the proportion of former CNA soldiers in their ranks.

The mere fact of having previously belonged to the CNA did not, of course, mean that the soldier would fail to become assimilated into his PLA unit. What may have been decisive in this respect, rather,

was the judgment which PLA leaders placed upon his political reliability. In Chapter 6 we will note the criteria PLA authorities applied
in screening captured Nationalist soldiers and the different procedures
by means of which they were incorporated into the PLA. It will
suffice now to note that the fact that a former CNA officer or NCO
was demoted to private when incorporated into the PLA was a good
indicator of its judgment of his present and potential reliability. Of
the sixty-one privates interviewed with our basic questionnaire, at
least thirty-one were former CNA officers or NCO's who had been
broken to private when taken into the PLA. Of these thirty-one,
twenty-four revealed out-group, and seven in-group identifications.

An out-group might be expected to develop particularly if a PLA
unit included any appreciable number of former Nationalist soldiers
who had been favorably disposed to the CNA or who were rated by
PLA instructors as poor material for potential conversion to communism. In studying our interviews the impression emerges strongly that
the PLA system for forming small groups of high solidarity and
morale was put to a severe strain by the attempt in the years preceding the Korean War to incorporate many former CNA personnel without weeding out the "unassimilables."

The development of out-group consciousness within a unit had
considerable significance. Once soldiers realized that personal discontents which they had suppressed were shared by others within the unit
and once they began to identify themselves with an out-group they
were less likely to "reform" their basic personalities in conformity
with PLA demands. The Chinese Communist system of indoctrination relied heavily upon bringing small group pressures to bear
against the individual who deviated from the prescribed norm. Such
pressures were more likely to be effective against the soldier who
could be made to feel that his discontents were those of an isolated
individual.

If the PLA had been willing and able to release the unassimilable
misfits from its ranks, the possibility of achieving ideal groups might
have been greater. However, this is by no means certain. A practice
of releasing political misfits—rather than transferring them to an even
more deprivational existence or executing them—might have undermined the efficacy of indoctrination techniques employed for inducing
the men to repress thoughts and behavior contrary to PLA norms. If

noncommunist soldiers knew that misfits would be released from service after a trial period of indoctrination, would they not have less interest in conforming to PLA demands? In this sense, the principle of the "captive group" seems essential to the PLA system of political indoctrination and group formation, which relied so heavily (as we shall see in Chapter 5) upon inducing the psychological mechanism of repression to achieve its pedagogical goals.

A more promising way out of this dilemma would have been greater selectivity in recruitment. Adoption of higher standards of admission coupled with preinduction political indoctrination might have succeeded in reducing the number of soldiers who were potential political misfits or, in PLA parlance, "stubborn elements" and "unregenerate reactionaries." There is some reason to believe that in the late forties PLA authorities were not unaware of this possibility. But adoption of policies for greater selectivity in recruitment of new soldiers evidently did not seem feasible at the time. The Chinese Communist leaders would have preferred to construct their armed forces of a politically homogeneous element of the population more receptive to learning the communist way of life. As we noted in Chapter 1, they compromised on this point for various reasons. The Korean War caught the PLA in a state of transition. Many more former CNA soldiers had been taken in than could be readily assimilated. Given time and favorable circumstances, the PLA might have been able to gradually replace many of the "undigestable," "unregenerate" former Nationalist soldiers with more carefully selected young recruits who had already received considerable political indoctrination in civilian formations before induction into the service. After the end of the Korean War, as will be noted in Chapter 11, the PLA did move in this direction.

This concludes our examination of the practices employed by the company political officer to develop positive attitudes toward the PLA. Now our focus will shift to the feelings of the men in small groups toward each other, and to how the leaders attempted to manipulate these feelings through criticism meetings.

5 *Criticism Meetings and the Morale Informants System*

Criticism meetings were effective for unifying unit members. It made one who had faults or had made mistakes decide to imitate the behavior of the men who had no faults, and made others careful not to make any mistakes.

Chinese prisoner

To expose one's errors before other men in the unit and to be criticized by them was really disagreeable.

Chinese prisoner, private

ATTITUDE REORIENTATION VS. BEHAVIOR CONTROL

We turn now to a closer examination of some of the important devices employed in the Chinese Communist Army to remold attitudes and to control behavior. Robert J. Lifton's study of Chinese "thought reform" is suggestive and illuminating at many points for understanding the general rationale behind indoctrination and control practices employed within the Chinese Communist Army.[1] Lifton focused on Chinese and foreign intellectuals who had been subjected to a particularly intensive, prolonged exposure to thought reform. Other Chinese social groups are subjected to less intensive forms of basic indoctrination which, nonetheless, utilize the same general principles and some of the same procedures.[2] It was obviously necessary to employ a milder variant of thought reform in large mass organizations such as the PLA. It would have been totally impractical in indoctrinating new soldiers and young cadres to attempt the same kind of intensive, prolonged treatment of each individual described by Lifton, which sometimes lasted for a period of several years.

Thought reform within the PLA, therefore, relied to a greater extent than so-called "brain-washing" of intellectuals on organizational controls and the manipulation of the feelings of the men in small groups toward each other. At the risk of oversimplifying matters, what took place in this respect within the PLA may be regarded as a form of group therapy in contrast to the individual psychotherapy of intellectuals described by Lifton. In addition, as Morris Janowitz has remarked,* though modeled on thought reform principles, the PLA indoctrination techniques described in this chapter obviously were not aimed exclusively at the conversion of the men but also at mobilization, even though temporarily, of the uncommitted.

The reshaping of the thought and behavior of soldiers was achieved on one of several different psychological levels. The most thoroughgoing means to the end to which PLA authorities aspired was the transformation of individual soldiers into good communists who would be positively motivated to perform the tasks assigned to them. To this end, indoctrination efforts relied heavily upon pedagogical techniques that were designed to induce the men to repress negative thoughts and feelings that stood in the way of accepting the values, standards, and attitudes implicit in the PLA soldierly model. Criticism and self-criticism meetings were among the major pedagogical practices used for bringing pressure to bear upon the men to abandon "negative," "reactionary" modes and to reshape their ideas and behavior along approved lines. At the same time, these meetings provided opportunities for uncommitted individuals to enter into group situations to strengthen their sense of commitment.

Criticism meetings helped to maintain control of thought and behavior in other ways as well. The political apparatus in the PLA utilized morale informants and other means to learn as early as possible whether conditions of service such as inadequate food, clothing, medical attention, and homesickness, were beginning to have an adverse effect on the morale of the individual. The results of this surveillance enabled the company political officer and his associates to utilize available resources to obtain improvement in conditions, if possible, and to utilize small group meetings and criticism meetings to encourage the soldiers concerned to view these problems from a perspective approved by the PLA.

The system of surveillance and criticism also provided a more subtle kind of protection. Within the communist movement the "polit-

---

* In a personal communication to the author.

ical health" and ideological soundness of its members has traditionally been viewed as potentially brittle, subject to abrupt lapses, and
even total reversals. Whenever concern over this possibility is acute,
as it evidently was within the PLA, authorities maintain a watchful
attitude for the slightest indication in the behavior and thoughts of
Party members and candidates that foreshadows breakdown of political reliability. The never-ceasing process of surveillance, self-
examination, mutual criticism, and self-criticism within the PLA had
the preventive function, therefore, of catching and eradicating minor
symptoms before serious lapses occurred. Anxiety concerning the
political health of Party adherents was understandably extended to
non-Party soldiers. They were supposed to be remolded into Party
soldiers, and therefore required watching for this reason. But also,
perhaps PLA leaders feared that if non-Party soldiers were permitted
to express their negative attitudes freely, this might have an insidious
effect on Party soldiers in the unit.

While criticism meetings were supposed to induce repression of
undesirable thoughts, they often failed to achieve a thoroughgoing
transformation of the individual soldier and instead brought about a
more limited type of psychological adjustment. Exposed to unpleasant surveillance and the risk of severe criticism, the individual might
indeed learn to control his behavior, to suppress various evidences of
negative thoughts, and to simulate good or adequate morale. But he
did not always genuinely repress and discard ways of thinking and
behaving that were condemned by the political apparatus; he merely
suppressed expressions of them that got him into trouble. The distinction between repression and suppression, between eradicating evil
thoughts and merely covering them up, is an important one for the
analysis of materials presented in this chapter. In contrast to the soldier who succeeded in repressing his negative tendencies and remolding himself along the lines demanded of him, the soldier who merely
suppressed his negative qualities was knowingly engaging in dissimulation under duress.

Under certain conditions, perhaps when they realized that more
thorough solutions were out of the question, PLA leaders were willing to accept the less thorough adjustment that the practice of dissimulation represented. They were aware that the men were only suppressing negative thoughts and behavior, for this was either plainly

visible to the trained eye or else it was reported to them by morale informants. Suppression was acceptable to most company political officers if a disaffected soldier simulated good morale actively by working hard, at least when under supervision, and performing his tasks more or less acceptably. Criticism meetings, therefore, served not only the goal of conversion but helped to mobilize and direct the uncommitted.

The practice of controlling one's behavior and simulating correct attitudes was not confined to ordinary soldiers. It was well known within the PLA that Party members, too, differed in the strength of their identification with communism. The homely analogy of "beets" and "radishes" was widely applied within the army for distinguishing between communist soldiers who were thoroughly converted, "beet-red" all through, and those red outside but white inside, who were called "radishes." [3]

It is of interest to note that some students of Chinese character structure believe that submissiveness to authority and the practice of "seeming compliance" to authority is a basic, widespread Chinese personality trait.[4] Relevant in this connection are the results of an experimental study of forced attitude change made recently by Paul Hiniker with Chinese refugees in Hong Kong, which parallel our findings on the difficulty the PLA experienced in bringing about a genuine change of attitudes in its soldiers. While it was relatively easy in Hiniker's study to induce the Chinese subjects to comply overtly with authority, it was at the same time relatively difficult to induce them to internalize the principles advocated by an authority. Hiniker concluded that "internalization" (genuine attitude change) by means of "forced compliance" seems to depend heavily upon the prestige of the authority in the eyes of the subject and may indeed require an intermediary stage of personal identification with the authority to become operative.[5]

We suggest that an "intermediary stage" of this kind is precisely what the Chinese Communists attempted to provide in the institution of the company political officer and lower-level politicized cadres. We noted in Chapter 4 the ways in which company political officers, often successfully, attempted to develop the friendship and respect of soldiers under them in order to facilitate their indoctrination and assimilation into the PLA system.

The effectiveness of thought reform in China as a whole as well as the difficulties it encounters were recently assessed by Franz Schurmann. He agrees that whereas the individual subjected to thought reform and similar processes may learn to speak and act like a communist, "it is more difficult to conceive of a fundamental moral and psychological transformation of the individual." Nonetheless, he suggests that thought reform "in all likelihood . . . has been widely successful in bringing about identity transformations in individuals." Schurmann believes that Chinese Communism succeeds in this respect insofar as it exerts sufficient moral and emotional appeals which, when added to the rational and practical elements of its ideology, must exert a profound impact on those exposed to them. Schurmann also emphasizes, as we do, the crucial role of the group in creating and maintaining "correct thought" in the individual.[6]

THE MORALE INFORMANTS SYSTEM

The company political officer spent considerable time observing the men working, marching, eating, and resting. He often dropped in on squad and platoon meetings; and, insofar as time permitted, he circulated throughout the company talking to soldiers individually or in groups in order to find out how they were getting along. The political officer's opportunities for direct contact and surveillance were limited, however, especially during combat. Moreover, he knew that the men were likely to control expression of disapproved attitudes when he was around. To a considerable extent, therefore, he relied upon platoon, squad, and group leaders for morale surveillance.

Our interviews provide considerable evidence that in the period under survey these cadres took the assignment of morale assessment and reporting quite seriously and did a good job of keeping themselves as well as the company political officer intimately informed of the state of mind and behavior of the men.

An interesting feature of the PLA's variant of morale surveillance was its reluctance to use non-Party men as informants. This stood in sharp contrast to the practice in the Soviet Army of using noncommunist soldiers, especially those in trouble with security authorities, to spy upon their fellow soldiers. Several respondents reported that junior cadres were not used in the morale surveillance apparatus if they were not Party members or candidates.

In units in which all or most military cadre positions were manned by Party members, the company political officer had little need for additional secret morale informants. (As we noted in Chapter 3, however, the Political Defense section at regimental level had its own secret informants within companies.) Under these favorable circumstances, each of the three group leaders within a squad was himself able to observe in detail the thoughts and behavior of the two or three men under his control. If the cadre structure within a platoon composed of three squads was fully politicized in keeping with the PLA model, the number of Party adherents—and morale informants at the same time—would number at least fourteen: platoon leader, assistant platoon leader, three squad leaders, and nine group leaders, together constituting over a third of the platoon strength of approximately thirty-eight men. However, the cadre structure, particularly in the less highly regarded units sent to Korea in March and April of 1951, was not always fully manned by Party men. Thus, a platoon leader from one of these units (in the 64th PLA Army) reported that only seven of the thirty men in his platoon were Party adherents.

Morale reports were either channeled upwards through squad and platoon leaders—except when any of these were not Party adherents —or given directly to the company political officer. Reports were made orally, especially at lower echelons of the company, or in writing. The frequency of reports varied, depending upon circumstances and the seriousness with which the morale situation was viewed. According to some of our respondents, daily reports were made. Typically, the political officer, after studying the reports, held staff meetings at company level, at which they were discussed and remedial measures considered. In a precombat situation, if reports indicated that unit morale was very low, the political officer might recommend that the unit should not be committed to battle until he had had an opportunity to hold meetings in order to improve morale. On occasion, the political officer spoke privately with individuals reported to have bad morale and tried to reason with them regarding the necessity of carrying out duties or engaging willingly in combat. If a man remained "stubborn," the political officer often criticized him or put him through a severe examination designed to expose the reasons for his bad morale. On other occasions, men who had displayed bad morale were disciplined either by having the case brought up in a group criticism meeting or by being punished—for example, by being made to dig two trenches instead of one, or by being ordered not to sleep at night but to reflect upon their conduct. (One respondent stated that, apart from being criticized, a man was not punished for having bad morale until the third report to this effect was turned in.)

It was evident from our interviews that a wide range of attitudes and behaviors was reported by morale informants as signifying bad morale: for example, chance "defeatist" remarks, griping, lack of positive morale, lack of zeal for work, silence, apathy, quarrelsomeness, criticism of leadership, dislike of life in the PLA, expressions of homesickness, etc.

A major threat to the surveillance and control system was the possibility that Party adherents acting as morale informants might deliberately withhold negative information on some of the men in their unit. This could occur if squad and group leaders developed comradely ties of an apolitical character with their men strong enough to interfere with their duties as morale informants. No evidence of a general tendency to do so was encountered in our interviews, though admittedly direct questioning on this point was not undertaken. Also, the possibility cannot be excluded that as conditions of combat deteriorated even further in late May and June of 1951—that is, after the time of our interviews—hard core cadre members at lower levels became demoralized and as a result became less faithful in their activity as morale informants.

In the period of Korean operations under survey, the morale informants seem to have done their work efficiently on the whole, even though sometimes without enthusiasm. The devices for ensuring the integrity of this function appear to have been adequate to ensure a flow of confidential information on the state of mind and performance of rank-and-file soldiers. None of the twenty-five or thirty cadre members interviewed on two different questionnaires intimated any appreciable decline in the efficiency of the morale informants system. On the contrary, several volunteered information indicating the contrary.

The main devices for ensuring the integrity of the system were exclusive use of Party adherents as morale informants; multiple and mutual surveillance (which gave independent observation and cross-checking of any single informant's report); holding small unit leaders, who were also morale informants in most cases, responsible for any morale breakdowns or desertions among their men; pressure from above to ensure adequate reporting of morale, coupled with the possibility of independent verification by the company political officer or by inspection units from a higher level.

The utility of these devices is indicated in the following statements:

If there happened to be any deserter in the squad, the Party men, the Youth League members in the squad and the squad leader were responsible for it, so that they were to be criticized for not having observed closely and educated him thoroughly.   [*political officer*]

The squad leader was held responsible for a man's desertion, so he did not overlook, but reported on, any slight misbehavior in order to discharge his responsibility.   [*private*]

Even the watcher didn't like to watch, not to speak of the men who were under surveillance. I was in the position of watching them as I was a Communist, and yet I disliked in my heart to watch them. I pretended to work faithfully because I couldn't disobey the superior's orders. If I reported incorrectly I would be criticized without fail.

[*assistant squad leader*]

The squad leader [the POW himself] and assistant squad leader watched the members of the squad and informed twice a week regularly to the platoon leader, who in turn told the political officer. When any change took place in the unit members, when their morale became high or low, the squad leader informed instantly.   [*squad leader*]

New soldiers gradually became aware that intimate details of their behavior, speech, performance of duties, and even facial expressions were being observed and that confidential reports were being turned in to the political officers. This was reported by all of the soldiers we interviewed. Awareness of the extent and nature of the surveillance to which they were subjected developed from the fact that a chance remark or negative action later became the basis for an accusation at a criticism meeting:

We knew well that we were observed. For instance, without thinking, a soldier told a veteran that the U.S. artillery was very terrible. Afterwards, a political officer told us about this. Judging by this, it was clear that the veterans were observing all our conduct and were keeping the political officers informed.   [*private*]

At first, the men didn't know that the political officers were observing their morale. After being criticized and advised once or twice, however, they came to know that their morale was being observed.   [*private*]

In some cases the men's knowledge of the identity of morale informants was facilitated by virtue of the fact that for several years before the Korean War, the identity of Party members and adherents within the unit was no longer a secret as it had been at one time. Often, however, they remained unaware, or else were not sufficiently self-conscious in the presence of likely informants to realize that their behavior was being observed and might be reported. The men were genuinely surprised, therefore, when confronted later with a specific accusation, even though they knew in general that surveillance was going on all the time. On occasion, the men realized that surveillance was being stepped up:

Some one anxiously said: "They are keenly observing me lately for some reason." Further, we said secretly when they observed us keenly: "For what purpose do you observe us? I will desert at a good chance today or tomorrow."   [*private*]

The sixty-one privates interviewed with our basic questionnaire were almost unanimous in stating that they, as well as most rank-and-file soldiers in their units, found it extremely unpleasant and distressing to be under constant surveillance. Feelings of *severe* anxiety and fear, however, were not generally provoked by the surveillance system until the unit experienced harsh conditions of combat. Then, as combat requirements became more difficult to satisfy and as the scale of threatened punishments became more onerous, the men were much more afraid of the system of surveillance.

Under milder conditions, the reaction of the men to knowledge of morale surveillance was more typically one of distaste and resentment: "If the men knew they were being observed, they felt disagreeable and couldn't help but murmur 's.o.b.'" [*private*]. Contributing particularly to this feeling was the uncertainty and tension the system created in the minds of the men. They could never know just what aspect of their conduct was being recorded or just when it would be singled out later for criticism. As a result they felt continually ill at ease:

It is very unpleasant to know that you are being watched secretly by others. Even though you think you are not guilty of anything at all, you are not sure what report the political officers may receive about you. So you feel very displeased over it. One would prefer to be beaten on the spot.   [*private*]

The feeling of insecurity and malaise which surveillance created was, of course, essential to the efforts made by PLA authorities to induce the men to repress or at least control disapproved behavior. Knowledge that the nuances of their behavior were being subjected to surveillance and that "negative" morale would be criticized and punished evidently did motivate most men to make a determined effort to alter or at least control their behavior. Information was obtained on this point from fifty-one of the sixty-one privates interviewed with the basic questionnaire. Most of them (forty-four) reported that the predominant reaction to surveillance among rank-and-file soldiers in their unit took the form of an effort to suppress evidence of negative morale and to simulate good morale:

When the men had good morale, they dug hard, sang a song, or talked with each other with smiles on their faces. When they had bad morale, they seldom talked with each other, seldom smiled or sang. So the political leader could judge morale at a glance. . . . The men knew they were under observation, feared it and were careful of their sayings and doings. We tried not to show signs of bad morale and pretended to have good morale, smiling while talking, because the political leader scolded us very often, saying that we had bad thoughts when we had bad morale.
[*private*]

When our bad morale was detected by them, we were scolded on account of bad thoughts. Consequently, we took care not to show signs of bad morale and merely made much noise to pretend diligence while working, but we didn't work and rested when they went away.   [*private*]

As soon as the political officers appeared the men pretended to be in high spirits and talked pleasantly with each other, even though they were quite demoralized and had been hanging their heads. . . .   [*private*]

Thus, the men gradually learned what types of behavior were regarded by political personnel as indicators of good and bad morale. They attempted to control their behavior and expressions accordingly. Having described the pervasive system of morale surveillance, which was essential to the effective operation of criticism meetings, we turn now to an assessment of the Chinese use of this familiar communist practice in their army.

CRITICISM MEETINGS

When the politicized cadre model of the PLA was achieved, even the smallest military subunit—the combat group of three or four men—was led by a Party adherent whose responsibility it was to mold the group in the prescribed manner. Group meetings could be held as often as several times a day to discuss various matters. If a soldier expressed worry about his home life, the group leader assured him that the government was taking care of his family. If a soldier had trouble with a member of another group, the affair was settled through channels by the group leader who reported it to the squad leader, who passed the report on to the platoon leader if necessary.

In addition to regular group meetings several times a day, under peacetime garrison conditions a "mutual criticism" meeting was held by each squad for approximately twenty minutes every night. At such meetings the work of the squad during that day was reviewed and a discussion took place as to who had taken an active part in the squad's work and who had not. If someone was thought to be guilty of "misconduct" in this respect, a discussion was held as to how best to correct his misbehavior.

In addition to these daily mutual criticism meetings, a "self-criticism" meeting was held within each squad once a week for one or two hours. The purpose of these meetings was to give individual soldiers an opportunity to confess mistakes in their conduct during the week. If anyone failed to confess a mistake, other members of the squad were supposed to expose it. Everyone criticized each other's conduct, and promises were made not to repeat mistakes. If a man failed to mend his ways after being criticized on three separate occasions at squad meetings, he was subject to criticism at a platoon meeting.

During garrison conditions in China, platoon affairs meetings were held once a week. The pattern of these meetings was similar to that of the squad meetings. Company meetings were held less frequently.

Our respondents indicated that such meetings were held less frequently after entering Korea. Particularly under combat conditions were meetings held irregularly. Sometimes criticism meetings had to be deferred until the unit was pulled out of the line or until a definite pause in combat occurred. While the main function of these meetings was to promote willingness to conform and group solidarity prior to combat, they were also used to some extent for handling minor disciplinary problems during periods of combat.

A broad range of behavior was brought under scrutiny in the criticism meetings. Problems of "daily life" brought up at these sessions included instances of quarreling, cursing, failure to study and work with zeal, failure to express opinions at meetings, dishonesty, negligence about sanitation, griping about lack of furloughs, homesickness.

Violations of military discipline were also frequently brought up at the meetings. Desertion, whether attempted or merely contemplated, was widespread under garrison conditions in China as well as in Korea. Improper care of weapons, equipment, animals, and nonobservance of, or griping against regulations and orders were also the subject of rebuke at criticism meetings.

The PLA's effort to regulate relations of soldiers with the civilian population, especially women, offered many occasions for criticism and instruction at these meetings. Chinese Communist leaders attached great importance to creating a new role in these respects that would serve to raise the prestige of the soldierly profession. In Korea, demoralization and fear of death were frequently taken up in these meetings. According to a political officer we interviewed, "the problem most frequently brought up [in Korea] was demoralization and lack of bravery in battle."

Though PLA leaders tried to impart a spontaneous flavor to the criticism meetings, they were in fact closely controlled and manipulated in a number of respects. Attendance at the meetings was not formally compulsory; it became so in effect, however, because the men feared that they would be criticized for being absent. Illness could be and occasionally was used as an excuse for not attending these meetings in Korea as well as under garrison conditions in China.

PLA authorities implicitly demanded and enforced, if necessary, the practice of everyone engaging in criticism of fellow soldiers who had misbehaved. A private reported that one could be criticized for "not expressing opinions at a meeting." He added: "The squad leader opened the meeting with a statement ending thus: 'I expect all of you to debate and criticize diligently.'" Another private reported:

Eight out of ten men disliked the political, military, and cultural instruction and did not study hard. Though I, too, disliked learning, I pretended to criticize those who disliked the instruction. We pretended to criticize each other saying that we had to study hard. . . .

While we did not directly question prisoners on the matter, several indicated that it was difficult to get soldiers to volunteer derogatory information against a friend at criticism meetings. Soldiers reluctant to engage in self-criticism were pressured into doing so by the "example" set by Party adherents who typically began these meetings by criticizing themselves. The pressure to engage in self-criticism was heightened by the knowledge that confidential morale observations were being made continuously. An individual soldier could never exclude the possibility that a negative report had been turned in which would form the basis for a public accusation at the criticism meeting if he did not take the initiative of criticizing himself. His inducement to engage voluntarily in self-criticism was also enhanced by the possibility that if a soldier held back and waited to see whether he would be criticized, Party adherents would become annoyed and take a more severe attitude toward his "crime." Therefore, while a soldier was not obliged to criticize himself if he thought he had not committed any errors, he was under strong pressure to find some fault nonetheless:

A squad leader or a group leader would call a meeting to order. Then, in general, a Party member would stand and criticize himself first, saying: "I committed a certain error at such and such a place, and I think I should be blamed in such and such respects. I will make efforts hereafter not to commit the error again." Each of us had to criticize himself in turn. In order not to be criticized by others, everybody criticized himself reluctantly. The men who were unwilling to speak were urged to speak by others. If a man refused to speak, he would be condemned eventually as an "ideological reactionary."   [*assistant company commander*]

Everybody had to criticize himself even though he had committed no error.   [*private*]

The men who believed that they had not committed any errors need not criticize themselves. But if their errors were known by others, they were exposed and criticized.   [*private*]

If the man at fault did not criticize himself but had his mistake pointed out by another person, he was likely to receive a punishment [instead of being let off with a promise to do better].   [*private*]

Party adherents were well aware that a soldier might engage in perfunctory self-criticism simply to "satisfy" requirements and to ward off punishment. To permit self-criticism to degenerate into a purely formal ritual would have robbed it of its value. Accordingly, in properly managed self-criticism meetings Party adherents insisted that self-criticism be performed with appropriate seriousness and emotional feeling.

An additional requirement was that a soldier's self-criticism had to be couched in politically acceptable terms. It was not enough for the soldier to be repentant and to say that he would try to do better in the future. He also had to show correct political insight into the nature and basis of his misdeed. Otherwise, from the standpoint of the political organization, his self-criticism lacked full therapeutic and pedagogical value and could be rejected as inadequate.

We cannot arrive at firm judgments on the degree to which these requirements were enforced, or on the quality of the self-criticism elicited from non-Party soldiers. It would seem, however, that until at least early spring 1951 self-criticism was generally kept on a high level from the standpoint of the authorities. Not only did a number of our respondents volunteer the information that perfunctory self-criticisms were not acceptable; this could also be inferred from the fact that practically all soldiers interviewed expressed a strong dislike for the mutual criticism and self-criticism meetings: "If the self-criticism were recognized as a good one, that would be all right. But if it was not good—not touching upon his other defects—another man would point out his other defects and criticize him. . . ." [*private*]

As already noted, one of the essential requirements of an acceptable self-criticism was that it should convey awareness that ideological deficiencies were at the root of seemingly nonpolitical misdeeds. Any effort by the soldier to explain his failures on other grounds was likely to make the self-criticism he offered unacceptable. The soldier had to take care not to offer an explanation of his misdeed that could be regarded as an effort to gain understanding and sympathy for his human weaknesses and limitations:

This happened while our unit was in Manchuria. A squad leader was arrested in the act of escaping to his home. A self-criticism meeting was held. The political officer spoke first: "Now a certain comrade was arrested in attempting to run away with his wicked idea, and this meeting is for him. He is going to criticize himself. Everyone here is requested to listen to him and criticize him, in order to teach him." Then the squad leader criticized himself: "I escaped, as I was seized by homesickness. At my home I have my old parents and little children. None of them can work. So I wanted to go home to work myself. Now I realize that I was bad. I will make efforts not to do it again." Other men got permission to speak one after the other: "He is covering his true motive. He escaped because he did not like to oppose the U.S. and help [North] Korea, not because of homesickness." "He escaped because he feared death." "He ran away because he still has the ideas of the CNA." After all, no conclusion was reached so he was turned over to the self-criticism meeting of the company, at which he spoke as follows: "The reason I ran away was more that I did not like to fight in Korea than that I wanted to go home. . . . Now I understand that I was very bad and I will discard bad ideas and dedicate myself to our country and the people, to atone for my sin." Then others said that he had confessed his true motive now. He was pardoned by the majority decision.   [*private*]*

Our findings regarding the quality of criticism maintained in the PLA stand in contrast to the greater ritualization of "confessions" permitted within the Malayan Communist movement, which Lucian Pye has reported.[7]

The attempt to introduce egalitarian features into army life included use of the small group to discipline the errant individual. By creating the impression that one was judged and punished by members of one's immediate group, PLA leaders hoped to utilize group pressures to facilitate control of the individual and his eventual identification with their way of life.

Under garrison conditions the small group was widely utilized as a disciplinary tribunal, but during combat operations its jurisdiction in this respect was limited to relatively minor infractions and mild punishments. Some group decisions on discipline were subject to approval on a higher level and, often, the group merely offered its recommendations to the regular disciplining authority.

In reality, it is unlikely that group judgments on these matters would often run counter to the desires of the political organization in any important respect. The presence of at least one Party adherent in each group safe-guarded against this. It would be entirely possible for the company political officer, if he were sufficiently interested in a case, to coach his Party subordinates beforehand on the group

---

* It should be noted that, as this private's account indicates, the PLA took a relatively lenient attitude towards attempted desertion and AWOL's under garrison conditions. The official attitude toward such offenses was *gradually* stiffened during the course of the Korean War. Still, the most severe punishments were reserved for frontline deserters.

punishment to be "arrived at" in the meeting. Only one of our sources stated that this type of stage management took place: "It is apparently ordained that the punishment be decided publicly [by the group], but in reality the political officers contact the Party men or the old Eighth Route Army men beforehand so that all authority of punishment is really invested in the political officers" [*private*]. It may be assumed that the company political officer and his superiors at higher echelons generally took the initiative in defining what should be the current attitude of small group meetings toward particular misdemeanors.

Fifty-nine privates were asked whether there was anything about criticism and self-criticism meetings which they and the men in their units liked or disliked. Almost all of them (fifty-five) indicated in unmistakable terms that such meetings had been disliked. The feeling of acute unpleasantness and humiliation at being criticized by others and forced to engage in self-criticism before the group was the reason given most frequently (thirty-nine privates) for having disliked this practice. Several of our respondents said they disliked the meetings because they lasted too long, were held too frequently, or were boring. It is noteworthy that relatively few privates (only six) attributed their dislike of the meetings to fear of punishment or increased surveillance as a consequence of being singled out for criticism.

The frequency with which our respondents mentioned the humiliating character of criticism and self-criticism parallels the findings reported by Pye on the reaction of Malayan Communists to this practice.[8]

Some of our respondents had responded more positively toward the practice of public criticism and self-criticism at an earlier stage in their service. However, the impression gained from our materials is that most of them had reacted negatively to it at a relatively early period. In fact, a pronounced aversion to being criticized or engaging in self-criticism had developed in many of them long before they became critical of other phases of the PLA system. Unlike other aspects of demoralization and disaffection which set in only after severe combat in Korea, the men's attitude toward criticism meetings appears to have been well defined under garrison conditions in China.

There can be little doubt that small group criticism meetings were an effective device for *mobilizing and controlling* the behavior of soldiers in the PLA.* The "public shaming" to which they were subjected in criticism meetings was so unpleasant an experience for most soldiers that they preferred, within certain important limits to be sure, to exercise self-control over their behavior in order to avoid being singled out at one of these meetings. On the other hand, criticism meetings were less successful in achieving the more ambitious goal of turning basic attitudes of the men in a more positive direction, i.e., conversion to communism. As noted earlier, most of these fifty-nine privates would have to be considered as rather difficult subjects for political conversion. Therefore, their experiences do not permit a rounded appraisal of the utility of the public criticism device— together with other indoctrination techniques—for producing loyal communist soldiers. The four privates who expressed a favorable attitude toward criticism meetings (and who were well assimilated into the PLA generally) enable us to glimpse the positive results that could be achieved by this device. As one of them put it:

I think the self-criticism meetings were very useful. If we did not have them, we would have no means of offering our views to our superiors, and freedom of speech would not exist at all. The men who committed errors used to mend their ways and lived in harmony with each other and they had no quarrels. . . . Of course, some men [but not this POW] hated these meetings.

Cadres who had risen from the ranks provided better evidence regarding the contribution criticism meetings could make to successful indoctrination. For some of them public shaming may have been so important an emotional experience that they experienced a sudden, marked change in orientation. This kind of experience in itself would not transform the individual into a well-indoctrinated communist, which is in any event a long, drawn-out process. But it might serve to give him a basic self-dissatisfaction and a strong desire to cooperate actively with group leaders in the reshaping of his personality and thoughts so that he could eventually become a good communist. In

---

* Since direct observation of life in the PLA has not been possible, judgments on this question have to be based upon estimates of effectiveness obtained from prisoners who were participants and upon inferences from statements on their attitudes towards these meetings and towards other aspects of the way of life in the PLA.

any case, whether shaming played an important role or not, criticism and self-criticism meetings probably helped in the gradual education and reshaping of these individuals who did become well-indoctrinated communists in time.

In interviews with twenty-five cadre members serving as military leaders in their units no evidence was obtained that any of them had experienced a sudden "conversion" as a result of being subjected to criticism meetings. Several of these respondents did state that criticism meetings were useful in the gradual reshaping of soldiers into communists. This goal, they pointedly observed, could be achieved only with great difficulty:

> I think it was the purpose of such meetings to make one improve day by day, to imbue him with communism in his daily life, and finally to make him a Party member and then a communist soldier. . . . These meetings were useful for preventing minor misdeeds . . . but they hardly had effect upon fundamental problems of thought; they might have such an effect, however, through long practice.   [*former Nationalist lieutenant*]

> I think such meetings were useful for correcting small mistakes but were not much good for correcting deep ideological faults. These were difficult to correct and took a long time.   [*platoon leader*]

There is much more evidence in our materials that criticism meetings were an effective device for inducing even those noncommunist soldiers who were labeled "reactionaries" and "stragglers in thought" to control their behavior along desired lines. This was the nearly unanimous judgment of the twenty-five PLA cadre members—many of them members of the political hard core—whom we interviewed on this point. A few felt that in this respect the beneficial effect of criticism meetings upon ordinary soldiers was only temporary and that after a few days the same errors cropped up again. But most of them regarded criticism meetings as definitely useful aides in controlling the men by inducing self-control:

> Most of the men stopped their minor misconducts easily [as a result of criticism meetings], so that these meetings were helpful to the cadres for leading the men.
> Criticism meetings were effective for unifying unit members. It made one who had faults or had made mistakes decide to imitate the behavior of the men who had no faults, and made others careful not to make any mistakes.
> These meetings were useful because everybody became careful in his

conduct for he was afraid of them. Though the "guilty" persons had complaints in their hearts, they pretended to work with zeal.

Such meetings were very useful, for others too—not to speak of the guilty person—became determined and cautious.

Lest the judgment of cadres on this point be regarded as unduly favorable to the PLA system, the testimony of privates should also be cited. Three-fourths of the fifty-nine privates interviewed on this question definitely credited the criticism meetings with having had a strong influence on their own behavior as well as on that of most privates in their units. (It should be recalled that all but four of these fifty-nine privates strongly disliked criticism meetings.) Several others conceded that these meetings were partially successful in this respect —that is, with regard to minor matters or with respect to only some of the men. Some typical statements by privates who disliked criticism meetings but regarded them as effective:

The self-criticism meeting was useful. On account of it, we came to heed our own behavior, to have occasion for self-reflection, and to eradicate reviling and assaulting from our army. The one who committed an error mended his deed to gain honor again and the other members were awakened in many respects.   [*private, conscripted in 1947*]

I can say that the effects of such meetings were remarkable. We learned what we had never known and improved our knowledge. Anyone who had ever committed a fault never did so again.
                              [*private, conscripted in 1949*]

It was very effective. That is, all the men who saw that scene [criticism and self-criticism] exercised self-discipline and never committed a fault; and it made the person in question improve himself not to commit it again.   [*private, former Nationalist private taken into the PLA in December 1949*]

It was effective superficially, for the man who had been criticized was careful because he was watched by the officers.
                    [*private, former Nationalist lieutenant taken into the PLA in May 1950*]

Such meetings were useful to some extent . . . however, the same errors were repeated without regard to such meetings.
                    [*private, former Nationalist lieutenant taken into the PLA in May 1950*]

The man who was criticized was careful not to commit the fault any more, but the other men who were present in the meeting forgot the lesson two or three days afterwards. . . .
                    [*private, conscripted in December 1950*]

Several privates explicitly observed that criticism meetings were not effective for changing one's basic ideology; in fact, none of the privates credited criticism meetings with so great an effect. Rather, criticism meetings occasionally had the opposite effect of promoting or strengthening anticommunist feelings among those who were bitterly and repeatedly singled out for attack. A number of cadres as well as privates referred to this unanticipated boomerang effect: ". . . But I am not sure whether ideological attitudes could be reformed or not [by means of criticism meetings]. The results were rather opposite from what they expected. . . ." [*assistant company commander, former Nationalist 2d lieutenant*]

Why was the system of criticism meetings able to induce self-control and dissimulation? The explanation which most readily suggests itself is that the men feared punishment if they were called upon the carpet before the group. But the fact is that very often the group—that is, the political organization which manipulated the group—limited itself to verbal reprimands and accepted the errant soldier's apology and promise to do better. The more severe forms of punishment stemmed directly from the PLA's formal disciplining apparatus rather than from criticism meetings. At most, fear of punishment as an ultimate sanction reinforced somewhat the immediate impact of the criticism meetings.

A more important factor accounting for the efficacy of criticism meetings in inducing men to greater self-control is suggested, of course, by the finding already noted that for so many soldiers it was unpleasant and humiliating to be publicly shamed. What is striking, however, is that the individual experienced humiliation of this kind even though he was not strongly identified with his immediate group. (Most of the thirty-nine soldiers who reported this kind of reaction to the criticism meetings had *not* been very well assimilated into the PLA or the small group life within their units.) We must look, then, to other factors in trying to account for the humiliation so many soldiers experienced in criticism meetings. Part of the explanation may be that Chinese culture had made the individual deeply sensitive to loss of "face" even in relatively impersonal settings.[9] The nature of our interviews was too crude a vehicle for probing into this matter.

But there is indirect evidence of the operation of deep-seated cultural and personal factors in molding attitudes toward PLA criticism meetings. Some of the statements of our respondents indicate that public criticism was extremely distasteful and humiliating:

> The criticism meeting was more severe than to be struck or scolded.
> *[private, former Nationalist private]*

> Once at a criticism meeting, a comrade stood up and said: "This soldier has said that he would like to have leave to return home. His attitude spoils the military spirit of our unit; it is injurious of our morale. We must clean up such ones from our squad hereafter." The person in question blushed deeply and seemed to have reformed himself since then.
> *[private, former Nationalist private]*

> As criticism exposed mistakes, it was feared and disliked more than a hard blow.   *[private, former Nationalist master sergeant]*

> . . . The other men who were present in the meeting thought it would be a shame for them to be criticized in that way and exercised self-discipline.   *[private, former Nationalist assistant squad leader]*

> Most of the former CNA troops, who had an unconditional hatred for the PLA . . . disliked the political officer because he watched their actions and if he noticed a fault or error he criticized or punished them in front of everyone giving them more agony mentally than to be beaten or cursed. . . .   *[private, former Nationalist platoon leader]*

Perhaps revealing of the degree of humiliation involved in such experiences is the fact that practically none of the fifty-nine privates volunteered the information that he had been personally singled out for attack at one of these meetings.

The effectiveness of "public shaming" as a method of controlling behavior in Soviet Russia has been discussed by Dr. H. V. Dicks.[10] While a reliable basis for comparison of the two armies in this respect is not available, criticism meetings were evidently used somewhat more widely and perhaps more effectively for this purpose in the PLA than in the Soviet Army.

By forcing soldiers to dissimulate, the political officers gained more than an acceptable performance from relatively demoralized personnel. Inducing individual soldiers to adopt a measure of self-control helped to avoid some of the dangers of having a lot of potentially disaffected noncommunist soldiers within a unit. The policy of denying the individual opportunities to express even minor discontents served to stifle the growth within him of worse forms of negativism. The working hypothesis behind this policy, we note, was exactly the opposite of the familiar belief that it is good to permit a man to "let off steam" occasionally.

Also, by forbidding open expression of one's discontent the PLA hoped to isolate each discontented individual psychologically and socially. This is another manifestation of the familiar totalitarian device of "atomizing" political opposition and depriving it of the possibility of developing an organized group basis. PLA authorities operated on the assumption that forcing men to suppress evidence of their bad morale provided a safeguard against the danger that discontented individuals would reinforce and possibly increase each other's discontent if they revealed their true feelings fully to each other.

Insistence that bad morale should not be openly expressed was probably strengthened by other considerations. It seems likely that Chinese Communist leaders shared the belief, held also by Russian Bolsheviks, that even a state of good "political health" on the part of a communist is subject to abrupt lapses and even total reversals. Such a belief is capable of generating deep-seated anxiety. The demand by political officers that disaffected soldiers suppress signs of "bad thoughts" and negative morale may have been motivated in part by a conscious or unconscious fear of a sudden lapse on their own part or on the part of their fellow Party comrades.

In any totalitarian or highly authoritarian organization in which nonbelievers are co-opted and made members of a captive group, as in the PLA, a policy of forcing dissimulation upon the nonbelievers may recommend itself to its leaders as a means of maintaining supervision at lower levels. Functionaries who directly supervise and lead the rank and file can fulfill their organization-defined role better if they are "freed" from witnessing extreme manifestations of the discontent of their charges. The self-conceptions and self-appraisals of functionaries are capable of being influenced by their subordinates' attitudes. By contriving to force rank-and-file soldiers to conceal bad morale and to simulate acceptable, if not good, morale the PLA system probably reduced somewhat the psychological strain and cross-pressures to which supervisory personnel were subjected from the demoralized men under them. Every military organization tries to find ways of preventing cadre members from being infected by the demoralization of the rank and file. The PLA relied less for this purpose on imbuing its cadres with the attitudes of military professionalism than do other armies. The unusual model of a politicized army created special problems in this respect and led its leaders to adopt unusual techniques to cope with them.

LEADERSHIP ATTITUDES TOWARD DISSIMULATION

Political personnel at company level certainly knew that the men were trying to cover up bad morale, but quite possibly they were not always aware of the full extent to which disaffected soldiers were feigning good morale. All twenty-four cadres interviewed on this point readily conceded that there was a tendency among the men under them to dissimulate. The two political officers in our sample had also been aware of this. As one of them put it:

I could tell the state of morale at a glance. When the men were of high morale they obeyed orders well; also they sang songs, joked among themselves and enjoyed mess hours. But when they were of bad morale they came to neglect their duties, never spoke; they became light eaters and kept their leaders at a respectful distance as much as possible. . . . The men knew that their morale was being observed. Devoted Communists didn't mind it, but those who had been land proprietors in the past and were former CNA officers were afraid of the observation and hated it. . . . Those who were ignorant and simple did not try to conceal signs of bad morale, but the bright tradesmen, the learned and the experienced who had roamed the world were careful not to show signs of their bad morale. . . .

An assistant company commander stated that the men tried to camouflage their bad morale even when suffering battle fatigue and fear of death. Several respondents implied that, though Party men and cadres themselves, they too had engaged in dissimulation. An extreme statement of this kind was provided by a company commander: "Old PLA and Party men seemed to have this tendency [to dissimulate] even more. At meetings they urged us to fight bravely for the purpose of keeping one's honor, but in truth they were cowards."

PLA leaders had to decide what policy to adopt toward dissimulation, a type of adjustment which fell far short of the positive motivation desired. The choice was between intensifying efforts to reshape the men into communists or settling for the immediate advantages of securing conformity and obedience. If priority were given to achieving the ultimate goal, mere dissimulation would not suffice and could not be tolerated; additional pressure and criticism would have to be applied in the hope of inducing total repression of negative tendencies.

The attitude of higher authorities toward the problem remains somewhat uncertain. The immediate burden of dealing with it rested upon the company political officers. They were directly confronted with the problem and had to decide whether disaffected soldiers who were suppressing negative attitudes and doing their tasks more or less adequately should be criticized nonetheless for lack of more positive motivation, greater voluntarism, and "activism." In this respect as in others, therefore, the company political officers mediated between organizational requirements and social realities. We infer from our interview materials that company political officers probably got little clear and consistent guidance from above on how to deal with this problem, and that their judgment and performance in this respect was influenced by various considerations. The level of tolerance they displayed toward dissimulation evidently varied from unit to unit; they must have found it difficult to strike an expedient and skillful mode of reacting to the problem.

Our account of the motives and calculations underlying a "tolerant" attitude toward the widespread practice of dissimulation is necessarily somewhat speculative. A political officer might decide upon a relatively severe, intolerant policy toward dissimulation when he thought this might succeed in forcing the men in his unit to repress disfavored attitudes, thereby facilitating remodeling of their personalities. But he might decide against taking a tolerant attitude toward dissimulation for an entirely different reason, namely fear of getting into trouble with superiors. After all, the trained eye of a higher political officer might easily see through dissimulation when he visited the company; or else the reports of morale informants and political defense agents, placed in the company by the regimental political office, might well contain such information. If higher echelons in the political apparatus were unwilling to accept dissimulation at lower levels, the company political officer's opportunities for a flexible policy were limited.

Intolerance of dissimulation might also be adopted simply because of the personal zeal of a particular company political officer. The descriptions of their political officers given by our respondents in Chapter 4 suggested that the zealous type of political officer was not uncommon in the PLA.

On the other hand, tolerant attitudes toward dissimulation were also evident and can be explained on various grounds. Most political officers probably knew that to get the men to carry out most tasks did not depend upon imbuing them with really good morale. Moreover, a certain amount of dissimulation was permitted simply because the political organization within a unit was not always up to par. Its efficiency was lowered when the cadre structure was not fully manned by Party adherents or when the ideological quality of Party members had degenerated, either because of demoralization or because soldiers had been recruited into the Party cadre apparatus who were not yet ready for such responsibilities. It is also likely that some members of the political organization accepted the practice of dissimulation because they realized that the poor political potential of so many of the raw recruits and former Nationalist soldiers, the difficult conditions of service, hardships of combat in Korea, and inadequate opportunities for indoctrination all combined to make it virtually impossible to give many soldiers a more positive set of motivations and to assimilate them more successfully into the PLA way of life.

Reality and pragmatic considerations of this kind might well have led political personnel at some point not merely to tolerate dissimulation but to tacitly encourage it. After all, the practice of dissimulation could be viewed as a source of strength since the environment was indeed oppressive. In a sense, the better the dissimulation forced upon the men, the better they performed their duties with at least some degree of voluntarism, and, therefore, there was less likelihood of the company political officer getting into trouble with his superiors. At some point, political officers may have realized that it was to their advantage not to attack and expose the men who were trying to feign good or adequate morale lest this remove remaining incentives to do a passable job, destroy unit morale completely, and force them to a greater reliance on outright coercion.

A convincing job of dissimulation might also be acceptable to the political officer who had achieved some detachment from the PLA system and was enforcing its demands in a formalistic manner rather than from personal zeal. Such an attitude might well have developed on a considerable scale among lower echelon political personnel who had come to the realization that they, too, were but pawns in the system, and that in effect just as they forced ordinary soldiers to dissimulate so too were they forced to dissimulate in front of their superiors. This attitude was described by an assistant company commander:

A soldier might be very enthusiastic about his work outwardly, but inwardly he might abuse us or the political officer. That is easily understood psychologically when we think of it from the soldier's standpoint. . . . They worked hard in our presence to show their enthusiasm outwardly. When we were gone, they abused us and complained. I understand such a man, because we did the same to our superior.

We have seen that criticism meetings, linked with the morale informants system, constituted a severe but on the whole effective pedagogical device for informing the simple-minded individual what types of behavior were to be avoided if he wished to stay out of trouble. These meetings enabled group pressure to be brought upon the errant individual. They provided uncommitted individuals with opportunities to participate in group activities in ways which might give them the satisfaction of belonging and gaining acceptance. In time, the practice of group criticism and self-criticism led some soldiers to adopt a more positive, cooperative attitude and to identify with the PLA's standards and incorporate them into their own way of thinking. Participation in criticism of others in the unit, which was incumbent on everyone, may have reinforced some individuals' identification with officially prescribed standards and demands, thereby also strengthening their involvement with the group life sponsored by PLA authorities. Finally, criticism meetings were a device for resolving some of the everyday tensions that are bound to develop within any group of individuals who work together.

6 *Leadership in Combat Units*

> . . . to subordinate the organs of the Red Army's political work
> to those of its military work . . . may lead to estrangement from
> the masses, to domination of the government by the army, and to
> a departure from proletarian leadership—in a word, to the same
> path of warlordism as that followed by the Kuomintang army.
>
> *Mao Tse-tung*

THE DUAL SYSTEM OF AUTHORITY

We noted in Chapter 3 that the political organization of the PLA
interlocked with the military command structure at each level down
through the company. There was, as a result, a dual channel of authority. We will focus on the workings of this system at company
level since it was here that members of the political organization
came into closest contact with the men.

Leadership functions were divided between the military and political co-commanders of a unit. But though their job titles were equivalent, the true balance of power between them favored the political
officer for a number of reasons. The company political officer had a
direct line of communication with the political officer at the battalion
level. While the military leader of the unit was excluded from the
political channel of communication and authority, the political officer
was officially authorized to participate in making military decisions at
company level. Throughout the PLA all *military* orders delivered to
any subordinate echelon had to have the signature not only of the
military commander of the unit but, as well, the countersignature of
the political officer at the same echelon of command. In contrast,
political orders to lower echelons did not require the countersignature
of the military commander.

In practice this generally meant that a military commander had to
obtain the consent of his co-commander, the political officer, in implementing military orders received from a superior authority and be-

fore initiating military action on his own. In time of emergency or when there was no time to consult the Party Committee or political officer, the military commander could use his own judgment and make a report of his action to the Party Committee later. A military commander might be discouraged from doing so, however, because in that case he would be wholly responsible for the matter. That this system could result in tactical inflexibility or delays on occasion seems likely, but investigation of this possibility fell outside the scope of the present study. One purpose of the system of dual command was probably to prevent unauthorized withdrawals or retreats by local commanders.

The relative power of the company political officer was buttressed by virtue of the fact that periodically he reported secretly on the company military commander to the Battalion Political Instructor. Moreover, in many cases company military commanders had not been in the Party as long as the political officer; and in some instances they had not yet been admitted into the Party.

· The assumption is frequently made by Western observers that any political commissar system must be a strongly divisive element which undermines unity of command, thereby leading to military inefficiency. Perhaps this judgment stems from imagining the chaos and friction that would occur if a political commissar system were suddenly installed in our armed forces. But to assume that it has a similar impact within communist armies seriously exaggerates its disruptive effects.

The employment of political commissars in a communist army does indeed have certain disadvantages and risks. These vary widely, however, depending upon historical circumstances and the type of commissar system employed. There are important variations of the commissar system, as we have already noted, which might be expected to affect its overall utility. In addition, as Colonel Robert B. Rigg has observed,[1] the particular historical development through which the Chinese Communist Army passed shaped its commissar system in a way that set it apart from the Soviet Army in important respects.

From the initial establishment in 1927 of "The Worker's and Peasant's Red Army," there was a close union of military and political ways of life in the Chinese Communist movement. As a revolutionary army that lacked for so many years a stable territorial base, the Chinese Communist Army was also simultaneously an agency for civil administration. Civil and military functions were closely welded not only within the Chinese Communist movement but also in the combination of duties performed by its high-ranking leaders. Over the years there developed in China a group of communist leaders who had had experience both as military commanders and as commissars. Only with the defeat of the Nationalist armies and the conquest of the Chinese mainland, shortly before the Korean War, did an opportunity arise for developing autonomous organizations for civil government and for the armed forces. The "civil-military" distinction, however, was slow in emerging. At the time of the Korean War the overlap of civil and military authority was still strikingly evident in the fact that each of the six administrative regions into which China was divided was ruled by a "military and administrative (political) committee." The chairman of these committees was in most cases simultaneously commander of the corresponding geographic "military area" as well as of the corresponding Field Army (or its military equivalent).

In contrast to the Soviet Army, which was created within a relatively short period of time from a heterogeneous mass of Tsarist and new revolutionary elements, the highest military talent of the Chinese Communists was developed within the Party over a long period of time while the Party was engaged in organized revolutionary activity. As a result, the post-revolutionary political and military leadership of the Chinese Communist movement was both more homogeneous and more unified than that of the Soviet Army in which political commissars were needed to watch over and control military officers, many of whom had been in the Tsarist army.[2]

What is true in this respect of the top military commanders of the PLA is true only to a lesser extent of the younger, less senior military leaders who commanded armies, divisions, and smaller units in Korea. It should be remembered that these combat leaders were not steeped in the same tradition of unified command that exists in Western armies. Rather, they had been conditioned from the time of their entrance into the PLA, and as they advanced into command positions, to accept the commissar system as an integral and valuable aspect of PLA organization. Their conception of the role of a military commander was significantly different from that which a unit commander in a Western army brings to his task. In the PLA military cadres were indoctrinated to accept the dictum that "politics is supreme." This meant not merely that military commanders should confine themselves to purely military command functions, but that they should accept the fact that even in the military sphere political officers had a legitimate supervisory and collaborative role to play. An assistant company military commander whom we interviewed put it in these terms:

My superior, the battalion commander and we, the military leaders [in the company] thought that politics came first. So we respected the political officers. Therefore we were afraid sometimes that they might rebuke us. . . . As we thought politics came first, the political officer had more authority. For instance, in the case of some military problem, even if the military leader insisted on working it out in a certain manner, if the political officer did not agree it couldn't be done. . . .

Acceptance of this system was furthered by the practice of drawing junior military cadres from Party ranks insofar as possible. Even if the military leader was not a Party man, there was no separate military tradition or organized body of sentiment to which he could appeal on behalf of his preference for keeping political considerations out of military affairs. A *non*-Party military leader who gave any indication of such sentiments would be very much isolated, and immediately subjected to close supervision and surveillance by political leaders. For this reason, it seems clear that any effort to modify the dual command system in favor of military leaders, and to introduce greater specialization of function and career, would have to come from military leaders who were Party members.

If a political officer were a dilettante in military affairs, his efforts to supervise or second-guess the military commander's conduct of operations were likely to be resented and to result in inefficiency. However, it was not often the case that political officers lacked military command experience. At the time of the Korean War there was as yet no rigid career specialization along separate political and military lines. In part, the reasons for its absence stemmed from the historical development to which we have already referred.

In addition to the weight of this tradition, PLA authorities were probably aware of the continuing desirability of staffing the political apparatus with men who had also had considerable military experience. Fragmentary information obtained from our interviews on the careers of individual political officers indicates that they were often recruited from among junior military cadres. It would also appear to be the case that during the course of his career a political officer often received alternating political and military assignments at company, battalion, and perhaps higher levels.*

As a result, at the time of the Korean War the PLA appeared to be surprisingly free of complaints that political officers were not equipped to offer military commanders seasoned military advice. While other complaints were made by prisoners we interviewed, in no case did a military cadre charge or imply that the political officer in his unit was an amateur in military affairs. The only instance of this was reported by a private:

> I think that the political and military commanders of the unit were not on good terms because they did not share the same opinion particularly at times of combat, as the political officer had no practical experience of combat while the military leader did. . . . The military cadres seemed to have no respect for the political officers.

What this suggests, of course, is that the predominantly favorable relations between political and military commanders may have deteriorated later insofar as the pattern of recruitment and the system of training created a new crop of political officers who lacked practical military experience. As the PLA loses even more its earlier character of a guerrilla force and changes into a more modern, mechanized army, a greater specialization of political and military careers is to be expected.

---

* Colonel Rigg, too, has noted that many higher PLA officers had served during the course of their career as political commissars as well as military commanders: "The Red Chinese Army officers did not always have a full quota of troops to command, so they occupied a variety of posts in the interim between battles. When they lacked commands they acted as commissars. What has developed in China is a group of army, group-army, and field army commanders who are *both commanders and commissars*. Many present-day PLA officers began as commissars and are now primarily commanders." Rigg, *Red China's Fighting Hordes,* pp. 23–24. It should be noted that in the Soviet Army a similar policy of interchanging military and political officers in order to erode military professionalism has been resorted to from time to time. T. W. Wolfe, *The Soviet Military Scene: Institutional and Defense Policy Considerations* (Santa Monica: The RAND Corporation, 1966), p. 36.

The assumption that serious conflict between the political and military commanders in a unit must have often occurred in Korea or that it could have been easily stirred up by means of psychological warfare neglects the fact that both had an important stake in cooperating with each other. The pressure to pull together must have been considerable, especially during battle situations. Not only was their survival at stake, but their reputations and careers within the PLA as well.

The importance of maintaining smooth relations between the political and military commanders of a unit was certainly not lost upon higher authorities. An agency was provided, as we have seen, in Party Committee meetings for discussion of differences that the unit political and military commanders were not able to resolve themselves. Moreover, according to an assistant company commander whom we interviewed, both military and political commanders operated under the general injunction not to hurt each other's feelings and to respect one another. If the political officer wielded somewhat more power in any showdown with the military commander, the temptation to abuse his position and to act arbitrarily was curbed by placing particular responsibility upon him for getting along with the military leader. Especially when the company military commander was also a Party member, which was usually the case, the political officer was forced to act with greater restraint. For the military cadre, being a Party member, also had access to the Party channel. In such cases, the issue between them was more likely to be settled on its merits rather than on the principle that a Party man is more likely to be "right" than a non-Party man. This, at least, was the contention of a battalion political officer:

The military and political leaders did not fear one another. Rather, when they had a disagreement on some matter, the person who was "wrong" feared the person who was "right," because they were both Party members and the "right" one could report the problem to the superior organization.

It is interesting to note that in this respect the political commissar system in the PLA worked differently than in the Soviet Army. In the Soviet Army the blame would almost always fall upon the unit *military* commanding officer.[3]

It was widely understood within the PLA that questions of individual personality and temperament were important in determining whether and to what extent the military and political co-commanders of a unit got along with one another. It is possible that frequent shifting of some political officers from unit to unit in peacetime, as reported by some respondents, was motivated by a desire to find political and military commanders who worked well together. Of course it is also possible that company political officers were sometimes shifted because they got along too well with a military commander and began to overlook his shortcomings. Information obtained from respondents regarding PLA policy on the length of time served by political officers with any one unit was fragmentary and inconclusive. In cases of chronic conflict between the political and military commanders of a unit, in which both seemed at fault, both might be reassigned.

It is likely, however, that higher authorities would not generally intervene unless friction between the co-commanders became overt to the point of affecting their prestige in the eyes of the men. Both the political and military commanders of a unit were under pressure to maintain at least outwardly harmonious relations and a public impression of mutual respect. That they generally succeeded in this respect during the period under survey seems clear from the testimony of privates interviewed with one of our questionnaires. These respondents frequently stated that the two commanders in their units seemed to be good friends, to respect each other, and to at least get along together outwardly. But the "harmony" between political and military commanders could also be superficial:

> We pretended to get along well to save our face. Really we were sometimes bored to death; neither liked to sit facing each other nor did we [the military commanders] like to listen to him [the company political officer]. . . .   [*assistant company military commander*]

> The political and military commanders seemed to get along well with one another. . . . In my opinion even if they had any difficulties with each other, they wouldn't have shown it before us because it would have affected our morale.   [*private*]

While extreme conflicts between military and political commanders were the exception rather than the rule for the period under survey, our materials do indicate that a number of difficulties arose as a result of the divided command structure. The division of authority was not as neat as it seems at first glance. Not only could there be no rigid separation of "political" and "military" spheres of responsibility in a military unit, but, as we have seen, the political officer actually had a supervisory responsibility over the military command channel. Consequently, the division of responsibilities between the two commanders of the unit remained ambiguous, subject to interpretation and variation in practice. Although most respondents felt that the political officer had more authority than the military commander, the terms of their relationship varied and in some cases respondents held that the military commander had equal or greater authority.

We may assume that possibilities of conflict between the two were reduced to the extent of their being able to work out in practice a clear understanding of their spheres of responsibility. The fact that the relationship between them was not more clearly defined by higher authorities tended to give greater scope to personal compatibility as a determinant of its success. As a battalion political officer remarked: "In general, their relation was not bad, but when their individual traits lacked harmony with each other and when they held to their own opinions, there could be conflicts."

The major conflict between the unit military and political commanders, other than in combat periods, sprang from disagreement as to the relative importance of their respective functions. This conflict most commonly manifested itself in competition for access to the men's time for purposes of training and indoctrination. The military commander wanted more time for strictly military training; the political commander stressed the primary importance of indoctrination and morale-building:

In general they got along well with one another . . . [but] political officers and military leaders did have conflicts over hours of training. Each tried to get more time for his type of training.
[*assistant company military commander*]

. . . If the company [military] commander wanted to have military training at a fixed time, and if the political officer wanted to give a political lecture at the same time, there could be a conflict on the problem of time. [*battalion political officer*]

Division of command responsibilities carried with it the possibility that one or both of the co-commanders of a unit would attempt to manipulate blame for personal advantage. Whether the combat deficiency of the men in a unit was due to military inadequacies, for

which the military commander was responsible, or to morale inadequacies, for which the political officer was responsible, could become
a bone of contention. Our interviews do not contain much material
on this point, but the following statement by a political officer has
perhaps broader significance:

When the men were demoralized, I said that the military leaders were to
blame for their failure of leadership, while the company [military] commander ascribed it to the failure of political officers in their political education. Thus we threw blame on each other, so that we were not very
good friends.

Another major area of potential conflict existed in the political officer's efforts to enforce the PLA code of soldierly behavior upon the
military commander. Thus several respondents reported friction between the two as a result of the political officer's efforts to prevent the
military commander from abusing the men or confiscating food from
civilians contrary to regulations.

We have noted that for various reasons the frictions latent in the
dual system of authority were kept to a minimum in the PLA at the
time of the Korean War. However, conditions affecting relations between political officers and military commanders have changed, especially at company level. In Chapter 11, we note developments in the
PLA since the end of the Korean War that have resulted in greater
tensions and conflicts between political and military cadres.

COMPOSITION AND QUALITY OF THE JUNIOR CADRES

In all armies combat performance depends critically upon the quality of leadership furnished by company-level officers and, particularly, by junior cadres at squad and platoon level. To this end many
armies cultivate and rely largely on military "professionalism"; soldiers possessing leadership qualities are selected and trained as combat cadres, and promoted, without particular concern for whether
they hold ideological or political convictions. Such a practice, however, was definitely contrary to the requirements of PLA organizational doctrine at the time.

Rejecting that model of military professionalism, the PLA attempted to recruit squad and platoon leaders from among soldiers
who, in addition to displaying leadership potential, could meet stand-

ards for entrance into the Party. The PLA goal was to merge the military cadre structure with the army political organization. An effectively politicized cadre structure was deemed essential to cohesion and combat performance. This was well understood by members of the PLA at all levels. As one leader put it: "If a method could be devised for destroying the political system within the PLA, the army would lose all tactical efficiency and would become merely a confused mob." The surveillance and control measures employed by the hard core cadre in small combat units was an important means of holding in check disintegrative tendencies present in situations of severe and widespread demoralization of the rank and file. Military pressure and psychological warfare against PLA units were unlikely, therefore, to achieve their ultimate objective—collapse of unit resistance—*until and unless* the hard core cadre within the unit was first weakened in numbers or in spirit.

Given the critical importance in PLA organizational doctrine of having the cadre structure in combat units manned by reliable, well-indoctrinated Party soldiers, it is of considerable interest to note the extent to which the various armies sent to Korea met this requirement. Despite the fact, as noted in Chapter 1, that the units selected for duty in Korea were the best in the PLA from the standpoint of political loyalty as well as military proficiency, the caliber of their junior combat cadres nonetheless fell short of the high standards set by PLA authorities. Relatively few military cadres at company level, and particularly at lower echelons, were Chinese Communists of the pre-1945 vintage. Of 70 company, platoon, and squad leaders interviewed with one or another of our questionnaires, only 9 had entered the PLA before 1946 and 2 during 1946. The remaining 59 had entered service after 1946: 13 in 1947; 24 (mostly former Nationalists) in 1948; 17 (mostly former Nationalists) in 1949; and 5 as recently as 1950.

Though these cadre members had been indoctrinated and were considered relatively reliable, many of them could hardly be considered to have attained the revolutionary idealism of the early Chinese Communist guerrilla forces. The shortcomings of the junior cadres in this respect reflected pragmatic compromises which circumstances had imposed on PLA authorities in the years preceding the Korean War.

From 1927–1937, when the Chinese Communist army was known as "The Worker's and Peasant's Red Army," it was in effect an armed revolutionary movement which had a relatively homogeneous political character. During the next eight years, when it was known as the "Eighth Route Army" and fought against Japan, it became saturated with "patriotic" elements and its class character was adulterated. Nonetheless, according to Colonel Rigg, it was still "nearly pure" from the standpoint of reliability. Then in 1946, with the beginning of the civil war with the Chinese Nationalists, when it was renamed "The Chinese People's Liberation Army" (PLA), its internal political composition began to become more heterogeneous. Chinese Nationalist soldiers and officers captured in the civil war were increasingly incorporated into the PLA, particularly in 1948–1949, for several reasons: to make up for losses, to safeguard against the danger that released prisoners might join Nationalist guerrillas, to utilize their military skills and experiences in the expanding PLA.[4]

It is of some interest to note the pragmatic criteria PLA leaders applied in screening captured CNA personnel in order to decide how to incorporate them into the rapidly expanding communist army. Generally speaking, PLA authorities judged that the political orientation and reliability of these former CNA personnel were related to the degree of resistance that had been offered by the Nationalist unit to which they had belonged. The greater the resistance offered before capture, the more anticommunist the Nationalist unit and its individual members were considered to be; and the greater the caution exercised in incorporating this element into the PLA.

On this basis, Chinese Communist authorities worked out criteria and procedures for incorporating former CNA personnel in three different ways, depending upon the circumstances of capture: [5]

1. *CNA units which negotiated a surrender of the entire group to the PLA without putting up a fight at all*: these units were shifted intact to the PLA with minimum alterations of their officers corps, but with superimposition of the usual political organization (i.e., Political Section and political officers).

2. *CNA units which, after offering some combat, surrendered to the PLA by means of an armistice negotiation*: these were retained intact for a short while, then their officers were gradually displaced with

members of the Communist Party. The former Nationalist officers were gathered into "liberal cadre training" groups for purposes of intense indoctrination; afterwards, many of them were reassigned to PLA units as combat leaders, but usually at a position equivalent to a lower rank. Privates from these former CNA units were sometimes mixed into existing PLA units. Thus, the original organization and composition of these CNA units which had surrendered was eventually broken up because they were not deemed reliable.

3. *CNA units which fought the PLA desperately and surrendered only because they were overpowered*: the personnel from these CNA units were considered even less reliable and, accordingly, the remnants of these former CNA units were dissolved immediately. Their personnel were used to fill in existing PLA units. CNA officers from such groups were not considered reliable and were frequently downgraded to privates in the PLA units to which they were later assigned.

The application of the first two of these methods of utilizing former CNA personnel resulted in the fact that an appreciable number of cadres holding positions equivalent to the rank of junior officers and NCO's at company and lower levels within the PLA were former Nationalist soldiers. Only partial data is available on the proportion of former CNA soldiers among the junior leadership corps in PLA units: of 70 cadres equivalent in position to junior and noncommissioned officers whom we interviewed with one or another of our questionnaires, 47 were former Nationalist Army soldiers while 23 had seen service only in the PLA. (Of the 15 company-level cadres in this group, 8 were former CNA soldiers.)

Former CNA personnel permitted to hold positions of leadership in the PLA were, as we have noted, selected on the basis of pragmatic criteria and heavily indoctrinated. Despite this, however, many of them were not regarded by PLA authorities as true members of the hard core in their unit. Former CNA personnel who attained cadre positions in the PLA equivalent to the rank of junior officers or NCO's were not taken into the Party immediately. Even those former CNA soldiers who entered the Party apparatus often remained on a probationary status and were not immediately accorded the status of full-fledged, trusted members. The urgent need for military skills and junior combat leaders in the rapidly expanding PLA had adulterated standards for selection of military cadres and, to a lesser extent, of Party candidates. The number of opportunists among these former Nationalists was probably not inconsiderable.

Movement upward in both military position and political status—and the two tended to be linked—was carefully controlled by PLA authorities. Our interviews did not cover in detail recruitment and promotion policies. Available materials indicate that several years could elapse before a former CNA soldier was permitted to move up gradually, step by step in military position, to enter the Party on a probationary status, and, finally, to reach the status of a full-fledged member of the controlling Party group within the PLA unit.

The use made of former CNA personnel was also related to the date of their capture and incorporation into PLA formations. Our materials indicate that former Nationalist personnel captured after the end of 1948 generally had not fared very well as yet in their careers in the PLA. Not only had they had less time for absorbing PLA indoctrination and for proving their merit, but it would seem that CNA troops captured after 1948 were often held in greater suspicion by Chinese Communist authorities on the ground that they came from the better CNA units still remaining to Chiang Kai-shek. In any event, a close relationship existed between date of incorporation and subsequent career in the PLA. Of 137 former CNA soldiers whom we interviewed with one or another of our questionnaires, 46 had been privates in the CNA and remained privates in the PLA. Comparison of former rank in the CNA with military position achieved in the PLA for the remaining 91 soldiers in our sample showed that officers and NCO's incorporated into the PLA after 1948 almost invariably suffered reduction in position (50 of 54) whereas almost half of the former CNA officers and NCO's (17 of 37) incorporated into the PLA in 1946–1948 retained or improved their position.

Recency of enlistment and Nationalist background, then, were severe handicaps to PLA authorities for producing a hard core cadre of the desired political strength. It may seem odd to consider soldiers who have been in service for several years and reached positions equivalent to junior officer and NCO as "recent" enlistees; but from the standpoint of Chinese Communist leaders new Party soldiers did not mature fully for many years. Their reliability had to be tested under different circumstances and remained uncertain. They had to be subjected to the close scrutiny of older Party members.

Another potential source of weakness in the junior cadres, from the standpoint of PLA authorities, can only be briefly noted since insufficient data on it was developed in our interviews. In accord with orthodox Marxist practice, the Chinese Communists regard the political reliability of an individual as dependent upon his class origin, unless he has been reformed. Accordingly, in the PLA close attention was paid to the occupational and socioeconomic backgrounds of personnel in screening and grading their political reliability. Class backgrounds other than workers and peasants were regarded with suspicion, though occasional exceptions were made in allowing persons with bourgeois backgrounds to become military cadres.*

The political reliability of cadre members could be affected if they or their families had suffered politically inspired deprivations for which they held the Chinese Communist regime responsible. Our materials on this important point were limited to 17 junior cadres.† Thirteen of the 17 respondents in this group reported having suffered in one or more ways as a result of Chinese Communist policies or actions. Six had had land taken away from their families in the course of the communist redistribution of land holdings in China. Four reported sentences of death, imprisonment, or beating imposed on a member of their family. Two more reported that heavy taxes had been imposed upon their fathers for being a "rich land-owner" or a "wealthy retailer." Another reported that his parents' house had been confiscated and that they had been forced to do compulsory labor.

Two others reported serious family losses due to PLA requisition-

* According to Belden, *China Shakes the World,* p. 480, the class character of the Chinese Communist forces began to be adulterated as far back as during the war against Japan when "patriotic" elements were taken in, apparently in considerable numbers. Rigg, *Red China's Fighting Hordes,* pp. 125–26, calls attention to a regulation adopted on August 4, 1950 by the Chinese Government Administrative Council, entitled: "Decisions Concerning the Differentiation of Class Status in the Countryside," which listed twelve occupational classes, starting with "poor peasant" and ending with "landlord or rich peasant" according to which soldiers were to be classified, presumably to assist in gauging their political reliability.

† These seventeen prisoners were interviewed with a supplemental special questionnaire designed to study the softening of the PLA hard core which had taken place as a result of Korean experiences. Respondents were asked whether they or their families had ever received any benefits or suffered in any way as a result of Chinese Communist or PLA policies and actions.

ing. Four reported that they had been divorced without their consent, or were worried lest easier divorce regulations introduced by the communists might have permitted their wives to divorce them without their knowledge. In contrast, only 3 of the 17 respondents reported any benefit to himself or to his family from the regime's policies. Two of these said they had been awarded land. It is possible, of course, that others had also benefited but were reluctant to mention it.

If these 17 respondents are at all typical in this respect, a surprisingly large proportion of the PLA junior leadership corps at the time of the Korean War had suffered in a direct manner from the communist regime's domestic policies.

In this chapter we have considered several basic organizational features of the PLA that affected the quality of leadership in combat units. Leadership functions and responsibilities were divided between military and political co-commanders of the combat companies. But the latent conflicts and disadvantages inherent in this system of dual authority that have materialized in other communist armies were not present to a marked degree in the PLA during the period encompassed by the study. We have considered some of the special historical circumstances that help account for this, circumstances that may not have persisted during the remainder of the Korean War and were certainly altered thereafter. We have also considered the composition and quality of the all-important junior cadres in PLA combat units at the time of our study. (In Chapter 11, we look at developments in the PLA after the Korean War.) Once again, special historical circumstances affected the ability of PLA authorities to fill cadre positions in combat units with the type of reliable Party soldier called for by the organizational model followed at that time.

7 *Motivation and Control of Combat Personnel*

> The function of the Party soldiers was to take the lead in everything so as to set an example to the rest. In combat they stood foremost and at the retreat they followed last.
>
> *Chinese prisoner, private*

PREVIOUS chapters have described various policies and practices employed by PLA authorities to mold the human material available to them into the kinds of soldiers, officers, and social groups called for by the Chinese Communist model. We also noted that the results achieved in this respect fell considerably short of this goal even in the best units sent to Korea. Such as they were, these armies had to be psychologically prepared for combat. In turning now to the more direct methods PLA leaders employed for motivating and enforcing combat, we shall note a great deal of pragmatism and carryovers from Chinese military tradition at work that were largely independent of the peculiarly communist character of the military model described earlier.

PRECOMBAT BRIEFINGS AND EXHORTATIONS

It was PLA practice before a combat action to prepare members of the unit by giving them a detailed briefing on the immediate tactical situation and the battle plan for the unit. Combat briefings of this kind had several purposes. They served to acquaint all soldiers in the unit with the nature and goals of the forthcoming action and to explain what their part in it was to be. These meetings also offered commanders and combat leaders an opportunity to create a sense of responsibility in each unit and in individual soldiers for contributing effectively to the larger operation. Still another reason for giving small combat groups so detailed an account of battle plans in advance of the action probably had to do with the primitive state of communications in the PLA, which did not permit ready transmission of orders once combat began.[1]

Responsibility for these precombat briefings rested with company political officers. This was part of the larger task, assigned to the political apparatus within the army, of securing cooperation at each level in implementing orders received from above and ensuring that each individual effectively discharged his duties. These briefings were typically preceded by a preparatory conference of the company's Party members. Following this, a meeting was held of the entire company or separately for each platoon and squad. The character of a group discussion was created by Party members. After announcing combat orders and giving instructions on how to implement them, the political officer and the unit military leader would ask the men to discuss problems connected with the execution of the order. Party members then would speak out, according to previous instructions agreed upon in their preliminary conference, directing and controlling the discussion in ways encouraging other soldiers to agree with and support the orders. It was hoped that the discussion could be managed subtly enough so that ordinary soldiers would believe they had taken part in making the decision that they were to carry out and thereby fight more bravely.

When combat circumstances did not allow enough time for this kind of meeting, Party soldiers were simply instructed on ways to lead ordinary soldiers who were under their jurisdiction.

In these precombat briefings information was usually given on the composition, character, weapons, and morale of the opposing unit, the relation of the forthcoming action to larger objectives, the difficulties likely to be encountered, and the grounds for believing that the PLA units would be successful in the forthcoming action.[2]

Combat preparation of this kind was useful. Detailed analysis of enemy forces and of the tactical problem often gave soldiers a greater sense of sureness. As one battalion political instructor we interviewed put it: ". . . when the men of the unit met with some difficulties [in the ensuing combat], they were not so discouraged as their mind had been prepared for them beforehand." [3]

It need not be assumed, of course, that the company political officer was privy to a full and accurate picture of the higher command's knowledge of the tactical situation and the overall PLA battle plan. On the other hand, a surprisingly large amount of reliable information on these matters was often given to ordinary combat soldiers in these briefings.[4] American intelligence officers gradually overcame their initial skepticism regarding the accuracy of Chinese prisoners' information on PLA battle plans. After the war, the official U.S. Marine historian was led to comment on the "paradox that the Chinese Reds, so secretive in other respects, let the man in the ranks know about high-level strategic plans. . . ." [5]

As already noted, precombat briefings were also designed to give the men a convincing basis for expecting that their unit could be successful in the forthcoming action. Certain themes appear to have been relied upon quite often in these briefings for purposes of morale-building. The most important of these themes, especially during the earlier and more successful period of PLA operations in Korea, was the assurance that *superior numbers* would enable the Chinese forces to overrun the opposing enemy unit. Other morale-building themes used in precombat briefings during the period under survey emphasized the PLA's considerable advantage in combat experience, the fact that the Korean people were supporting them, the low morale of opposing forces, and the inferiority of opposing forces in close combat skills.

At the conclusion of these precombat briefings the men were urged to distinguish themselves and their units in the forthcoming action in order to win honors and awards for themselves and their families. They were also called upon to fight bravely for the "sake of the people," China, Mao Tse-tung, and, at times, even Stalin. Efforts to arouse hatred against the enemy were also an important part of precombat exhortations.* Political officers and other Party personnel were required to engage in exhortations of this kind. Instructions were issued to them regarding the general nature of the exhortations to be made, and lower level political personnel were reminded from time to time of the importance of the task.

Party members, too, were usually exhorted by the political officer in the preliminary meetings from which non-Party soldiers were barred.

* We did not directly question the prisoners on this point; and, possibly because of the awkwardness of the subject, few of them volunteered any information.

Thereafter, all soldiers were gathered together in company, platoon, and squad meetings which were stage-managed in order to whip up group spirit and to elicit spontaneous expressions of determination.

Something of the content and flavor of the exhortations by political officers in these precombat meetings is conveyed in the following accounts provided by some of the men we interviewed:

They used to say: "You should distinguish yourself for the sake of the people, following the principle of the revolutionary hero."

They stimulated our fighting spirit by lectures. They said: "Now the enemy military force is such and ours is so and so. Accordingly, we are bound to win this battle. Those who give distinguished service in the battle shall be rewarded, and being reported to superiors, their exploits shall be commended officially. Comrades be courageous."

He gave a special instruction to the effect that since the coming combat was quite an important one he hoped all of us would fight bravely and distinguish ourselves surmounting every obstacle; and he hoped that we would execute the honorable mission that our superior had assigned us by assaulting the enemy as human bullets when we were near to enemy positions. . . .

He encouraged us saying: ". . . If you fulfill your duties and fight bravely we are sure we will win the battle. We can finish the war shortly. Your distinguished services and honors will shine on your head, and your family will be commended officially as an honorable soldier's family when the news is reported to your native place."

He said: "While we were under the Nationalist regime in the past we were persecuted and exploited in extreme fashion. America helped and controlled the CNA. It caused our hard and bitter life in the past. You should fight bravely for the honor of the Chinese, of Mao Tse-tung and Stalin. If not, you will be more miserable than you were in the past. . . ."

He said: "You must do your best to make great gains of which you can be proud before other units."

Following the exhortation, platoon or squad meetings ended typically with all unit members taking a formal oath. The oath was intended to promote mutual identification and loyalty among the soldiers in a combat unit and to commit each of them before his fellows to fight bravely with them in the coming engagement. One of the prisoners in our sample, a political officer himself, recalled the following as being a typical oath taken on these occasions:

A SOLEMN PLEDGE TO KILL THE ENEMY

We eight members of the squad hereby solemnly promise to be determined to kill the enemy by helping the leader in this combat and achieve merits to our most glorious honor.

(1) I will fight bravely without being afraid of enemy fire and make our firearms effective to the greatest extent.

(2) I will overcome every difficulty. I will not be afraid of great mountains to cross or of long marches. I will fight bravely as usual even when I have nothing to eat for a full day.

(3) We will be united and help one another, observe one another, so that we may not retreat even a step.

(4) We eight members of our squad without fail will kill and wound more than three enemies for the people of China and Korea and for our leader.

(5) Should we fail to do these, we wish to be punished. [In case of a Party man he adds, "I will be faithful to the Party as a Party member."]

	Squad Leader _____		Thumb Print
	Name	Date	Signature
Vice S. Leader	_____		Thumb Print
	Name	Date	Signature
Private	_____		Thumb Print
	Name	Date	Signature

Simple exhortations of this type are not characteristic of practices followed in the armies of more highly industrialized and developed societies where, indeed, they would probably be dismissed by the men as a ridiculous appeal to heroics. It would be a mistake, however, to assume that such propaganda was viewed as gauche by the relatively unsophisticated Chinese troops. There is considerable evidence, rather, to the contrary. While the testimony offered by prisoners who had been Party members and combat leaders may have to be discounted somewhat, statements of the following kind made by former Nationalist soldiers, who had been demoted to privates in the PLA and had never been fully assimilated, cannot be ignored:

Putting trust in the political officer's words of this kind, the members of the unit were in high morale and fought full of vigor. So I think it was not a little effective in strengthening the combating power.

. . . everybody made an effort not to act against their oath.

After these special instructions, most soldiers achieved a good result and fought bravely.

There is evidence also, as one would expect, that the positive impact of exhortations declined, especially on non-Party personnel, as the military situation of the PLA deteriorated. Appeals to bravery and "solemn oaths" were more effective in the early stages of the war, before Chinese troops had tasted the murderous concentration of UN firepower. Against the latter, the political officer's words were often of no avail:

> Most of the men trusted what was said and did as they were told. . . . This sort of talk helped to build up fighting spirit among the privates. It made a big difference in the first PLA attacks and combats, but later it began to have less and less effect. This was because they had a taste of enemy artillery barrage from air and ground. [*platoon leader*]

> . . . We did not know about American military power or weapons, and as we heard the speeches of the political officer, our morale was high and soldiers fought well. But when we crossed the 38th Parallel and came south of the Han River, the power of the enemy weapons was so strong that our comrades were being killed off. Seeing this, our soldiers lost courage in spirit, and morale was getting bad. Since that time none of our speeches affected them. [*assistant company commander*]

In units that had been subjected to considerable hardships, the morale of Party soldiers serving as combat leaders of the platoons and squads was also often affected. Under these circumstances even they could not be aroused by the precombat exhortations:

> Such eloquent words had no effect upon the fighters, for they knew how excellent the weapons of the enemy were. . . . Even on the old Eighth Route Army men and the Party members, they had little effect for these men, too, entertained much fear in their heart. [*private*]

> These efforts of the political leader had no effect at all. During this combat the troops retreated or surrendered as they pleased, just as the enemy barrage began. There was not one man who, after hearing the political officer's lecture, attempted to defend his position to the last as the political officer told us to do. [*private, former Nationalist private*]

Short of desperate situations of this kind in which even Party members and combat leaders became utterly demoralized, the system of precombat exhortation evidently retained considerable value. The effectiveness of combat propaganda cannot in any case be adequately gauged merely in terms of the number of individual soldiers who were positively affected thereby. Skillful and determined squad and platoon leaders can raise the fighting performance of ordinary soldiers who lack positive motivation of their own. This is true in all armies, but it took on a special character in the PLA because of its effort to fill all cadre positions down to squad and subsquad levels with Party soldiers or candidates. Since combat leaders of small units were generally Party members or candidates, the fact that *they* were inspired, even under adverse military circumstances, by precombat exhortations strengthened the overall performance of combat units:

The efforts of the political officers gave courage to the communists and members of the [Communist] Democratic Youth League, who fought bravely taking the lead of the common soldiers at the risk of their own lives. . . . [*private, former Nationalist sergeant*]

After such lectures these Communist Party men really came not to fear death; they launched a hand-to-hand struggle in combat achieving great results. [*cultural leader*]

These lectures were very effective, we had no chance of starting an offensive and were always on the defensive; but listening to these lectures many of the unit members became excited. Fanned by military spirit to distinguish themselves, some of them held up grenades and rushed against enemy tanks. But most of these fervents were members of the Party.

[*private, former Nationalist private*]

COMBAT LEADERSHIP BY POLITICAL OFFICERS AND CADRES

During periods of combat, the military commanding cadre of a company was primarily responsible for leadership and direction of the unit. Company political officers and their assistants also had important duties to perform but they were not usually concerned with on-the-spot supervision or detailed conduct of frontline operations. Instead, as many of our respondents indicated, the political officer was likely to remain at the company command post or at other points to the rear from which he could supervise supply, care of the wounded, and burial of the dead, watch for stragglers, direct reserve platoons, and remain in readiness to contact battalion headquarters for further orders.

Ideally, it should not have been necessary for a company political officer personally to provide frontline combat leadership for the troops. This was the function discharged normally by platoon and squad leaders, as well as subsquad group leaders, who were supposed to be well-motivated political soldiers. Our interviews indicate that in the PLA, more so than in the Soviet Army, those soldiers who were supposed to serve as combat "models" did indeed provide strong combat leadership and were not simply a propaganda myth.* Membership in the Party apparatus was not simply a formality; these political soldiers indeed functioned as a hard core in their units. Prior to the Korean War the PLA seems to have been successful to a considerable extent in its effort to recruit more active, energetic, and skilled soldiers as combat leaders and, simultaneously, to enroll them in the Party. Indoctrination and intimate participation in the politicized group life of the unit appears to have imbued these combat leaders with a stronger set of motivations than might otherwise have been the case. As a disaffected private who had been a master sergeant in the Nationalist Army put it: "The function of the Party soldiers was to take the lead in everything so as to set an example to the rest. In combat they stood foremost and at the retreat they followed last. . . ."

There were exceptional circumstances, however, when company political officers were expected to undertake a more direct military function in combat. Thus, if the company commander became a casualty, the political officer might temporarily take over his duties. As we stated previously, few political officers were without considerable military experience of their own; as a result, their assumption of combat direction on the battlefield would not necessarily reduce the quality of military leadership.

In some instances company political officers or their assistants took over leadership of small combat units within the company. This could occur when experienced platoon and squad leaders were lacking, when otherwise competent combat leaders became demoralized or were unable to inspire their men, when the fighting power and

---

* Information on this point about the Soviet Army is from the study by Dicks, Shils, and Dinerstein, *Service Conditions and Morale in the Soviet Armed Forces* (Santa Monica: The RAND Corporation, 1951), see especially p. 66: . . . In the Soviet Army itself, the passionate, fervent Communists, the genuinely convinced men—aside from *Zampolits* [political commissars]—apparently have not succeeded in performing the function of the "hard core" which the extreme Nazis carried out in the German Army. Our information, such as it is, indicates little contagious enthusiasm and strengthened morale flowing from the Communist Party members to the other members of a military unit, nor do we have any evidence that the Communists—aside from *Zampolits*—have stiffened resistance by threatening the weaker soldiers. We have no indication as to whether the Communists have played an especially active role in units which have important or particularly dangerous assignments. Soviet propaganda claims that Communist Party members do play this role, but our data are noncommittal.

morale of the rank-and-file soldiers was so poor (as in the case of raw recruits) that only the immediate presence of higher officers might succeed in rallying them to battle.

Some indication of the varying circumstances under which company political officers undertook to provide direct combat leadership, and of the attitude and policy of higher commanders toward this practice is given by the following material from some of our respondents.

Two platoon leaders in different regiments of the 192d Division, First Field Army (half of whose units were composed of green recruits of poor morale), both reported that their company commanders and their chief and assistant political officers each led one platoon, commanding the attack at the head of the platoons. The result of this, reported one of these platoon leaders, was that "the squad leaders and platoon leaders took courage, thinking they must fight bravely while the company commander and political officer led the men at the utmost head." According to the other platoon leader: "It was very useful as a stimulus to the morale of the men."

A private (125th Division, 4th Field Army) reported that many political officers in his outfit were killed in battle "because they spent much of their time with the men in the front line to lead combat themselves and to encourage the men." A company political officer (118th Division, 4th Field Army) reported that all leaders up to and including company commander had been ordered at one point to assume combat leadership at the utmost front line in order to raise the men's fighting spirit.

A cultural leader (platoon grade leader, 195th Division, 1st Field Army), "two-thirds" of whose unit was composed of inexperienced, poorly trained recruits with low morale, reported that ordinarily the fighting spirit of the men could not be raised by the platoon or squad leaders who themselves had low morale. The company commander was forbidden by battalion and regimental leaders from leading at the front on the ground that it would be difficult to replace him. Therefore, in order to stimulate morale, the company political officer went to the front with the assistant company commander. When the situation became critical the battalion commander and battalion political instructor, who ordinarily stayed on the third line with a reserve company, went forward to inspect and to encourage.

In addition to participating directly as combat leaders on occasion, political officers attempted to boost morale by visiting frontline positions. Some of our respondents reported that political officers frequently accompanied company and battalion military commanders on such visits. But this was by no means the universal practice. On occasion, the failure of political officers to visit the front was resented by the men, particularly in view of the exhortation to heroics which they had made prior to combat:

> When the battalion and company commanders came to the front line, the men's morale was raised high. On the other hand, not being able to see the battalion and company political officers on the front line, the men cursed them inwardly: "Those people who told us to fight bravely when there was no combat never have even come to the front line."
>
> [*platoon leader, 4th Field Army*]

> The men hated very much the battalion and company political officers who were always in the rear on the pretext of watching for stragglers.
>
> [*platoon leader, 3d Field Army*]

COMBAT SURVEILLANCE AND ENFORCEMENT

In situations calling for an attack, as we have noted, combat leaders served as "models" to inspire rank-and-file soldiers to aggressive assault tactics. In other tactical situations the task of combat leadership was to firm up the resistance of the rank and file, to prevent them from behaving in an "individual" undisciplined manner, from retreating, panicking, or performing other acts of cowardice. For this purpose strong emphasis was placed upon mutual supervision and surveillance during combat. Depending upon the quality of the personnel filling the cadre positions in a combat unit, tendencies toward unit disintegration under unfavorable combat conditions could be more or less effectively controlled. With well-motivated Party adherents straddling the cadre control structure of a unit down to the subsquad level, each group leader had only two or three non-Party rank-and-file soldiers to watch over and control.

Our respondents frequently noted that this surveillance and control system had been quite effective in combat. Disaffected soldiers were afforded few opportunities to desert to the rear or to voluntarily surrender to the enemy. The severity of the surveillance tended to isolate the individual soldier and to prevent him from coming together with

like-minded members of his unit to discuss and plan desertion or surrender.

The surveillance network within combat units could easily be
transformed into a method for *combat enforcement*. From an early
stage after Chinese intervention into the Korean War, members of the
hard core surveillance apparatus in some units were empowered to
take direct coercive action to enforce combat and prevent desertion.
Several interviewees mentioned that even while the PLA was advancing on the battlefield generally, special units had been set up to catch
deserters running away from the front and to pick them up in rear
areas. Sometimes precombat exhortations given the men by their political officers were combined with explicit threats of death to those
who retreated without orders. Other respondents reported that if the
men feared to advance, the political officers "gave us combat enforcement, holding their pistols."

Under ordinary conditions while still in China, attempted desertion
was apparently common. A number of the prisoners interviewed had
made unsuccessful attempts of this sort; they reported that relatively
mild punishment—severe criticism or a short term of imprisonment—was inflicted on first offenders. Only repeated offenders were
executed. The attitude toward desertion in Korea was stiffer, but
even here our respondents indicated that the death penalty for desertion was an ultimate rather than immediate punishment. The likelihood of summary execution for attempted desertion was greater during combat and in critical circumstances. It should be remembered
that the findings presented here cover only the period up to approximately late April and mid-May 1951; immediately thereafter, prior
to the inception of truce negotiations, the military situation of the
PLA further deteriorated and there may have been greater reliance at
that time upon explicit threats of execution.

If fear of extreme punishment was not always utilized as a deterrent, the tightness of the surveillance and control system in any case
gave would-be deserters few opportunities to carry out their intention.
This is indirectly conveyed by the answers 86 prisoners (63 privates,
23 cadres) gave to the question: "What made you follow the PLA to
the last, undergoing so many hardships in this war?" (See Table 2.)
The deterrence effect of the surveillance system was the consideration
mentioned most frequently—by 83 percent of the privates in the

TABLE 2

REASONS GIVEN BY EIGHTY-SIX CHINESE PRISONERS
FOR HAVING FOLLOWED THEIR UNIT TO THE LAST [a]

	Privates *(63)*	*Cadres* *(23)*
Surveillance ever-present, gave no opportunity to desert [b]	52 (83%)	10 (42%)
Desertion to rear futile; would be caught and returned to front line	13	4
Discouraged from deserting due to difficulties anticipated from not knowing Korean language or geography; did not know where to go	16	5
Fear of being shot or abused if captured by UN forces	14	5
No opportunity to surrender because mostly in rear area or ill	9	3
Did not intend desertion; taken prisoner unwillingly [c]	0	7
Able to desert without too much difficulty	7	1
Other answers (e.g., desertion in China futile due to communist control over all localities)	5	4

[a] More than one reason was given by a number of prisoners.
[b] Among those giving this reason, 18 privates and 3 cadres stated in addition that they feared execution by PLA authorities if caught deserting.
[c] These replies indicated positive motivation for continuing combat until forcibly captured.

sample, and by over 40 percent of the cadres at company and squad level. The replies to this question, while giving some indication of the relative importance of the surveillance system in discouraging desertions, cannot be used for confident generalizations about the PLA as a whole.

Most of these eighty-six respondents, particularly the privates, evidently had been highly demoralized for some time prior to capture. One would expect highly demoralized soldiers to be deterred from desertion more by the surveillance and control system within their unit than by fear of possibly harsh treatment at the hands of enemy forces. Fear of harsh treatment in the event of capture probably characterized soldiers who were not yet severely demoralized, who still retained some allegiance to their unit, or who accepted the propaganda theme of enemy atrocities as a convenient means of rationalizing their forced acceptance of combat duties which the hard core cadre imposed on them.

We gained the impression from the prisoners interviewed that belief in good treatment by UN forces had often emerged belatedly, in direct response to the increasing or sudden desperation of the soldier's military situation. As in other kinds of desperate situations when an anxiety-ridden individual's hopes come to dominate and shape his expectations, the belief in good treatment was in a sense "born of necessity." The closer the soldier came to death or capture, the more willing he evidently became to believe the promises of good treatment made in United States psychological warfare. While these impressions emerged strongly from the interview materials, they remain hypotheses which it was not possible to verify. Nonetheless, statements by prisoners such as the following one are highly suggestive of the way in which beliefs regarding postcapture treatment developed in response to the situation: ". . . the fear of being killed if I would surrender made me follow the PLA to the last. But immediately before I surrendered, the men in the unit in general said that the enemy do not kill prisoners, so I surrendered."

The emphasis given here to the importance of situational factors in inducing a change in beliefs does not of course imply that assurances of good treatment in psychological warfare were of no consequence. Assurances of this kind, even though based on facts and skillfully publicized, may have no immediate effect in increasing the belief in good treatment among those enemy forces that have not suffered as yet the corrosive effects of prolonged military hardship and defeat. Nonetheless, such assurances serve as useful "preparatory" communications; they may have a delayed effect later on, serving to expedite the desired change of beliefs and behavior when the situation of the soldier and his unit has deteriorated.

COMBAT EVALUATION AND AWARDS

The awards system was ingeniously structured to permit both a very wide distribution of decorations and a finely graduated differentiation of status and prestige. It is interesting to note that in the Soviet Army the official policy of few and sparsely awarded tokens of merit was changed only in World War II. An elaborate hierarchy of military decorations was created at that time, and the whole apparatus for status differentiation within the Soviet Army made rapid strides thereafter.[6]

The awards system in the PLA had the simple purpose of stimulating all kinds of desired behavior. What distinguished the PLA in this respect was the crudity of its awards system, when viewed from a Western standpoint. PLA leaders openly exhorted their men to do meritorious deeds in order to win fame, honor, and material prizes. And, without attempt at subtlety, they did not hesitate to utilize ceremonies at which awards were given to engage in pedagogical instruction and to exhort other men to emulate the prize winner.

Chinese Communist authorities evidently regarded the awards system as being a particularly important part of indoctrination, training, and morale-building programs. Such was the zeal with which, according to our respondents, the political apparatus tackled this problem that life in the PLA appeared to be given over to a never-ending, all-inclusive process of performance assessment. Everyone in the cadre hierarchy was engaged in rating his subordinates and in turn being rated by his immediate superiors. Reports were submitted at frequent intervals, verbally as well as in writing, from each echelon to the next higher level. Performance assessment was applied to minute peacetime and noncombat chores as well as to behavior during combat operations. Understandably, however, the system worked in a more orderly, regularized, and formal fashion outside the sphere of immediate combat.

Immediately following a combat engagement, when a unit was pulled back several miles from the front in order to rest, one man in each squad was designated to recommend men in his squad for merits. These men, together with their company commanders, served as a "committee of examination" to examine and grade meritorious deeds. Results were reported to political officers for their approval. The more important the award the higher the headquarters which must approve the recommendation.

Awards were announced by the political officer at "recognition meetings" which included the membership of the entire company (in some cases only the squad). Recipients came before the assembled group one by one, a red flower was pinned on the soldier's breast, and they were saluted by the entire group. The political officer praised the recipient's meritorious service and exhorted others to make him their model. A speech of the kind typically given by the political officer on such an occasion was furnished by one of the prisoners interviewed:

The comrade performed his duty without regard to life or death for the sake of our unit and our country in the face of great difficulties. I ask that all the men also show merit following the example of this comrade.

When lack of time did not permit such a ceremony, the political officer personally called upon the individual soldier to praise him. If the political officer was preoccupied or absent, the military commander of the company acted in his place.

An open attempt was made to regulate the social respect given a soldier and his family according to the level of his performance. It was evidently assumed that most soldiers would be influenced by the prospect of grants of honor and deference. They were encouraged to do their best not only in order to merit praise before the entire unit, but also in order to have their deeds publicized back home in their local communities and, in cases of an outstanding merit, throughout the province or even the whole of China. The prospect was held out that a meritorious soldier might bring honor to his family and achieve special forms of deference—for example, he might be rewarded by being allowed to sit with high-ranking military leaders or even to shake hands with Mao Tse-tung:

The political officer said: "The comrade has achieved meritorious service at the risk of his life for the fatherland, people, himself, and his family. This is a glory not only for himself but also for his family. The local government (of the soldier's residence) shall be informed of the meritorious services of these comrades. Their families shall be treated well. Newspapers shall talk of their glorious deeds. A label, 'Glorious House of a Soldier,' will be placed on the gate of their house. The people in the community will offer their gratitude and respect to the families of these soldiers. You other soldiers should also perform meritorious deeds for yourselves and your families."

The political officer said: "If you, our comrades, fight bravely and achieve meritorious conduct, you will be given special treatment. . . . And you will be seated side by side with leaders at such entertainment as plays, guided to the front seat and treated specially in other ways."

The political officer said: "Since meritorious deeds are to be reported to Premier Mao Tse-tung, this would be not merely your own glory, but also your family's. . . . Moreover, the merits will be announced among the whole army and reported even in the newspapers in China, so that your name will shine for a long time."

Those who achieved the Special Merit received the privilege of a personal meeting with Premier Mao Tse-tung.

While the PLA was not unique in providing a hierarchy of finely graduated awards, perhaps unusual was the opportunity offered a soldier to accumulate smaller merits into progressively larger ones. Thus the more important merits could be won not only directly, by a particularly outstanding deed, but by accumulating a certain number of lesser merits. The "commendation award," the lowest award, was given for faithful achievement of duties and seemed to be the counterpart of the "good conduct" medal in the U.S. Army. The third class merit was usually given for positive performance of daily tasks; three of these automatically qualified the recipient for a second class merit, which was otherwise given directly for a brave assault on the enemy. Three second class merits, in turn, earned a first class award, which was otherwise given directly, for example, to a soldier who attacked enemy tanks in hand-to-hand combat and destroyed one tank. The accumulation of three first class merits, in turn, yielded a "special merit," which was otherwise given directly for capturing enemy soldiers, inflicting a great loss of tanks or casualties, or shooting down an enemy plane. The special merit was the highest merit award in the PLA and qualified the recipient at the same time for the title "combat hero." There were different grades of the combat hero corresponding to the organization of the PLA: Regimental, Divisional, Corps, Field Army, and National.*

The awards system reinforced indoctrination efforts designed to instill in the men the officially prescribed conception of the soldierly role and to get them to behave in everyday life along desired lines. In fact, few directives and injunctions were not reinforced by incentives and rewards. If the authorities wanted to promote mutual helpfulness

---

* This consolidates material from a number of respondents. A somewhat different version of the awards was given by other prisoners interviewed. PLA military publications, which presumably contain information on the subject, were not utilized. For a brief account of PLA decorations, see Rigg, *Red China's Fighting Hordes*, pp. 110–12.

within units, to improve soldier relationships with civilians, to encourage the taking of enemy prisoners, etc., they reinforced their verbal injunctions with a specific reward for that conduct. If during military operations, as in Korea, the highest priority was placed on getting supplies to the front, special incentives and merits were held out to transport units for successful performance of their tasks.

Material rewards or prizes were offered in addition to honorific awards and medals. Commodities needed in everyday life—for example, cigarettes, tooth brushes, soap, handkerchiefs, towels, pencils, paper, underwear, stockings—were frequently given to award winners. When circumstances permitted, special meals and entertainment were given to high award winners. Sometimes, money was given or promised:

I saw a piece of washing soap given to the winner of the minor meritorious award. A soap, a pencil and letter papers were given to the winner of the major meritorious award. . . .

The man who was honored by the regimental merit would be entertained by the regiment for six or seven days during which he could drink liquor and eat delicious meals. The man who was awarded the divisional merit was to be entertained at the division for a month during which he could get a delicate diet and wine. The man who got the army's merit would get a furlough for two or three months during which he could ride in an automobile and fly in an airplane to interview the Red boss, Mao Tse-tung, with whom he could chat and eat.

The political officer told us that should a man achieve a meritorious exploit on the battlefield . . . his family would be awarded a military emblem; a family having no land to plough would be given land; a family having no movable property would be subsidized with money.

The political officer said: "If you fight bravely and distinguish yourselves . . . your family will be commended officially as an honorable soldier's family and will be treated well—that is, it will be rationed food and distributed cotton cloth."

While a soldier's opportunities for promotion were furthered by winning an award, information obtained from our respondents does not indicate that promotion followed automatically. But the award winner at least received a higher priority for promotion when a vacancy occurred. Many respondents reported that their political officers held out the possibility of promotion as an inducement.

Recruitment of new members for the Communist Party was also

closely tied in with the awards system. Party committees within the units were always interested in identifying likely candidates for Party membership. There was an urgent need for combat leaders on squad and platoon levels who combined military skill with political reliability. Therefore, privates who achieved meritorious deeds were closely scrutinized as possible candidates for the Party. Entrance into the Party was frequently held out as an inducement by the political officer in his precombat exhortations for bravery. The achievement of merit awards did not automatically qualify the recipient, but it was taken into account in recommending a soldier for Party candidacy. For soldiers already in the Party, as one would expect, advancement within the political apparatus of the army depended to some extent upon the record they made and the merit awards they accumulated:

The political officer said: "If you accomplish your duties bravely and achieve a great exploit, you, my comrades, will be able to become members of the Communist Party. . . ."

Everybody who accomplished meritorious services got a priority to join the Party. . . .

The political officer said [at an awards ceremony]: ". . . These comrades have done great works for the people and will be promoted to higher political positions gradually."

The awards system was also utilized to promote unit pride and to strengthen group solidarity within units. In presenting an award at a unit ceremony, the political officer often praised the recipient for the honor he had brought to his whole squad, platoon, company, battalion, regiment, division, and corps as well as to himself. A variety of unit awards were available, too, for rewarding the group as a whole for its performance:

When a squad or a platoon distinguished itself, the company political officer reported to Divisional Headquarters on it; then Divisional Headquarters awarded the unit a title or a flag depending upon the greatness of the meritorious conduct or bravery. There were such titles as Black Night Squad, Hero Squad, Night Combat Squad, etc. On the flags presented there was a brocaded mask flag.

Distinguished service by a unit could also be rewarded by naming the unit after its leader if he was killed in action.

One of the highest unit awards was the title, "Iron and Steel Brigade," which was given for outstanding combat performance. It could be awarded after a major engagement on the decision of the divisional political secretary. A more common method of awarding it was for an army commander to present it to a divisional commander *prior* to an expected engagement. The divisional commander in turn called in his regimental commanders, informed them of the honor, and told them that he would award it to the regiment which fought best in the coming action. The regimental commanders then exhorted their troops. In this manner, unit awards were utilized to promote competition between different units within the same division. A unit so honored, and only that unit, learned a special marching song. Units winning the "Iron and Steel" designation were regarded as crack units having high morale; and perhaps for this reason they were sometimes taken into the confidence of PLA authorities more closely than other units.

Much less use was made of the argument that a soldier's *postwar* welfare depended upon the achievement of meritorious deeds while in service. The reason for avoiding this subject is not difficult to infer. There was no regular period of military service in the PLA at that time, and no easy way of obtaining a discharge. For all practical purposes, once a soldier was taken into the army, whether as a volunteer, conscript, or as a Nationalist prisoner, he remained in service indefinitely until he died or lost his value to the PLA.

The effectiveness of the awards system both in fostering identification with the group and strengthening combat motivation was probably somewhat greater in the PLA than in other armies. Except when they were subjected to extremely severe conditions of life, work, and combat, many soldiers in the PLA were evidently attracted by the prospect of honor and material rewards for meritorious behavior. It would certainly seem to be the case that they were motivated thereby to a degree that would be unusual in the U.S. Army. Cultural differences may have a bearing on this, especially as regards the apparently greater sensitivity of Chinese soldiers to overt manifestations of social respect and to the importance of family in social life. The material prizes offered by the PLA seem trivial by Western standards but, of course, such matters are relative and depend upon the standard of living. Perhaps the utility of material awards can be better appreciated by Western observers if one were to imagine that the U.S. Army offered as prizes not tooth brushes, underwear, and stockings, as in the PLA, but automobiles and retirement pensions.

Respondents who testified to the effectiveness of the awards system included, it will be noted, some who were not members of the in-group within their unit:

The men who witnessed this scene [the awarding of merit prizes, including monetary awards to transport prize winners] were stimulated to work hard in order to distinguish themselves, and be favored with such privileges.   [*private, former Nationalist captain, identification with out-group*]

When the award-winning soldier returned to the front line [after a furlough], many merits of order were shining on his breast. Seeing him, other soldiers made up their minds to do a distinguished merit, considering it an exquisite glory.

[*private, former Nationalist corporal, identification with in-group*]

Such a prize-giving system was quite effective upon the men, who came to think that such commendation was an honor not only for themselves but also for their families. Their families were respected and admired by the people.

[*private, former Nationalist private, identification with in-group*]

It was really effective upon the men. Most soldiers made efforts to perform meritorious deeds to obtain good treatment for themselves and their families. Those who had performed meritorious services got freedom of speech and action to a certain degree. Compared to others, they got more commodities, higher pay, and were respected by others. Their families were respected and also treated well by their local governments and people. The men came to know these facts clearly.

[*cultural leader of platoon rank,*
former Nationalist 2d lieutenant]

Because of these prizes and such praise, the members of the unit exerted themselves to accomplish distinguished service and brave exploits in combat. . . .

[*supply cadre, assistant company commander rank, veteran*]

The men respected and envied those who were rewarded; their morale was stimulated, and they envied that those who were rewarded would be able to see chairman Mao Tse-tung and shake hands with him when the war was over.

[*cultural leader of platoon leader rank, procommunist attitudes*]

The efficacy of material rewards in raising combat motivation was also indirectly emphasized in the grim observation, volunteered by several respondents, that looting was a primary incentive for Chinese troops in battle:

They were encouraged to break through the enemy position to kill and wound the enemy and take his rations, clothes, boots, fountain pens, cigarettes, lighters, and watches.

[*battalion commander, former Nationalist 2d lieutenant*]

The men fought bravely in order to distinguish themselves for the sake of the people, following the principle of the hero. But their real purpose was to get the enemy's biscuits, canned food, chocolates, and clothes after the attack.   [*cultural instructor, 2d lieutenant rank*]

The directness and lack of subtlety with which honor and material prizes were offered to soldiers for good performance of combat and noncombat duties did not seem to prejudice the efficacy of the awards system. It must be remembered that most of these soldiers were drawn from the poorly educated, economically deprived peasantry. The more sophisticated former Nationalist soldiers, who had the benefit in many cases of broader experience and urban backgrounds, were more likely to see through the obvious peddling of honor and prizes in return for good deeds. The negative attitude of these former CNA soldiers is typified by the phrase "childish means" which they frequently applied to the PLA awards system:

It had a strong effect on the old Eighth Route Army men and the Party members, who were determined to try to get such rewards. But to us who were from the Nationalist Army it seemed to be but a child's play. We laughed at it and sometimes scorned them.

[*private, former Nationalist private, identification with out-group*]

Party members and fervent Reds wished to get such titles and medals. But noncommunists would laugh at their childish means.

[*assistant company commander, former Nationalist 2d lieutenant*]

Our interviews suggest that the awards system was less effective in Korea than it had been in China, and its value declined further as the military situation of the PLA in Korea deteriorated. Our interviews indicate that many Chinese soldiers—including an appreciable number of relatively new Party soldiers serving as squad and platoon leaders—soon came to view the task demanded of them in Korea as totally unreasonable. Once the early successful Chinese offensives ground to a halt and the full firepower of the UN forces was felt, the motivational value of the awards system began to drop sharply:

While in the rear when I saw a man with the Hero medal I envied him and wished I had the medal too. But when we were in the frontline combat area, such vain ideas were swept away. I thought then that if I were to die, there would be no more Hero, no more medal!

[*private, former Nationalist private, identification with out-group*]

However, I never envied such a thing [awards] at all. I thought that while there is life there is honor. How should we know honor after death? If anyone died in order to get it, nothing would be so foolish.

[*private, former Nationalist private, identification with out-group*]

Most of those who were rewarded for their meritorious deeds were Party men or procommunists and they were proud of the award. The other men thought it without interest and a token of early death to be awarded.   [*captain, former Nationalist captain*]

Two other factors of lesser importance contributed nonetheless to the reduced efficacy of the awards system in Korea. Many of our respondents noted there had been a partial breakdown in the implementation of the awards system. Awards continued to be made in most (but not all) units; but the actual delivery of medals was in many if not most cases postponed until the soldier returned to China. Perhaps more important than this was the fact that many fewer material prizes could be awarded in Korea, because of the difficult supply problem, than had been the case in China. The practice of rewarding meritorious soldiers with better and more food, for example, could hardly be continued on the same scale in Korea. A number of respondents explained their coolness toward award winning by noting that everyone, award winner or not, got the same two meals a day in Korea.

The motivational utility of the awards system was further handicapped in that promises of material aid to the families of meritorious soldiers tended to lose their efficacy. Mired down in Korea, uncertain when and if they would ever get back to China, soldiers often felt there was no way to verify whether promises to aid their families were being or would be kept. Aware of this, PLA authorities occasionally attempted to provide "evidence" to show that promises of special material benefits for families of merit-winning soldiers were being kept. But in one instance, at least, the attempt was clumsy and backfired:

About a month after each formal official commendation, the political officer says without fail that a letter has arrived from the father of a comrade who was praised about a month ago. After gathering together all the members of the company he reads the letter which usually says: "After you joined the PLA, we were given enough land and a house. We are in easy circumstances at present. I expect you not to worry about your family. I hope you will fight bravely. As soon as the good news of your meritorious deeds was delivered, not only the local government but also all the village sent flowers and entertained us at dinner. Their great gratitude and respect is too much for me. Your meritorious service is a great glory not only for yourself but also for your family. I, your father, expect you to fight more bravely for our fatherland and people. You ought to return the favor." Laughable to say, the letter is a false one. It has no envelope. After reading it to us, the political officer usually puts it in his pocket. If it is a true letter, he would return it to the man addressed, I think.   [*cultural instructor of platoon leader rank, former Nationalist 2d lieutenant*]

As in the case of other motivational practices that were employed, the value of the awards system for raising combat motivation cannot be measured simply in terms of the number of rank-and-file soldiers favorably affected. To evaluate the awards system in these terms would overlook the fact that its primary function was probably that of motivating the hard core soldiers who filled the cadre positions. As already noted, Party soldiers served as combat leaders and "models." It is of great significance, therefore, that according to the almost unanimous testimony of prisoners interviewed, the awards system strongly influenced the combat motivation of these key personnel. Even under relatively difficult military conditions, the morale of Party soldiers evidently remained high and they were stimulated to fight bravely by the prospect of winning awards.

This is not to say, of course, that their readiness for combat was due exclusively or even primarily to the awards system. What is clear, rather, is that the prospect of awards effectively reinforced the motivation of these Party soldiers, partly no doubt because they were already well incorporated into the group and identified with its goals. Non-Party soldiers, unaffected by precombat exhortations to heroics and by promises of honor and prizes, made ungrudging admissions that the Party "fervents" were positively stimulated and fought bravely: "The Party members fought bravely in fact after being given such special instruction; however, the majority of the men joined combat reluctantly." [*private, identified with the out-group*]

Our interviews did not produce systematic data on the frequency and distribution of awards among different categories of soldiers. But it is clear that to a disproportionate extent awards, and especially the higher ones, went to commanders and junior cadres, all of whom were likely to be Party members.

If Party men reaped most of the awards, it was not necessarily because of favoritism. In fact, they *were* the bravest fighters, the most active, hardworking, and loyal elements in the PLA. Recruitment into the Party was based partly upon these criteria; the award-winning non-Party soldiers of today were likely to become Party soldiers tomorrow. On the whole, there appears to have been little resentment among non-Party soldiers that Party fervents got most of the awards and the higher merits. In order to experience such resentment, some sense of identification with and desire for participation in the PLA system would have had to be present. But many of these non-Party soldiers stood so much outside the group life of their units; they shared so little its ideals and aspirations that they were not caught up in the contest for awards.

The possibility of resentment was further reduced by virtue of the fact that the system of awards had conspicuous democratic and egalitarian features. There was only one system of awards, theoretically open to all; there were no special merits reserved exclusively for Party soldiers. And the same type of award ceremony was held whether the recipient was a cadre or private, a Party or non-Party soldier. In this connection we may recall the widespread agreement among our respondents, noted in Chapter 4, that company political officers had been ready to praise all those who performed well.

But not all non-Party soldiers were equally detached from the group life of the PLA. Many former Nationalist soldiers felt that career opportunities in the PLA were unfairly blocked by the stigma of having belonged earlier to the CNA. To have been a former Nationalist soldier often made one an object of distrust and suspicion in the PLA. With few exceptions most former CNA soldiers could work their way only gradually into the inner group of their unit. Soldiers who shared such aspirations, who stood on the outside but who would have liked to be in, and who had made some effort to achieve good deeds in order to advance themselves, undoubtedly experienced occasional resentment of the award winners or became embittered. Still, judging from available materials, those who felt discriminated against by the distribution of awards evidently constituted a small group. Remarks of the following caliber were infrequently offered by prisoners whom we interviewed:

Old Eighth Route Army Party men were able to get official commendations easily; so they made much effort . . . but it was difficult for ordinary men in the unit to get official commendations. I don't know why. And, consequently, they had discontent and complaints in their heart and were displeased. The partiality sometimes had a bad effect on them.

[*assistant squad leader, former Nationalist master sergeant*]

We have dealt in this chapter with various methods employed by the PLA for motivating and enforcing combat. We have left for separate treatment in the following two chapters the question of the character and efficacy of the broader war indoctrination these troops received before they were sent to Korea.

8 *War Indoctrination*

> . . . guerrilla troops should have a precise conception of the polit-
> ical goal of the struggle and the political organization to be used in
> attaining that goal. . . . In a war of long duration, those whose
> conviction that the people must be emancipated is not deep rooted
> are likely to become shaken in their faith or actually revolt. With-
> out the general [political] education that enables everyone to under-
> stand our goal . . . the soldiers fight without conviction and lose
> their determination.
>
> *Mao Tse-tung*

CHINESE COMMUNIST experience emphasizes, as the quotation
from Mao Tse-tung indicates, that thorough indoctrination of soldiers
on the origins and war aims of a conflict is essential in sustaining
their morale and combat performance through difficult and prolonged
military operations. This proposition would seem so self-evident as to
be virtually a truism; and yet, on this very question of the importance
of war indoctrination, both theory and practice have varied in
modern armies. It may give us a better perspective on the Chinese
Communist experience, therefore, if we review briefly some of the
evidence concerning the significance of war indoctrination for the
U.S. Army during World War II.

Intensive surveys were made during the war of the morale and attitudes of American soldiers. The results of these surveys led some
scholars to suggest that political and ideological considerations apparently played only a minor role in stimulating the morale and combat performance of the American soldier. The publication of these
official wartime attitude surveys in the multivolume study, *The American Soldier,* did indeed produce much intriguing evidence of the
largely apolitical motivations of soldiers in World War II.[1] While the
authors of *The American Soldier* gave a cautious, balanced interpretation of their findings, their results and those of other studies of mili-

tary psychology * were widely taken as supporting the general proposition that intimate comradely ties within small military groups—and, related to this, the spirit and attitudes of military "professionalism"—are far more important sources of good combat motivation than a soldier's understanding of the origins of a war and war aims. The proponents of this thesis do not ignore the fact that soldiers with bad morale often question the legitimacy and justification of the war ("Why are we here?" "What are we fighting for?"). But this is regarded as more an expression of bad morale rather than its cause. According to this view, the really important bases of combat morale and motivation lie elsewhere in the nature of the small groups to which the individual belongs and the relation of these combat groups to the larger organizational structure.

There is much to be said for this thesis. Yet, as the authors of *The American Soldier* themselves suggested [2] and Edward A. Shils and Hans Speier subsequently emphasized in two independent appraisals,[3] appreciation of the importance of small group comradeliness for military morale should not be allowed to obscure its relationship to political convictions and the importance of these convictions, too, for military morale. Thus, tacit acceptance by soldiers of the legitimacy of a war may itself be an important precondition for the formation of, and participation in, small group ties in military units. A soldier's tacit patriotism and his acceptance of the legitimacy of a war, although not in themselves producing strong combat motivations, nonetheless contribute indirectly to his combat readiness by furthering a "general readiness to accept commands" and by providing "the rudiments of one of the most important preconditions for the formation of primary groups. . . ." They do so, Shils suggests, by providing ". . . *a set of generalized moral predispositions* or *sense of obligation*. The latter need not be strongly present in consciousness but some measure of identification with the collectivity and some sense of generalized obligation and readiness to acknowledge the legitimacy of its demands in numerous particular situations must exist.

* Particularly important in this respect is the pioneering research with German prisoners of war in World War II by Dr. Henry V. Dicks, a British psychiatrist. See, for example, his "German Personality Traits and National Socialist Ideology," *Human Relations,* Vol. 3, No. 2, June 1950. Another basic reference is Edward A. Shils and Morris Janowitz, "Cohesion and Disintegration in the Wehrmacht," *Public Opinion Quarterly,* Vol. 12, No. 2, Summer 1948.

Thus, for example, the soldiers who thought first of getting the job done must, in some way, have accepted the legitimacy of the 'job' and felt some degree of obligation to carry it out." [4]

The understanding of the complex basis of military morale conveyed in these appraisals of U.S. Armed Forces in World War II is suggestive for the present study. It would be imprudent, of course, to apply this theory of morale mechanically to an army like the PLA, since it differs so much in its origins and character from Western armies. This brief digression regarding combat motivations in the U.S. Army, however, does serve to remind us that the bases and dynamics of morale are complex and are not presently capable of being reduced to simple cause-effect relationships between well-defined variables. As Shils and Speier have implied, "comradely ties" and "political convictions" about a war evidently are not entirely separate and independent variables; rather, they interact with each other in subtle ways. Combat motivation or morale is in any case not determined solely by comradely ties or political convictions. Other factors—equipment, the quality of leadership—may also affect combat motivation. Moreover, combat morale is not simply a dependent variable in its relation to political convictions and comradely ties. There can be reverse effects: Once combat morale has deteriorated, it can begin to undermine the individual's political convictions about the war as well as his comradely ties with other soldiers. While it is true that adverse combat conditions may initially heighten a soldier's identifications with his group, nonetheless the anxieties, deprivations, and fatigue associated with severe, prolonged combat may eventually loosen both the soldier's identification with the comradely group and his acceptance of the legitimacy of the war.[5] This kind of feedback effect is, indeed, strongly suggested by our materials on morale trends within the PLA during the Korean War.

Prior to sending their forces into Korea, Chinese Communist leaders expended considerable effort in attempting to instill in their soldiers an understanding and acceptance of the official account of the origins and nature of the war and of the legitimacy of Chinese and North Korean war aims. There is no question but that PLA authorities acted on the assumption that successful war indoctrination would significantly enhance the cohesion and morale of their combat forces. Their earlier experiences must have given PLA leaders tremendous confidence in the importance of this factor. Successful political indoctrination of the masses had after all been essential in creating a revolutionary army and in carrying operations against the Chinese Nationalist regime to a successful conclusion. Suggestive of the quality of this experience is Lieutenant Colonel Robert B. Rigg's vivid account of the impact which indoctrination had on Manchurians who were unwillingly conscripted and impressed into the Chinese Communist Army in 1945–1946, at a critical point in the civil war:

They were sullen groups whose obedience was initially brought about by the bayonets that ringed them in. Some deserted; others were shot for trying. Some surrendered to the enemy in subsequent skirmishing; but most of them were guarded, quickly trained, handed guns and told to shoot—or be shot by the Kuomintang enemy. They were not the best soldiers. . . . But several things impressed them. For one, they never had heard so much talk in an army before—about a cause and about the purpose for fighting. Talk, talk, lecture, literature, slogans, songs. The commissars drummed and droned the cause of the crusade. Chinese or Japanese armies of the past had never been like this. Chang Tso-lin's and Chiang Hsueh-liang's war-lord armies had molded soldiers, but never by talk. . . . Whatever there was to dislike about their unsought military service, the new Manchurian soldiers had to admit that *this* army had a purpose, or at least it announced one.[6]

Once military preparations for intervening in the Korean War were seriously under way, therefore, we may assume that PLA authorities turned to the task of indoctrinating their troops at the same time convinced of its importance and confident of their ability to overcome whatever doubts their men felt as to the wisdom and outcome of this decision for war.

INDOCTRINATION THEMES

Many of the PLA units that were designated for duty as "volunteers" in Korea had been engaged in economic development projects in various parts of China. After being alerted and deployed to Manchuria, they went through a period of special training which, in many cases, lasted for two or three months.

Political indoctrination designed to prepare troops for participation in the Korean War usually went on concurrently with military training. It received considerable emphasis. As much as several hours a day were devoted to political indoctrination at a time when special intensive military training was being given. Many prisoners whom we interviewed observed that political training was considered as important, if not more important, than military training.* At first much of the political training was of a general character. This was consistent with PLA policy to conceal from most of the forces being moved from various points in China to assembly areas in Manchuria the fact that they might be sent to Korea. Once in Manchuria no uniform policy appears to have been followed in preparing troops psychologically for their entry into Korea. Some contingents were heavily indoctrinated; others were told only just before crossing the Yalu River into Korea; still others apparently were not told they were entering Korea until they had actually crossed the Yalu.

There are various possible explanations for the lack of a uniform policy on this matter. The problem of desertion was apparently fairly widespread even while in China. PLA authorities may well have felt that to tell the troops that they were being shipped to Korea might have seriously aggravated the problem of desertion. It is also possible that some units were not told where they were going for security reasons, to deny enemy intelligence opportunities for information on PLA intentions.

In some units, on the other hand, PLA authorities obtained a statement from each soldier that he was willing to participate as a "volunteer" in Korea while the unit was still in Manchuria. Recalcitrant individuals were "persuaded" by manipulating the small group to which they belonged in order to arouse pressure for conformity. A platoon grade cadre from the 39th Army, 4th Field Army reported that toward the end of a three-month period of military and political training, around the 7th or 8th of October, the men in his unit were asked to sign up as "volunteers" for the Korean War. The voluntary aspect of the signing-up was purely formal:

If one actually didn't sign he was called up by his squad-leader, platoon-leader, assistant [company] political officer or [company] Party Branch Committee and asked : "Why don't you join it? Are you afraid of death?

---

* Unless otherwise indicated, the materials from which this account of the war indoctrination of PLA troops is reconstructed are from prisoner replies to several questions on this subject in one of our questionnaires, and from incidental information obtained in other interviews we conducted.

Do you dislike the war, etc.?" And then they explained to him what it meant to join. Thus they could not help joining it.

An assistant company commander in the 38th Army, 4th Field Army, recalled that at the time when the Americans pursued the North Korean Army back into North Korea:

We had a staff meeting almost every day in Manchuria. "Do we join the Korean battle or don't we?" About 70 percent of us agreed to fight. . . . At the time, about 30 percent of us denied it, and they were criticized and confuted as cowards, afraid of war, reactionaries who cannot fight courageously for the fatherland and people. . . .*

Turning now to the specific content of the indoctrination we note, first, that Chinese leaders did not pass over the inherently difficult questions of the *legitimacy* and *wisdom* of engaging United States forces in a war beyond China's borders. They did not attempt to dispose of the question whether the Chinese decision to intervene in Korea was justified by making generalized allegations that United States forces were "aggressors" or fabricating charges of actual aggression against Chinese territory. Rather, they gave their troops a detailed rationale for the decision to take part in a war outside their own borders. Similarly, they dealt with the second question regarding the wisdom of doing so by a reasoned argument for expecting military success.

Thus, the indoctrination given troops to prepare them for participation in the Korean War followed two main lines. One set of themes, intended to legitimize intervention in Korea, presented the Chinese Communist view of the origin of the war, the nature of the enemy, and the character of his war aims. Another set of themes appraised the relative strength of the two sides in such manner as to give PLA troops confidence in their ability to win the struggle. These two sets of themes emerged clearly and consistently from the statements recalling their indoctrination made by prisoners we interviewed.†

* The situation described by this informant, in which soldiers were permitted to discuss and oppose entry into the Korean War, would be unthinkable in the Soviet Army of World War II. (Herbert Dinerstein in a personal communication to the author.) The contrast with the Soviet Army noted here indicates, once again, the greater use of egalitarian or pseudodemocratic devices in PLA group life.

† This reconstruction relies primarily upon replies of respondents to questions which specifically asked them to recall what their political officers had told them about the war in Korea, why the PLA had to intervene, etc.

LEGITIMACY OF THE INTERVENTION

The effort to justify PLA entry into the Korean War made use of the following major themes:

1. South Korea started the war by invading North Korea;

2. A "civil war" ensued between "democratic" North Korea and "reactionary" South Korea;

3. North Korea was about to win the "civil war" when the "aggressive," "imperialistic" United States sent in overwhelming forces and drove the North Korean Army back;

4. The United States has "aggressive" designs against China and plans to attack Manchuria as soon as completing the conquest of North Korea;

5. The Chinese Communist government has to send PLA troops into Korea to frustrate the intention of the United States for aggression;

6. North Korea is a "brother" country of China and, like China, has a "democratic" political organization. The North Koreans helped the Chinese Communists win their struggles against the Japanese and the Chinese Nationalists. For these reasons, the PLA should help North Korea in its present struggle against the "aggressive," "imperialist," and "reactionary" forces of Syngman Rhee, the United States, and its UN "puppets."

In addition, a number of minor themes were also employed:

1. The United States is attempting to follow in the footsteps of the Japanese who first invaded Korea, then used it as a bridgehead for invasion of Manchuria and China in an attempt to enslave the entire Chinese people;

2. The United States has aggressive plans also against the Far East as a whole, Russia, and the whole world, which will be put into effect if the United States "invasion" of Korea and its plans against China are not thwarted;

3. If the United States "aggressors" are not stopped in Korea they will attack other members of the "democratic" (Communist) camp which will resist and, thus, World War III would break out. Therefore, to fight in Korea is to fight for "world peace" as well as "peace" in Asia;

4. The United States has already "aggressed" against China by

bombing and scouting Manchurian territory (Antung) and by "occupying" Formosa.

In brief, then, the PLA entry into the Korean War was justified on two general grounds: (a) the desirability of a strategy of "aggressive defense" against a more or less imminent United States attack upon Manchuria; (b) the necessity to help an "ally," North Korea. The latter was presented as a moral and political imperative rather than a legal obligation stemming from treaty provisions.

CONFIDENCE IN VICTORY

Indoctrination emphasized specific components of Chinese Communist military strength which, it was said, gave it an edge over United States forces. Political and moral advantages, such as the "support of the Korean people," "the support of 'Democratic' [Communist] nations," and a "righteous cause" were also claimed. However, these nonmilitary bases for confidence in victory were definitely of secondary importance to themes which emphasized PLA military strength:

1. PLA numerical superiority;
2. Superior PLA war tactics;
3. Chinese Communist troops braver, better motivated, and more experienced than U.S. troops.

In addition to these three major themes, PLA military strength was conveyed by a number of minor themes:

1. PLA weapons adequate (or good) in number and quality;
2. PLA will be supported by Korean people;
3. PLA has support of "Democratic" (Communist) nations;
4. PLA will win because it has a "righteous cause."

Prisoners asked to recall what they had been told when being sent to Korea replied, typically, as follows:

The political officers mentioned . . . with regard to the PLA's excellent prospects for winning the war: its superiority in number and quality of troops over those of the U.S. Army; its superiority in operations and tactics due to its abundant experience in combat as compared to the U.S. troops.   [*private, 26th Army, 3d Field Army*]

Even at the front line they talked to us about the tactics of the U.S. Army . . . as being very childish. The U.S. troops can only push back and forth on the road; they have been well fed and well clad so that they lack perseverance and are weary of the war.

[*private, 20th Army, 3d Field Army*]

Seeing that there are only 50,000 U.S. troops in Korea at present, and their weapons are not particularly excellent, our mere appearance in Korea will put them to rout as far as Pusan, only to flee away to Japan thereafter.

[*private, 26th Army, 3d Field Army*]

The political officer spoke as follows . . . [with reference to] the reason why we will win this war: "As China has a population of 400 million, we could expand our army as much as we please. In the matter of weapons, too, we have sufficient weapons to overcome the U.S. troops. We are a righteous army which is supported and aided by many Democratic nations led by Russia. . . ."

[*captain, 66th Army, attached to 4th Field Army*]

The political officer told the men . . . [with respect to] the favorable conditions which will lead us to victory: "(a) We are supported by the Korean people while the UN forces are not welcomed by them; (b) We are overwhelming in number, well-trained, courageous, so that we can overcome the hardships. On the other hand, the American soldiers are afraid of battle for they have led a luxurious, easygoing life; (c) Our tactics are splendid; the PLA troops are especially accustomed to mountain combat; but the enemy's tactics are very crude; (d) The enemy has many weapons which, however, are useless against bayonet charges." In short, the PLA can win this war, the political officers said.

[*private, 40th Army, 4th Field Army*]

Several observations may be made about the nature of this attempt to instill confidence in victory in the troops who constituted the initial military force sent into Korea in the late autumn of 1950. It is noteworthy that little effort was made to prepare these soldiers psychologically for the hard fighting and military difficulties they were to encounter later in Korea. Rather, PLA propaganda deliberately created the expectation of an easy and quick victory. At times this expectation was explicitly spelled out, and in any case it was unmistakably implied in the one-sided propaganda picture given of PLA military strength and United States military weakness.

A desire to instill confidence in junior grade combat leaders and soldiers may have motivated the decision to present so optimistic a picture. For example, the statement by a company political officer: "Our Regimental leaders said that we would come back home in triumph in a month after we reached Korea. Of course this was to encourage the lower leaders and the men. . . ." At the same time the possibility must be considered that the confident tone of propaganda directed to the troops indeed faithfully reflected the expectation of PLA authorities regarding their prospects for military success in Korea. The arguments employed in troop indoctrination to instill confidence in victory clearly reflected PLA military doctrine at the time. This was the same military doctrine that had led to striking successes in the civil war against Nationalist forces. The impression fostered among the troops going into Korea was that they would win as they had won before, with the same weapons and tactics; nothing new was required. There was nothing in troop indoctrination at this time to suggest that PLA authorities were concerned with the possibility of encountering unusual difficulties in applying the same doctrine and tactics in Korea.

The optimistic content of the war indoctrination received by the Chinese Communist forces accounts in large measure for the fact that it was initially successful to a marked degree. Our interviews indicate that, although sent as "volunteers" to intervene in a foreign conflict beyond China's own borders, most of the soldiers had accepted the justification and rationale offered them in official propaganda. The weakness of the justification for intervention in the Korean War was not widely perceived at first by the troops and did not seriously affect their morale for a while.

It is indeed a sobering fact that the justification given for the decision to intervene was initially successful with most of the PLA combat troops. This success was achieved despite the frank avowal to the troops that they were participating as "volunteers" in a conflict outside China's borders in order to deter a would-be "aggressor" from attacking China later on. This fact may lead some to conclude that the resources available to Chinese Communist leaders for persuading their troops to engage in military forays beyond Chinese borders are so great that it is useless to contest the war indoctrination that precedes and accompanies moves of this kind. This may well be the case, but the Korean experience cannot be taken as proof of this proposition since the United States did not attempt to contest, with appropriate counterpropaganda, the war indoctrination PLA troops were receiving while still in Manchuria. Similarly, although large numbers of Chinese troops were known to be in North Korea for weeks before the PLA launched its first full-scale offensive in late November 1950, evidently no effort was made by United States psychological warfare personnel to counter the indoctrination these troops had received. While it would be naive to exaggerate the impact such efforts might have had, it is also unwarranted to assume that they would have been entirely useless if part of a well-planned and implemented psychological warfare campaign.

We turn now, in the following chapter, to a point of much greater significance: When the initial promise of a relatively quick and easy victory was disproved by events, Chinese soldiers began to question and reject the legitimacy and wisdom of intervention in the Korean War. Loss of confidence in victory and general erosion of all the other major components of the indoctrination they had received contributed to loosening group solidarity in small combat units. The weak legitimization of the Chinese intervention played a belated, secondary role in the process of demoralization which was, to be sure, caused primarily by harsh, prolonged combat experience in the rugged terrain and winter climate of Korea. In the absence of foreign invasion of Chinese territory, the decision to intervene in the Korean conflict could no longer be adequately justified to hard-pressed, suffering combat personnel. As the fighting became severe and costly in human terms and as the war dragged on the Chinese leaders found that they had a less firm and increasingly less convincing base on which to mount their appeals for additional sacrifices against a well-equipped foe who had not, after all, invaded China.

9 *The Erosion of Morale*

Sometimes a unit possessing the spiritual element can defeat an enemy possessing excellent weapons. At the time we crossed the Yalu [autumn 1950], the morale of the PLA was excellent. But as time went on, being attacked continuously on both sides from modern aircraft and field artillery, we suffered many casualties. Consequently, when we reached the 38th Parallel we began to be demoralized and, now, the PLA has been utterly demoralized.

Chinese prisoner

THE PLA achieved significant military successes in its initial offensives in late November and December 1950. These successes served to confirm the expectation of quick victory that formed the keystone of the war indoctrination given to the "volunteers." The confidence that had been placed in Mao Tse-tung's military doctrine appeared amply justified.

However, by the end of January 1951, the "panic and inertia" of the U.S. Eighth Army was halted under its new commander, General Matthew Ridgway, and it was given the mission of remaining in Korea to fight a war of attrition against the numerically superior forces.[1] This strategy required new tactics. Henceforth the primary objective became to inflict maximum casualties on enemy forces rather than to hold or win territory. The firepower of UN forces was further increased and concentrated. New defensive tactics of "rolling with the punch" of Chinese offensives were put into operation. In limited offensive operations of its own the Eighth Army took precautions to safeguard its flanks and rear. The battle line moved forward and backward. Forced to operate in the relatively narrow Korean peninsula the Chinese armies found themselves confronted for the first time by position warfare and a firm battle line. The Eighth Army frustrated all Chinese efforts to create a fluid battlefield situation more suited to exploitation by the guerrilla type tactics employed by the PLA. The inability of the Communist forces to push the Eighth Army out of Korea became increasingly evident.

As the PLA's military difficulties and casualties mounted, the positive effect of its war indoctrination on the troops quickly wore thin. The military facts of combat in Korea no longer fitted the pattern of expectations which PLA propaganda had aroused within its forces. The promise of a relatively quick and easy victory proved to be unfounded. It became painfully obvious that UN forces enjoyed important military advantages, especially in modern weapons and mechanization, that PLA weapons and tactics were inadequate, that the repeated PLA offensives failed to achieve decisive results, that Chinese Communist forces were suffering a high rate of casualties. Thus, as the bitter winter wore on exacting a heavy toll of casualties and demoralization, it became evident that the PLA was not fighting as well as it had been expected to. This realization was widespread among combat cadres as well as rank-and-file soldiers. It also permeated veteran soldiers and party members at least at company levels and, to a lesser extent, at battalion and higher levels.[2]

Of eighteen veterans (mostly cadres at company level) interviewed on this point, all but one stated without qualification that the PLA had not fought as well as had been expected in Korea.* Most of these veterans elaborated their opinion by referring to the fact that the quick victory expected and promised by their leaders had not materialized. Several added that the *best* armies sent into Korea initially by the PLA command had failed in their objective of throwing UN forces out of Korea and had had to be reinforced by other armies:

At the beginning of our participation in this war, high-ranking leaders said we would expel the U.S. Army from Korea and return home in three months. Nevertheless, even now we not only cannot accomplish our purpose but also have been dealt severe blows several times. Judging from this, it's clear that the PLA has not fought as well as its leaders expected it to.   [*platoon leader, 26th Army, 3d Field Army*]

. . . they dispatched at first the best army in the PLA—the 4th Field Army, especially the 38th, 39th, and 40th Corps which were called "Iron Troops"—to the forefront. Perhaps they did so in the hope of winning a rapid victory. Now the best troops are annihilated or nearly annihilated; this forced the PLA to send replacements from the 1st and

---

* These eighteen PLA veterans were interviewed on a special questionnaire; since none of them were captured later than mid-May 1950 their experiences and opinions do not reflect the increased severity of the punishment inflicted on PLA units by UN forces in late May and June.

2d Field Armies. From this I think it is evident that the PLA didn't fight as well as expected by its leaders. The men at first believed what the leaders said, but now the men do not believe it; the leaders find it very hard even in training the men. I think this is because the PLA didn't fight well in general; it suffered high casualties and its faith in victory has been weakened. *[former company political officer, acting assistant battalion commander, 40th Army, 4th Field Army]*

These eighteen veterans were asked to analyze *the chief difficulties experienced by the PLA in Korea.* Fourteen listed UN air power as the leading factor. Lack of mobility and firepower were the next frequently mentioned difficulties of the Korean campaign. Several emphasized the handicap of operating in unfamiliar terrain without knowledge of the local language. Each prisoner's answer reflected his own experience; the importance attributed to firepower, of course, might well have been greater among PLA prisoners captured later when heavier concentrations of UN artillery were brought to bear:

The chief difficulties in Korea were (1) shortage of provisions; (2) frostbite or illness due to lack of footwear; (3) limitations on military operations due to nonsupply of weapons and ammunition; (4) restriction of our military operations to nighttime only, which was equal to being half defeated. Summarizing these difficulties, we know that they were all caused by the enemy's command of the sky which contrasted with our lack of an air force. *[sergeant, 26th Army, 3d Field Army]*

The first difficulty was that the firepower of our weapons was poor while the enemy's was strong. The next was that due to the air attacks we had to march on the mountain lanes only at night, sleep in the air-raid shelters, eat and dress not as we should—even the amount was insufficient. *[company political officer, 40th Army, 4th Field Army]*

These statements of difficulties the PLA had encountered in Korea cannot be regarded as being atypical or as exaggerations contrived to please the interviewer. What the prisoners told us reflects the sober official battle reports prepared at the time within PLA units. Although it is not well known in the West, the fact is that Chinese Communist forces in Korea typically engaged in operations analysis of a remarkably objective and painstaking character. On this score, Lynn Montross, the official historian of the 1st U.S. Marine Division, has noted: "Contrary to expectations, Chinese military critiques [contained in captured PLA documents] have been candid in admitting failures and unsparing in self-criticism." In support of this point

Montross quotes at length from the captured operations summaries of three PLA armies that had engaged in combat with the U.S. Marines in the Chosin Reservoir area.[3]

Let us turn to a more detailed examination of the erosion of morale that took place under the difficult conditions described by our informants.

LOSS OF COMBAT MOTIVATION AND INCREASED RELIANCE UPON COMBAT ENFORCEMENT

We should recognize at the outset that what is remarkable is not that PLA morale should sag under the adverse conditions of combat encountered in Korea, but that the PLA's control devices should succeed as well as they did in maintaining cohesion within units and in extracting performance of combat duties. The remarks of a few of our respondents will suffice to illustrate the impact which sustained severe military pressure had on morale:

> The issue of a military engagement depends greatly upon the firing power of weapons, but fighting spirit—the spiritual element—is also important. Sometimes a unit possessing the spiritual element can defeat an enemy possessing excellent weapons. At the time we crossed the Yalu [autumn 1950], the morale of the PLA was excellent. But as time went on, being attacked continuously on both sides from modern aircraft and field artillery, we suffered many casualties. Consequently, when we reached the 38th Parallel we began to be demoralized and, now, the PLA has been utterly demoralized. It's not too much to say that the PLA has lost the courage to fight continuously at present.
> [*private, 50th Army, 4th Field Army, captured March 12, 1951*]

> We had more political training [prior to entering Korea] than military training. . . . The political officers gave the men high morale . . . but when we were driven by a strong enemy this kind of training became less effective.   [*company commander, 38th Army, 4th Field Army,*
> *captured March 7, 1951*]

> After crossing the Yalu, as we met with increasing difficulties, the men were so demoralized that it might be safely said that they were thinking only of deserting. Even some of the Party men who had not been in the Party long disliked fighting. . . . Except for the "positive" men among Party members, the combat strength of the men was very meager and weak.   [*platoon leader, 64th Army, 1st Field Army,*
> *captured April 24, 1951*]

In my opinion, the PLA cannot fight better in the future than they have because most of the junior leaders have lost their belief in victory and have had their faith in communism shaken. They sustained a big blow from the U.S.A. which had the newest weapons and strong firepower. Consequently they had to reconcile themselves to being killed. . . . I have to wonder why the Russians don't fight themselves and why only the Chinese should be sacrificed in Korea. Consequently such a death is less valuable. The men came to think like this and, once their fighting spirit was reduced, we cannot hold it and as a result can hardly expect good combat results.   [*company political officer, 40th Army, 4th Field Army, captured March 10, 1951*]

As these statements indicate, the bases for relatively strong solidarity and positive combat motivation, which PLA units had enjoyed earlier, were gravely weakened by March–April 1951. The PLA command had to place greater reliance thereafter upon organizational devices to enforce combat. The possibility of extracting minimum performance of combat duties from demoralized and dispirited troops rested increasingly upon the efficiency with which hard core cadres applied techniques of surveillance, combat control, and direction.* Simultaneously, in order to stem the weakening of morale and the temptation to desert, propaganda to the troops stepped up charges that UN forces treated prisoners harshly and threatened would-be deserters.

Combat morale was often so low that it required the immediate presence and active leadership of higher leaders at the front line to control troops and obtain performance of military duties. Exposed to increased combat risks, combat cadres and positive Party members suffered higher casualties. This observation was made by half of the eighteen veterans on a special questionnaire and evidently reflected a condition generally prevalent among frontline combat units.† It will suffice, for illustrative purposes, to cite a single cadre on this point:

When combat is furious, or morale is low, the company commander [ordinarily stationed in front of his rearguard platoon] leads in front of the foremost platoon; in such cases, too, the battalion commander takes the lead in front to encourage the men. . . . The casualties among com-

* For an elaboration of combat enforcement practices see Chapters 6 and 7.
† The representative character of these nine prisoners of war is suggested by the fact that, between them, they came from seven different armies and nine different divisions. On the implication of a high casualty rate among the hard core for unit combat potential see Chapter 10.

manders were high . . . because of their taking the lead in front. . . .
[*battalion commander, 64th Army, 1st Field Army,*
captured April 23, 1951]

LOSS OF CONFIDENCE IN WEAPONS, TRAINING, AND TACTICS

Well before Jacob Malik, Soviet Ambassador to the United Nations, suggested cease-fire negotiations in a talk on June 23, 1951, most combat soldiers and many cadres in the PLA had already come to view the war as an unequal, senseless struggle. Approximately a hundred prisoners (captured mostly in March and April 1951) were asked to comment on the adequacy of training and preparations for the Korean War. Almost all of them gave strongly negative answers, which are summarized in Table 3. This result is impressive even when allowance is made for (1) the possibility that the morale of soldiers who are taken prisoner is likely to be worse than that of many of those who are not captured or who die in battle; (2) the possibility that a soldier's opinion on such questions is likely to become more negative after he becomes a prisoner than while he is still fighting.

These ninety-eight prisoners came almost entirely from units sent into Korea in the late autumn of 1950. Thus, they came from what were considered to be the *best* PLA armies and units. The armies that were sent in as reinforcements in the spring of 1951, which are underrepresented in this group of prisoners, included a much larger percentage of raw, relatively untrained conscripts. This is among the reasons for believing that prisoners captured after the interviews for this study were made, that is in May and June of 1951, presented an even more negative appraisal of their training and preparations than the ninety-eight prisoners in this group.

Many of these prisoners either flatly stated or clearly implied that PLA training and preparations had been totally inadequate to cope with the UN forces in Korea. They complained that they had hardly received any special military training. Some noted that their units had been engaged in economic reconstruction tasks in various parts of China until designated for duty in Korea.

The disparity in weapons and materiel had exercised a profound effect on these prisoners. They saw the great advantage in weapons and equipment, and to a lesser extent in tactics, enjoyed by U.S. forces as reducing the PLA to the status of an old-fashioned army.

TABLE 3

RATING OF ADEQUACY OF PLA TRAINING AND
PREPARATIONS FOR THE KOREAN WAR
By 98 PLA POWs [a]

Soldier's rating of training and preparations	*Rank-and file soldiers*	*Squad and group leaders*	*Platoon leaders and higher cadres*	*Total*
	(49)	(23)	(26)	(98)
Totally inadequate	41	22	23	86
Partially inadequate	5	1	1	7
Partially adequate			2	2
Totally adequate	3			3

[a] Eighty of these prisoners were interviewed with one questionnaire, the remaining eighteen with another. In both cases an "open-end" general question was asked and the respondent was permitted to answer freely. The generally representative character of replies is suggested by the large number of PLA unit memberships covered by these ninety-eight prisoners.

Not only ordinary soldiers but many PLA combat cadres, at least on company level, also shared this belief. Of the many references to the fact that the PLA was simply outclassed by the "modern," "scientific" foe it faced, the following may be cited as typical:

I think it is quite impossible that with manpower alone China can defeat the U.S.A., which fights scientifically with the newest weapons of army and aircraft. Our weapons were mostly old style ones, especially we did not have many heavy weapons and no aircraft. . . .

[*squad leader, Party member, 40th Army, 4th Field Army*]

Judging from my own experiences, the training and preparations of the PLA are inadequate and insufficient to fight this Korean war. . . . All this while [while engaged in railroad repairs in China], we were never trained to cope with up-to-date warfare. . . .

[*battalion commander, Party member, 64th Army,
1st Field Army, entered Korea in February 1951*]

I think we were poorly trained and prepared. We didn't get any military training in the PLA; we had no combat experience. Most of our weapons and equipment were old-fashioned; we had no weapons such as airplanes, artillery, and tanks which are indispensable weapons in modern warfare.

Instead we fought only with human wave tactics; great numbers of men have been sacrificed. It was indescribably miserable.

[*private, in PLA since 1947, 42d Army, 4th Field Army*]

In the Red Army we were trained according to old-fashioned tactics. Men were to be used as weapons of attack. But this training was quite useless when we fought against the U.S. Army which was armed with modern, scientific weapons and tactics. . . .

[*private, former Nationalist taken into the PLA in 1949,
4th Field Army*]

The most severe and frequent criticisms were:

(1) PLA training in "human wave" tactics was "outdated," "unsuitable";

. . . in China I learned only how to handle a rifle. . . . While the U.S. Army fought with mechanized weapons, the PLA intended to fight only with human bullets.   [*private, 38th Army, 4th Field Army*]

(2) PLA political training was overemphasized at the expense of military training;

Since I became a prisoner [from the Chinese Nationalist Army] to PLA in December 1949 . . . we hadn't any military training. We just reclaimed lands for cultivation, etc. Except for this, we spent time in vain for so-called political training, such as reading newspapers, political lectures, etc.   [*private, 50th Army, 4th Field Army*]

(3) PLA combat training of small groups of three* in rushing, throwing grenades, and use of the bayonet was inadequate;

. . . for military training groups of three men went up into the hills to practice going near enemy lines and attacking. . . . But coming to Korea it was all of no use in front of U.S. artillery attacks.

[*private, former Nationalist taken into the PLA in 1948,
38th Army, 4th Field Army*]

(4) The PLA did not train men adequately for defense against air attacks;

While we were in Manchuria our superiors deceived us, saying, "Dig fine trenches and we will have no fear of enemy planes. They cannot capture us" . . . we got no training for air raids.

[*private, former Nationalist taken into the PLA in 1948,
38th Army, 4th Field Army*]

* This refers to the standard organization of the squad into small groups of three for combat purposes, the so-called "3-3" principle. See Chapter 3.

(5) The PLA did not give men training for mountain combat;

Since I came into Korea, the whole area was mountainous and we had to march only at night; we never had such training at all in North East China.   [*private, conscripted into the PLA in 1949, 38th Army, 4th Field Army*]

LOSS OF CONFIDENCE IN PLA MILITARY DOCTRINE

As remarks of the kind just quoted imply, PLA military doctrine was discredited in the eyes of the Chinese soldiers by what they had experienced in Korea. It is of particular importance to note that disillusionment with Mao Tse-tung's doctrine extended to combat cadres. Questions on this point were included in the special interviews with the eighteen veteran members of the hard core in order to get at the impact of Korean War experiences upon their basic military and political orientations. Despite the limitation of numbers, the eighteen interviews do provide a basis for fairly confident generalization on certain points.

The eighteen hard core prisoners (mostly junior combat cadres at company and lower levels) were virtually unanimous in reporting that they and their fellow soldiers had come to question the applicability of PLA military doctrine to the conditions of combat and the nature of the enemy in Korea. While few cadres higher than company-grade rank were available for these special interviews, indirect evidence obtained from junior cadres indicated that some of the higher-grade leaders, too, must have had the same doubt. Just how high dissatisfaction with military doctrine went in the PLA hierarchy and the precise conclusions drawn cannot be estimated on the basis of available materials.

As indicated earlier, much of the propaganda aimed at instilling confidence in victory in the troops prior to sending them into Korea had been grounded on PLA military doctrine. The plausibility of indoctrination at that time was heightened by the prestige which the doctrine had gained as a result of Chinese Communist military successes against the Japanese and, particularly, in the smashing victory over the Nationalist forces in the recent civil war.

In a number of respects, however, the conditions of combat against a different enemy in Korea did not favor the successful application of the PLA military doctrine. The novelty of these combat conditions was recognized, implicitly or explicitly, by most of the ninety-eight prisoners interviewed and emerged with particular clarity in our more detailed interviews with the eighteen veterans.

These veterans noted that the PLA was forced to fight in the narrow space of the Korean peninsula, whereas its previous military experience had been gained in the vast expanse of China that provided virtually unlimited space for maneuver. At the same time, they observed, the PLA's effort to drive the foe off the Korean peninsula had been severely hampered by the fact that the opponent's sources of supply lay *outside* the peninsula. U.S. forces could give ground on the peninsula without jeopardizing their supplies; indeed, such retreats only served to shorten the 8th Army's supply lines. For the *first* time in its experience, therefore, the PLA found that lack of naval and air power was a severe handicap to the accomplishment of its military objective.

Finally, our respondents regarded the weapons inferiority of the Chinese forces as critical. The PLA had hoped to overcome this disadvantage in several ways. A form of "human wave" assault was employed on the tactical level to exhaust enemy ammunition, absorb his firepower and, finally, overrun key tactical positions by sheer manpower superiority. Guerrilla tactics were adapted to modern battle in order to envelop enemy units by the method of "short attack," relying upon surprise, superior mobility, and the ability to infiltrate in and around enemy forces. Finally, psychological warfare tactics were employed to confuse enemy troops and to reduce their will to resist.

Despite initial successes with these methods for overcoming the enemy's superiority in weapons, the PLA found that their effectiveness sharply declined for the following reasons:

1. The concentration of firepower which UN ground forces were able to achieve and maintain, despite the fiercest Chinese assaults, was unique in the experience of the PLA.

2. The PLA's experience of enemy air power in Korea was also unparalleled. In addition to inflicting casualties and physical destruction, UN air power had far-reaching disruptive and psychological effects, and imposed serious constraints on the tactical alternatives and mobility of Chinese ground forces.

3. UN forces finally succeeded in confronting the PLA with a con-

tinuous and firm battle line along the Korean peninsula. By "rolling with the punch" of Chinese offensives and by pushing ahead only very cautiously in its own offensive operations, the Eighth Army safeguarded its flanks and rear against tactical maneuvers favored by the PLA. After January 1951, the Eighth Army prevented all Chinese efforts to create a fluid battlefield situation more suited to exploitation by PLA envelopment and guerrilla tactics.

4. The PLA found that it lacked adequate mobility to cope with its opponent. It was unable to exploit local breakthroughs achieved at great cost because of its own supply difficulties, the greater mobility of UN forces, the fact that UN airpower restricted PLA movement virtually to nighttime, unfamiliarity with Korean terrain aggravated by lack of knowledge of the Korean language, and poor military communications.

5. PLA military tactics required the economic and moral support of the civilian population. But in Korea the traditional practice of obtaining food and other supplies locally became increasingly difficult as indigenous Korean stocks dwindled. This imposed a greater strain on the PLA supply system and increased its vulnerability to UN air interdiction. Nor could Chinese forces count upon the friendliness and positive cooperation of the Korean population.

6. Compared to the spectacular successes it had achieved in the Chinese civil war, Communist psychological warfare produced only limited results in Korea. The task facing PLA experts in psychological warfare was more difficult this time because they were now facing a highly professional army with a different national origin in a political setting that did not offer the same opportunities for propaganda exploitation that had been present in the civil war. Efforts to confuse, subvert, and demoralize UN forces by means of the same ingenious propaganda techniques that had worked so well in the civil war produced disappointing results in Korea.

PLA military tactics designed to overcome enemy superiority depended critically upon the high morale of its combat soldiers. Since Chinese leaders regarded morale as fundamentally a political matter, they placed great stress upon political indoctrination. If the old 8th Route Army—from whose successes and experiences the PLA military doctrine emerged—can be regarded as having been uniformly well indoctrinated, the Chinese armies which participated in the

Korean War must be rated appreciably lower in this respect. The political composition and character of the PLA had changed significantly during and since the Chinese civil war. As we have already noted in Chapters 1 and 6, the PLA faced the major task of assimilating and indoctrinating large numbers of former Nationalist soldiers and recruits. Although some progress was made, the job was far from complete when the Korean War broke out. As a result, the "spiritual" power of the PLA—an advantage on which the PLA prides itself and on which it relies to overcome enemy advantages in other respects—proved inadequate under the stress of military disadvantages and hardships encountered in Korea. The corrosive impact of novel conditions of combat upon confidence in military doctrine is indicated in the following comments:

> After they experienced combat with U. S. A. in Korea, all the leaders up to and including the company commander proposed, at a meeting at the Regimental command post, that a recommendation be made to Premier Mao: "While the enemy can operate day and night, we have to fight only at night under various bad conditions. Such unfavorable conditions can be overcome only by reinforcements of airplanes and artillery. We hope such reinforcements will be given us as soon as possible." Such a recommendation was proposed not only once but each time when there was a meeting. Leaders of regimental commanders rank also agreed with our opinion and felt that they could not expect victory in their operations unless the problem were resolved. . . . They [PLA leaders] tried to defeat the enemy's firepower with predominance of manpower. This was also the same tactic used in the last phase of the anti-Nationalist [civil] war. But I think such a military idea is no good. . . . It was possible in the Chinese civil war but is impossible in a modern scientific war, I think. These views of mine were shared by most lower-level leaders and the men in the PLA, although they could not dare to make them public.
>
> [*assistant battalion political officer, demoted to company political officer, 40th Army, 4th Field Army*] *

> The principle of winning victory by means of numerical superiority in men over the enemy's superior weapons can be maintained only when the enemy's superiority in weapons is not too great. In present day combat especially with the overwhelming weapons of the enemy this principle will only cause many casualties and failure. . . .

> Judging from what our officers said about our also having planes, tanks, and armored vehicles, they must have known that they had to get a

---

* This statement is noteworthy, too, for the evidence it contains of the freedom with which lower leaders communicated their viewpoint and recommendations to higher PLA authorities.

new way of fighting to stand against the U.S. Army which was equipped
with weapons of the newest type.

[*private, an old PLA veteran who remained a forthright*
ideological communist, 42d Army, 4th Field Army]

"Human wave" tactics are supposed to overwhelm the enemy's firepower with predominance of manpower and thus win the victory. From
my first experience in the present war, I found that this tactic had no
sense and no value. It also cannot be approved from a humanitarian point
of view. In actual combat it was nothing but a mass loss of lives and defeat.   [*squad leader in PLA since 1947, Party member,*
40th Army, 4th Field Army]

The training I got was in guerrilla tactics, which can be successful
when the army is closely connected with the civilian population and when
the soldiers are familiar with the area and terrain. Coming to Korea, however, we found that the Korean people were not so glad to meet us. And
we were strangers to Korean village conditions. So the old guerrilla tactics
were not suitable in this war.

[*assistant platoon leader, 26th Army, 3d Field Army*]

In the past when PLA fought against the CNA, it was siege warfare,
but what we are fighting now in Korea is a war of maneuver. Of course,
you can call the PLA's guerrilla tactics also a war of maneuver . . . but
as it doesn't make use of modernized mobile units, it cannot produce any
effect against a modernized enemy with plenty of mobility.

[*company political officer, 40th Army, 4th Field Army*]

In the past, the 8th Route Army used mainly a tactic of extermination
by means of envelopment, but we found by actual experience in Korea
that our forces lacked ability to maneuver—almost all of us marched on
foot—while enemy forces were mechanized and had great maneuvering
ability. In consequence, the enveloping tactics of the past seemed to have
become useless. . . .

[*platoon leader, Party member, 64th Army, 1st Field Army*]

THE LEGITIMACY AND WISDOM OF INTERVENTION

We noted in the preceding chapter that the PLA indoctrinated their
troops for participation in the Korean War by saying, in effect: "We
are morally justified to intervene *and* strong enough to win a relatively quick and easy victory."

Our interviews strongly suggest that most PLA troops sent into
Korea as part of the intervention force in the autumn of 1950 initially
accepted the official view regarding the origin of the war, the need to
help North Korea, the desirability of fighting an "offensive defense"

against U.S. forces before they had an opportunity to invade China. Practically all respondents offering a judgment on this point agreed that "most" soldiers at first had believed PLA propaganda on these matters because it sounded "plausible" or was skillfully presented.

The weaknesses implicit in the official case for intervention were temporarily overshadowed by the promise and expectation of a quick and easy victory. Not surprisingly, the overall impact of indoctrination on the troops was shaped more by arguments of Chinese military strength, designed to promote confidence in victory, than by moral justifications.

When events in Korea exposed PLA military weakness and the war dragged on, rank-and-file soldiers and a large proportion of lower-level combat leaders began to have second thoughts regarding the wisdom and justification of the decision to intervene in the war. It is difficult to estimate from our materials to what extent a similar shift in attitudes occurred among cadres above company level.

As might be expected, poorly assimilated soldiers tended from the beginning not to accept the case for intervention, or were quick to question and reject it after experiencing hardships of life and combat in Korea. On the other hand, soldiers who were natives of Manchuria may have accepted more readily the "legitimacy" of the Chinese intervention. Several prisoners who were hard core Communist cadres remarked that among the reasons why the 4th Field Army had been the initial force sent into Korea was the fact that it included many Manchurians. These soldiers were expected to fight better because they presumably would regard the threat of American "aggression" to their homeland as being more imminent. Several prisoners reported that belief in the official propaganda line on the origin of the war and the threat of aggression had been particularly strong among Manchurian troops.

The erosion of morale was cumulative and followed a logical pattern of its own. Loss of confidence in victory led many soldiers who had previously accepted their war indoctrination to reexamine and reject the official case on behalf of the legitimacy of intervention. The demoralization they were experiencing sharpened their critical faculties. They now belatedly discovered the flaws in the official case for intervention and saw more clearly the facts which contradicted it. The major weaknesses in PLA war indoctrination were articulated so well by our respondents that they can be reconstructed quite easily from the interviews:

1. The fact that there had been no military invasion of Chinese territory helped in time to undermine the effort to justify intervention in terms of an aggressive war of "defense." It is true that prior to sending their forces into Korea, Chinese Communist leaders had repeatedly charged the United States with air violations of Manchurian borders and had labeled President Truman's "neutralization" of Formosa on June 27, 1950 as an aggressive act. Nonetheless, PLA authorities evidently did not deem these charges important or credible enough to serve as the major justification for intervention. Rather, they were only minor themes in the propaganda preparation of PLA forces for intervention in Korea.

2. The fact that the action of the United States in aiding Korea had the official backing of the United Nations was not generally known among Chinese troops in the early stages of the war. It became known later and appears to have been of some importance, especially among noncommunist soldiers, in undermining the PLA's case. That a supranational authority sanctioned and had "legitimized" the action of the United States and its allies, and disapproved Communist China's intervention in Korea seems to have gradually impressed some soldiers. Few Chinese soldiers initially knew very much, if anything, about the United Nations. Allied psychological warfare use of the symbol "United Nations" could hope to overcome this gap only to a limited extent. It took some time before psychological warfare officers could find means of communicating effectively with illiterate and semiliterate enemy soldiers, and developed more effective techniques for projecting the prestige of the United Nations in their leaflets. The fact that various members of the United Nations furnished frontline combat forces was probably important in this respect.

3. The reputation of the United States as a nonaggressive, humanitarian power influenced an important minority of PLA troops, especially former Chinese Nationalist troops. Some of the prisoners interviewed traced favorable predispositions of this kind to personal contacts with U.S. forces in China during World War II. The fact that only recently, following World War II, had the United States withdrawn sizable military forces from China made it difficult for some

Chinese soldiers to accept the official charge that America harbored aggressive designs upon Chinese territory. The fact that following Chinese intervention in Korea the United States still did not directly attack Chinese territory seems to have further reduced the credibility of the official charge of aggressive American intentions.

4. The fact that North Korea started the war by attacking South Korea was not initially known by most soldiers in the PLA. Many of them were unaware of this explanation of the origin of the war until some time after they were in Korea. From UN psychological warfare leaflets and, perhaps particularly, from Korean civilians many Chinese soldiers learned and accepted the fact that it had actually been North Korea which initiated the war by attacking South Korea. But this knowledge probably did little to undermine the PLA's case for intervening in the Korean War. For the issue of war guilt was obscured by the Communist presentation of the Korean War as a "civil war" between the North and the South. Since, according to the Communist line, the United States and United Nations had "interfered" just when North Korea was about to win, the PLA was "justified" in entering Korea to help the North Koreans. However, when military reverses and heavy casualties created demoralization within the ranks, many Chinese soldiers found themselves increasingly out of sympathy with the official line that it was necessary to help the North Korean "brother." Willingness to sacrifice for the North Korean "brother" quickly wore thin under adverse military conditions once it was learned that little "brother" had started the war himself.

It is interesting that Communist Party members in the PLA who became disillusioned over the course of events in Korea were more prone to question the *wisdom* of the initial decision to intervene in Korea than the justification offered for doing so. As well-indoctrinated Party members they could accept the dialectical propaganda thesis that the imperialist class enemy, the United States, was necessarily the "aggressor." But at the same time, they could criticize Chinese intervention in the Korean struggle on grounds of expediency rather than morality. There is evidence of this among at least the lower Party cadres:

China has experienced continuous warfare for scores of years and, though one year has elapsed since the Chinese Communists unified China, the people are still living in miserable conditions. So I think it was fundamentally a bad idea for the PLA to enter another war when it must stabilize, strengthen, and improve everything concerning government, economy, and military affairs.

[*company commander, Party member since 1949, 4th Field Army*]

At first I thought it was reasonable [to enter the Korean War]. But now I think they were mistaken . . . it isn't long since the Chinese revolutionary power unified China, built a firm foundation, and established domestic peace. Despite this, they fight against the U.S.A. in Korea with very poor training and preparation. It means, rather, that they are weakening Chinese revolutionary power and engulfing it in dangerous circumstances. . . .

[*squad leader, Party member since 1950, 4th Field Army*]

COMBAT PROPAGANDA HANDLING OF SETBACKS

In giving news of current military operations PLA combat propaganda typically focused on favorable results achieved by communist units. This took the form mainly of statistical summaries of casualties inflicted and trophies taken. Successful communist units were held up as an example to the rest of the army. With few exceptions, the prisoners we interviewed noted that news of casualties and reverses was almost uniformly suppressed. Two political officers whom we interviewed described their own propaganda efforts in the following terms:

During the half month before I was made captive, I twice gave news of war developments through the squad leaders. The speeches that I transmitted then were mainly about the military results achieved by the 4th Field Army to which I was attached. I did not transmit news of an unfavorable character; but I told the men of disadvantageous conditions— for example, difficulties, ammunition, provision, etc.

They [political officers] never gave the men news of an unfavorable character but of success only. For example: "We have killed and wounded or captured 16,000 men of the enemy at the first combat; 40,000 men at the second combat; 12,000 men at the third combat; 50,000 men at the fourth combat. We have damaged or taken as booty from the enemy 11,000 automobiles, 300 tanks, 145 airplanes, 500 artillery and mortars, over 100 radios, and 80,000 rifles."

Difficulties of a transparent character—supply shortages—were acknowledged but held to be of a "temporary" character. The men were exhorted to wait patiently and to do their best for a while until

A Chinese Communist prisoner, wounded in both legs, is lifted by two fellow prisoners as they make their way to a rear area hospital in Korea.

shortages were overcome. Similarly, Chinese retreats and withdrawals—which could hardly be concealed or ignored—were usually explained in strategic and tactical terms. Thus, the PLA was represented as retaining the initiative even in "retreat" and as utilizing the "retreat" as a tactic which would contribute to the eventual defeat of the enemy forces. The precise explanation offered for a retreat seems to have varied with circumstances. Our respondents indicated that their leaders had explained retreats in the following ways:

1. The retreat was ordered by superiors for tactical reasons; the men must not question it; PLA leaders had a plan for victory.

2. The retreat was undertaken voluntarily in order to give the units an opportunity to rest, regroup, and heighten their morale after a combat. (Such an explanation was probably frequently used on occasions when the PLA command rotated frontline troops who were not at the moment under severe pressure from opposing forces.)

3. The retreat was caused by an insufficiency of manpower; retreating units would join other troops in the rear and then attack. (This explanation was probably used in conjunction with the familiar PLA tactic of "melting away" without offering much resistance to a strong enemy force.)

4. The retreat was a clever maneuver designed to lure the advancing enemy into a trap; "after dispersing the enemy power," the PLA would attack at the flanks and carry out an envelopment action. (The maneuver described in this explanation was indeed a favorite Chinese Communist guerrilla tactic. But it is possible that PLA propagandists also found it a convenient explanation at times for covering up retreats that did not have this objective in question.)

PROMISES OF AIR AND MECHANIZED SUPPORT

It may be assumed that the PLA high command closely observed the negative impact of military frustration and cumulative losses on confidence in victory and the prestige of its military doctrine. Although the old theme, "PLA numerical superiority will defeat the better weapons of the enemy," persisted in troop propaganda for a while, it was gradually replaced by another propaganda theme: "The PLA, too, will soon have better weapons" (air force, infantry weapons, and mechanized support). Implicit in this shift of themes, as some prisoners remarked, was the admission that their military doctrine had failed in Korea and that new military foundations would have to be created for a Chinese "victory."

A partial admission to this effect was conveyed in the indoctrination given the second wave of Chinese armies brought into Korea in February, March, and April 1951. (These were comprised mainly of the 12th, 15th, and 60th Armies of the 2d Field Army; the 63d, 64th, and 65th Armies of the 1st Field Army; and the 47th Army of the 4th Field Army.) While the theme of PLA "numerical superiority" was still held up to these troops as a basis for confidence in victory, admissions were made that difficulties had been encountered by the Chinese armies initially dispatched to Korea in the autumn of 1950. The indoctrination at this time also included reference to tactical lessons learned in Korea, under the impact of UN air and weapons superiority. And, most significantly, promises were made that this second group of Chinese armies would get air and mechanized support to match that of the UN forces, which would assure a communist victory:

At first, before we started [from China for Korea], our superiors told us that though the U.S. troops had mechanized weapons and good skill, their planes could not do us much harm as we would fight in mountainous areas and at night instead of day, and as combat would be with enemy infantrymen who were sons of rich families, who had had no experience of difficulties and who were very weak in fighting spirit. . . .
[platoon leader, entered Korea in March 1951,
64th Army, 1st Field Army]

We were told before we left China about the military lessons learned in Korea as a result of the 4th Field Army's combat experiences, as follows: (a) Because the enemy bombing and artillery fire is powerful and accurate, when a unit occupies a position the men should not gather there but disperse except for leaving some troops to hold the position. (b) Because the enemy troops fear close range combats the most, we should not start attacking the enemy until we approached as close to him as possible. (c) We should do our best to restrict combat to nighttime, if possible.
[platoon leader, entered Korea in March 1951,
65th Army, 1st Field Army]

Before and after we, the 18th Army Group, 2d PLA Field Army, joined the Korean War, our higher leaders said that soldiers of the 4th Field Army had not been able to fight well because of fear, as air supremacy had been held by the enemy, but that we didn't need to worry about

this in the least . . . [because] the Russians had given us infantry weapons and 3,000 trucks . . . and in the very near future would send air force and artillery to support us. . . .
[*company grade cultural cadre, entered Korea in March 1951, 61st Army, 2d Field Army*]

A similar shift could be detected in combat propaganda addressed to units that had comprised the initial intervention force and had been in Korea throughout the winter. When the morale of these units began to sag, political officers were apparently instructed to make promises of forthcoming air, tank, and artillery support. Sometimes these promises were only of a general character, but more often specific commitments were given that in the "coming spring offensive," the "May offensive," or "the next offensive," the PLA would have air and mechanized support: "Since the Hwangchoryong combat, our supreme leaders always said that our air force and mechanized units would come to Korea soon. . . ." [*platoon leader, entered Korea in the late autumn of 1950, 26th Army, 3d Field Army*]

The credibility of promises of air support may have been enhanced by virtue of the fact that some soldiers knew, from personal experience, that a certain number of men from their unit—the better educated, healthy, and vigorous, and well indoctrinated—had been reassigned some time before for training as air force personnel.[4]

While promises of air support temporarily boosted morale, the problem was aggravated with time when these promises remained unfulfilled. Many soldiers and younger combat cadres then felt deceived by their political officers and leaders; they assumed a more distrustful attitude toward their announcements. This problem was relieved later, as we shall note, when increased Soviet assistance finally became evident.

Younger, less firmly indoctrinated Party soldiers were often also adversely affected by these developments. There is less evidence in our interviews that the disillusionment over unfilled propaganda promises extended to more senior hard core Party members. In this connection it should be noted that while combat propaganda was ostensibly directed to rank-and-file soldiers, its failure to sway them cannot be regarded as the sole criterion of its effectiveness. Particularly in adverse military situations, the major task was to maintain the motivation of the controlling and directing cadres. Insofar as this objective was achieved, the PLA command could count upon the cadres to extract by organizational techniques a minimum performance from even highly demoralized rank-and-file members.

In any case, official propaganda continued to be effective to some degree with those rank-and-file soldiers who had earlier developed strong identification with their units. We have referred to these soldiers in Chapter 4 as members of the "in-group" within their unit. Their acceptance of combat propaganda was furthered by their positive attitude toward the company political officer who often served as the channel for official accounts of how the war was going. Our interviews indicated that members of the in-group were much more likely to have a favorable estimate of the political officer's trustworthiness in these matters than members of the "out-group." Thus, twelve of fifteen privates who were identified with the in-group in their unit had regarded the company political officer as trustworthy, whereas twenty-seven of forty-six privates who were members of the out-group had come to feel that the political officer was untrustworthy.

The deepening realization that "false promises" had been made regarding Korea was reported by our respondents to have been an important basis for losing faith in the political officer's word. Other reasons given for losing confidence in the political officer were: (1) the crudity and deceitful nature of communist ideology (charged mostly by former Nationalist soldiers); (2) violation of promises regarding favorable conditions of life and service within the PLA.

Our interviews also suggest that loss of confidence in the political officer's word was in turn closely associated with a loosening of the individual's positive ties with his unit.

PROMISES OF SOVIET AID

"Soviet aid" was one of the important themes relied upon in PLA troop propaganda to counter loss of confidence in victory. This theme, as we have seen, was closely associated with promises of future air and mechanized support. There was no perceptible effort to disguise the fact that the modern implements of war which the PLA so badly needed—tanks, airplanes, vehicles—would have to come from the Soviet Union.

The main lines which troop propaganda took on the role of Russia in the Korean conflict have been reconstructed from accounts provided by our respondents.[5] In the early stages of Chinese military victories in Korea, when visible signs of Russian military assistance were in any case at a minimum, the political officers said relatively little about Russian aid. The general expectation was conveyed, more by innuendo than by direct statement, that as an ally of and "eldest brother" to Communist China, the Soviet Union would not let the PLA down if things went badly in Korea. But political officers scrupulously avoided concrete and specific commitments on this point. When combat troops, disturbed over the weapons superiority of the enemy, asked their political officers what measures were being taken to redress this inequality, the answer was given that Russia had very many airplanes and artillery and that though the PLA itself did not have any it would (somehow) be able to obtain them in the future.

The question of direct Russian military participation in the Korean War was not pressing at this time, since the PLA was doing fairly well by itself. Troop propaganda did not have to deal too explicitly with this question for the time being. Instead, it called attention to the political and moral aid which Russia was lending China on the international scene. That Russia was militarily powerful and that it protected the rear of the Chinese armies was also noted. There was apparently some concern among troops at this time over the possible use of the atomic bomb by the United States. To combat such anxiety, political officers sometimes told the men that Russia, too, had the atomic bomb and would use it if the Americans did. Apart from this, the only expectation of direct Soviet participation created in propaganda to the troops was that the Soviet forces would go into action if Soviet territory itself were directly threatened, for example, by an invasion of Manchuria. Given time and mounting difficulties, by early March 1951 even hard core Party soldiers began to doubt these vague promises of Russian assistance which were unaccompanied by any visible signs of help.

With the arrival of the second wave of Chinese armies into Korea in March and April, however, concrete signs of Russian assistance were now directly visible on a wide scale. For one thing, some of these troops had exchanged their old weapons for more modern Russian infantry arms—carbines, automatic rifles, heavy and light machine guns—before entering Korea.[6] By early spring 1951, too, many soldiers had seen at firsthand, or had heard eyewitness accounts of communist planes, airfields, and air force personnel near the Manchurian-Korean border. Such concrete evidence of Russian aid of course lent weight and credibility to the promises made in troop propaganda:

> The unit members believed what their leaders told them, especially after we got the Russian infantry weapons.
> *[battalion commander, 64th Army, 1st Field Army]*

> At first the men didn't believe it [promises of Russian help] too easily, but since the recruits arriving from China told them that they had seen airplanes, automobiles, and anti-aircraft guns, the men gradually began to believe what the leaders or political officers told them about the question of Russian aid.   *[political officer, 40th Army, 4th Field Army]*

Nonetheless, Chinese units continued to lack adequate air and mechanized support. Our respondents reported that it became clear to the second wave of Chinese troops at their first combat that the promise of such support made to them in Manchuria was not being fulfilled and, further, that without air and mechanized support the more modern infantry weapons issued to them did little to redress the American advantage.

At this time the major theme in troop propaganda concerning Russia was that Russian assistance in infantry weapons would surely be followed by delivery of Russian airplanes, tanks, automobiles, technical assistance. While PLA propaganda committed itself firmly to this general promise, it remained deliberately vague on the key question of the quantity and speed with which Russian weapons would be available. The vagueness was pointedly recalled by a number of the veterans we interviewed. The noncommittal nature of official propaganda presumably reflected a policy directive, for there was much talk of forthcoming Russian help among the rank and file and, apparently, unrealistically optimistic expectations were circulating with which the political authorities did not wish to be identified. By taking a sober, noncommittal attitude on specific questions of the amount and speed of delivery of Russian equipment, the political apparatus within the PLA may have tried to safeguard itself from becoming a target of resentment later on when extravagant hopes were disappointed:

. . . But the political officers did not mention how and to what extent Russian aid would be given to the PLA because they were afraid that they would lose face if it were not to be realized in the future. Some privates were expecting much from Russian aid and were fond of talking about it.   [*battalion commander, 64th Army, 1st Field Army*]

When questioned by the rank and file as to why the Russian air force was not supporting Chinese troops, political officers replied merely that the "time has not yet come."

If PLA propaganda could not be more specific in indicating when Russian help would make itself felt at the front, they could and did refer to the fact that technical assistance and instruction were being given to the Chinese by the Russians. It was said that Soviet instructors were helping to train tank troops and artillery in Manchuria, and that a Chinese Communist navy was being created with Russian help in Port Arthur and Dairen.

The failure of the Soviet Union to aid more directly and effectively in Korea may well have had a significant impact on Party soldiers in the PLA. The number of veterans we were able to interview on this point was very small; moreover, since none of these eighteen interviews were with prisoners captured later than the beginning of May 1951, the full extent of Chinese Communist disillusionment with the Russians in the next few months may not be reflected in our materials. On the other hand, the possibility must be considered that the considerable communist buildup achieved with Soviet assistance during the prolonged period of truce talks, may have reversed to some extent the disillusionment with Russia described in these pages.[7]

REINTERPRETATION OF WAR GOALS AND MILITARY OBJECTIVES

PLA leaders attempted to counter the widespread loss of confidence in victory within combat units in other ways. Initially the troops had been told that the objective was to drive UN troops out of Korea within a short time. When it became obvious that available military resources were grossly inadequate for this task, more modest statements of objectives began to appear in the late winter and spring of 1951.[8]

This shift occurred gradually and can be reconstructed in general terms from the information provided by our eighteen special informants. First, propaganda to the troops frankly admitted that the PLA was faced with a longer war than initially expected. The implication was that the war had temporarily become a "protracted war." Without discarding the objective of ultimate military victory, troop propaganda attempted to explain away "temporary" setbacks as part of a new attrition strategy. This theme was then coupled with the assurance that such a strategy would gain time to enable the PLA to develop modern military forces that would enable it to fight under more equal conditions. Second, by mid-spring 1951, the initial objective of throwing the UN out of Korea by military means was replaced by the hope that a favorable political settlement would be obtained; the "attrition" strategy was then presented as a means to this more limited goal. The gradual introduction of this substantial modification of the PLA's war goals into troop propaganda was alluded to by our respondents in the following terms:

When we first joined the Korean War we fought with the purpose of driving U.S. troops away from Korea by attacking and advancing continuously step by step. But recently, they [political officers] said that the aim of the PLA was not to occupy a town or a bit of land, but to inflict as many casualties as possible on the enemy, weaken it and win the victory, and that for this reason even if we should have to withdraw to the Yalu it did not matter so long as we killed many of the enemy and could win the ultimate victory. . . . At first the [PLA] superiority of numbers was considered to be the direct factor to win victory, but now it is considered to be the means to obtain the time to learn the military skills and to get the modernized equipment necessary to win a victory.

> [*assistant battalion commander, formerly a company political*
> *officer, 40th Army, 4th Field Army, captured April 24, 1951*]

The military leaders of the PLA told us that "In this war, we are aiming at either of the following: (a) to defeat the U.S. troops thoroughly and drive them out of Korea; (b) to defeat the U.S. repeatedly and make them want peace."

> [*battalion commander, 64th Army, 1st Field Army,*
> *captured April 23, 1951*]

We have traced the erosion of morale and described some of the consequences. Demoralization of rank-and-file soldiers forced PLA leaders to rely increasingly on the cadres to keep the soldiers in line and to enforce combat. Accordingly, an even more serious development was that loss of confidence in weapons, training, and tactics gradually extended to combat leaders. The junior combat cadres began to view the war as a grossly unequal, senseless struggle. It became evident to them that Mao Tse-tung's doctrine of protracted war could not be successfully applied in the present struggle, which had to be fought on a continuous front in a narrow peninsula against a determined foe who possessed superior weapons and modern equipment. For the first time in their military experience, Chinese Communist leaders found that lack of naval and air power was a severe handicap to accomplishment of their military objectives.

Under these circumstances, we have seen, Chinese combat morale was not able to stand up indefinitely to the strain of a prolonged war outside China's borders that entailed high sacrifices. It can be assumed that this lesson was not lost on Communist China's military leaders, and that they will not lightly risk a repetition of it.

10 *The Erosion of Organizational Controls*

> If a method could be devised for destroying the political organization within the PLA, the army would lose all tactical efficiency and would become merely a confused mob.
>
> *Chinese prisoner*

A CASUAL observer of the Chinese armies in the spring of 1951 might well have concluded that a tightly-knit group of Party fanatics in each unit was successfully imposing its will upon the mass of rank-and-file soldiers. Even to ordinary Chinese soldiers who were outsiders within their units it often seemed that Party soldiers enjoyed close and harmonious relations. Our interviews, however, revealed that these cadres were subject to a variety of strains and pressures that affected the quality of their comradely relations.

Apparently unknown to many privates was the fact that members of the in-group in their unit also dissimulated, though not to the same extent as ordinary soldiers. The attitudes of outsiders to the company political officer and to the PLA system, reported in Chapter 4, were shared to some extent by company-level cadres. Thus, of eighteen cadres interviewed with our special questionnaire, five displayed a negative attitude and four a mixed orientation to their political officers. (Eight were favorably disposed toward them; no answer was obtained from the remaining prisoner in the group.) Many of the complaints of these cadre members were similar to those held by privates. They felt that the political officer had a "bad" character, that he criticized and abused those under him, that he lied and could not be trusted, that secret surveillance and criticism meetings were unpleasant:

I had been in the PLA for a long time and had been a Party member. Accordingly I knew that what they [political officers] said was different from what they did. So I didn't believe them. What they said did not reflect their own opinion but originated from their superior's instructions. . . . [*assistant squad leader, Party member*]

As the assistant political officer was hot tempered, used to scold the men, and was much too verbose (his speeches always lasted more than an hour), most of the men did not respect him. Even the Party men disliked him. . . . [*assistant squad leader, Party member*]

Almost everyone tried to hide his low morale from the political officer, disliking to face criticism, which they thought a humiliation.
[*platoon leader, faithful communist*]

The company political officers were quite ignorant and their ignorance created trouble from time to time. . . . The chief political officer was quick-tempered; his assistant was stupid. The battalion political instructor was intelligent in some ways. But he was so quick-tempered that he was somewhat hysterical in dealing with the junior staff. But they controlled the members of the Party and the unit through the organization. Consequently we treated them well outwardly, but we did not respect them at heart. . . . [*assistant company commander, non-Party member*]

The ordinary soldiers in the unit tried to hide their bad morale. They worked hard in our presence outwardly to show enthusiasm. When we went away, they abused us and complained. I understand such a man because we do the same to our superior.
[*assistant company commander, probably a Party member*]

Several aspects of the PLA system weighed particularly heavy on lower-level cadres in the combat units. The morale doctrine implicit in the PLA's approach, in common with that of the Russian Bolsheviks, recognized no limits to what a communist could accomplish if his political ideology was strong enough. The result was a pronounced tendency to demand of the individual, and especially of the communist cadre, more than seems humanly possible. Practical experience in leadership and management did not necessarily modify these demands. For, indeed, experience showed that "miracles" were accomplished by men who had been called upon to "overcome all difficulties."

Related to this was the communist definition of morale in political terms and the practice of accounting for shortcomings in an individual's performance in terms of his political deficiencies. Ample evidence of this was available in our interviews. "Whenever an error was found," concluded one respondent, "they [PLA leaders] took it as a disease of thought." Another respondent noted: "The political officer said we had bad thoughts when we had bad morale." Even applications for permission to get married and a soldier's fear of death were regarded by the political organization in the PLA as evidence of weak ideology.

This attitude was carried to extremes. Cases of severe combat fear, psychophysical shock, and psychiatric breakdowns, as well as instances of malingering and self-inflicted wounds, were dealt with on the basis of this political definition of morale and performance. Respondents reported that men suffering combat breakdowns under intense artillery and air bombardment were condemned before others in their unit as "ideological reactionaries." Soldiers suffering severe, incapacitating fear at the front line were sometimes cursed and beaten for having bad political views. Once their unit reached a rear area, these soldiers were often singled out for attack in criticism meetings. Sometimes they were placed in the front line. In brief, all but cases of severe psychiatric disorders resulting in total incapacitation, which were sent back to field hospitals, were defined and treated in political terms.*

There was, as we have seen, little sympathy in the PLA with the view taken in Western armies that every man has a breaking point. Rather, PLA authorities acted on the assumption that human failures, even under the most difficult combat conditions, were always due to personal deficiencies of a political character. If one's political ideology was firm enough, one would never flinch from a task, no matter how dangerous and hopeless it might seem.

In an atmosphere dominated by these attitudes, the men were certainly not pampered; but neither was recognition given to the fact of human limitations. When the demands imposed on them were not grossly unrealistic and when things went reasonably well, soldiers in the PLA might well experience a tremendous sense of their own power and worth at having performed difficult tasks well. But in situations of continued extreme stress, the unreasonable demands and political evaluations made by PLA authorities exacerbated the problem of maintaining group solidarity in the small combat units.

The resulting damage was particularly costly to the PLA insofar as it affected Party soldiers in cadre positions who were entrusted with

---

* Materials on the attitude toward soldiers experiencing severe emotional stress and combat breakdowns were obtained from a number of special interviews on this subject.

leadership and control functions. Hard core cadre members who came to feel driven by the system, whose deficiencies in performance were dealt with unsympathetically and regarded as evidence of personal political shortcomings, often became detached and lost their identification with the PLA system. This loosening of ties usually manifested itself initially, as one would expect, at the lower cadre levels in a unit where combat stress and failures were more immediately and directly experienced.

Members of the cadre structure in combat units, who carried on surveillance and control of rank-and-file soldiers, were themselves the target of a similar system from above that was hardly less pervasive or less relentless. A major gripe of junior cadres against the PLA system was "lack of personal freedom." This was the most frequently disliked aspect of military life among the eighteen prisoners interviewed with our special questionnaire for the hard core.*

By lack of personal freedom respondents meant the undue demands upon their time, surveillance, thought control, denial of initiative and independent judgment. Several respondents commented that Party members and cadres had even less freedom than ordinary soldiers, and that former CNA soldiers given cadre positions were closely watched:

There wasn't any individual freedom at all. Also, I disliked that they controlled even the men's thoughts. Party members had less freedom and for one who was raised up to the position of battalion political officer, there was no freedom at all. The mission of such a man was just to communicate to inferior leaders the superior leaders' decrees, just like a transmitter.

> [*former assistant battalion political officer demoted to company
> political officer for dropping behind his unit during a march*]

Though they made me assistant company commander they always supervised me. It was very unpleasant.

> [*former CNA company commander, not a Party member*]

Instances in which disaffected members of the hard core took action against the PLA, for example, by deserting or by surrendering

---

* In answer to another question on aspects of life in the PLA that were *liked,* the following were mentioned in order of frequency: no beatings or scoldings—13; equality of cadres and ranks—8; plentiful food—6; good discipline—2; good system for handling differences and complaints—2; educational opportunities—1; elimination of corruption—1. Two of the 18 respondents said they did not like anything about life in the PLA.

their units or groups, were still rare in the period of the war under survey. Though experiencing a considerable degree of defeatism and antipathy toward the PLA system, these men apparently continued to carry out their functions of leadership and surveillance, though perhaps at a lower level of efficiency. The system of mutual surveillance among the leadership group, together with other factors, was apparently an effective deterrent, at least in the period under survey. Nonetheless, a serious problem of depletion and replenishment of hard core cadres was beginning to emerge as intensive combat continued during the spring, and it is to this critical development that we now turn our attention.

We have already noted that the politicization of the military cadre structure even in the best of the PLA armies sent to Korea remained incomplete and uneven, particularly at platoon and squad levels. Implicit in this fact were important vulnerabilities that gradually materialized as the Korean War dragged on and grew more costly. The caliber of leadership and control of small combat units declined markedly as the PLA ran out of skilled, and well-motivated junior combat leaders. As noted at various points in this study, and particularly in Chapter 9, many soldiers and cadres interviewed with our questionnaires volunteered information that Party adherents who had formed the hard core cadre in their units suffered heavy casualties, particularly at company and lower echelons, and that many of them had become demoralized and lost their ideological fervor.

Very close attention was paid to these matters by PLA authorities prior to the Korean War and during the course of the war. The ideological firmness and morale of combat leaders was under continual assessment. Casualty and strength reports made special provision for reporting on the status of Party soldiers in each unit. For it was well known within the PLA that the combat potential of a unit depended directly upon the number of determined Party soldiers within it. It can be assumed that the progressive physical and moral attrition of junior hard core cadre members, reported by our respondents, did not escape the notice of the PLA high command and must have been a matter of considerable concern.

These developments in Korea might have had less serious implications if hard core replacements could have been easily provided. But there is little indication in our materials, specific or otherwise, that this was the case. Reliable, tested Party soldiers were badly needed as platoon and squad leaders even *before* the Korean War. Some recruitment of Party members and combat leaders from the rank and file occurred on the battlefield. But this must have been minimal after a while in Korea, given the high state of demoralization and disaffection among ordinary soldiers. Hard core replacements could have been obtained, and apparently were to some extent, from cadre training units and by stripping other units not committed to or withdrawn from combat. But if carried too far, this policy was shortsighted. Not only would the affected units become unsuitable for combat, but their progress in training and even their cohesion and control might be jeopardized. Finally, whether training and indoctrination programs even on an intensified basis could have provided enough new Party combat leaders to replace heavy losses in Korea is problematical. The longer the Korean War lasted and the higher PLA casualties mounted, the more difficult it must have become to make good communists out of conscripts and former CNA elements. Good communists and hard core leaders are not made overnight.

For this reason if for no other, the PLA high command may well have calculated that if the gamble of its massive spring offensives failed, it would be well to seek a cease-fire or an end to the war. Nonetheless, Chinese leaders could hardly have anticipated how serious would be the plight of their armies after their spring offensives came to a close. As we have already noted in Chapter 1, the Eighth Army's counteroffensive in late May 1951 hit the Chinese armies before they could carry out their usual tactic of withdrawing to rest, reorganize, and resupply once their offensive had spent itself. The counteroffensive on the ground and heavy blows from the air imposed a severe strain on the ability of the already weakened and demoralized cadres to maintain control over their units. That the remaining cadres were unequal to this task was clear from the precipitous, disorganized flight of the Chinese communist forces. We quote again the passage from Montross:

It was more than a CCF withdrawal; it was a flight of beaten troops under very little control in some instances. . . . And where it had been rare for a single Chinese soldier to surrender voluntarily, remnants of platoons, companies, and even battalions were now giving up after throwing down their arms.[1]

The effect of this picture of disintegrating armies and loss of control on top-level Chinese leaders may be surmised. A request for a cease-fire, indirectly and delicately voiced by Jacob Malik, the Soviet Ambassador to the United Nations, came on June 23 some three weeks after the collapse of the last PLA offensive.

11 Developments in the PLA Since the Korean War

> Pursuit of the joint goal of "revolution and modernization" has produced two styles of leadership—the "mass line" and technical-scientific styles. Personalities adhering to those styles have motivations and outlooks marked by different experiences and now distinguished by mutual antipathy and conflict.
>
> *John Wilson Lewis*

> From a sociological standpoint, the red and expert contradiction is the most important in China today.
>
> *Franz Schurmann*

THERE CAN BE little doubt that events of the spring of 1951, which we have described, had a traumatic impact on the PLA leadership. The costly, unequal combat of these months revealed major deficiencies in military technology, organization, and doctrine. It exposed PLA leaders, as Ellis Joffe has noted, to "manifold problems of modern warfare for which their rich storehouse of experience provided no solutions; and it dramatically demonstrated the limitations and liabilities of their hitherto successful strategy and tactics." [1]

Certainly, PLA leaders had every incentive to learn, and to learn quickly, from the "advanced experience" of the Soviet armed forces and to benefit from the Soviet aid and advice that was now available. These were the years, it must be remembered, of Sino-Soviet friendship. Despite differences with Stalin, Chinese Communist leaders retained respect and loyalty toward the Soviet Union. The civil war over in 1949, the Chinese Communists turned to the task of organizing the country and constructing a socialist state. To this end they decided to emulate the Soviet model. For the first five years of the 1950s, in Franz Schurmann's words:

They tried to create a second soviet union on Chinese soil. They translated thousands of Soviet writings on every conceivable subject. They modelled their entire institutional structure on that of the Soviet Union. They adopted an economic strategy directly copied from the Soviet Union; permitted the Russians to draft their First Five Year Plan; and made Russian the first foreign language of the country.[2]

The PLA benefited enormously from Soviet military assistance, and with the large stocks of Russian equipment, for which Peking paid, came the more intangible, double-edged influence of Soviet advisers, teachers, manuals, and writings.

We called attention earlier in the study (particularly on p. 51), to important differences in the scope of political controls in the Soviet and Chinese armed forces and their divergent approach to discipline and comradely relations in small combat groups. Here it suffices to recall that the Soviet military model allowed greater scope for military professionalism, particularly at the important company level, within a context of somewhat looser political controls. The Soviet system permitted greater reliance on "unity of command" as opposed to the Chinese stress on a "collective leadership" by military and political leaders at each level within the army under the aegis of the Party committee at that level.

In 1954–1955, following the end of the Korean War, when the PLA was modernized, many distinctive features of the egalitarian military model described in Chapter 3 were discarded or modified, and it began to resemble the Soviet Army. These changes in the character of the PLA had adverse consequences that were further complicated by upheavals in the domestic policies and ill fortunes of the regime, and by the rapid deterioration of the Sino-Soviet relationship in 1957–1958. As a result serious conflicts over policy developed between Party and army leaders, stemming in good part from the irrationalities of the Great Leap Forward and the People's Communes. In 1959, the Party purged some of the top military leaders and decided to reimpose the earlier military model on the PLA. Once again, priority was given to establishing tight political control within the armed forces, and to the ideals and practices of the older revolutionary military tradition as against the greater "professionalism" that had been copied from the Soviet military model.

The years following the end of the Korean War have been active and turbulent ones for the Chinese Communist regime and for the Chinese people. We must restrict ourselves to major developments in the nature and organization of the PLA, and to their possible implications for the strength, cohesion, and combat power of the PLA. Let us begin by returning to the battlefield of Korea in June 1951.

FROM A REVOLUTIONARY TO A PROFESSIONAL ARMY

If the Chinese forces, badly mauled by General Van Fleet's May counteroffensive, were momentarily on the brink of disaster in June, PLA leaders moved quickly to reorganize and strengthen them. Helpful in this respect was the slackening of military pressure by UN forces, especially on the ground, once truce discussions were under way. By this time Communist leaders had set aside thoughts of a military victory over the UN forces. They were seeking, instead, as favorable a compromise settlement as possible and evidently felt themselves under no great pressure to terminate the war quickly. Instead, they imposed on the truce negotiations a form of "struggle" designed to extract every possible advantage.[3]

In the meantime, to improve their bargaining position and to increase their options, they brought in still more fresh units from China, proceeded with a major buildup in their air strength, and reorganized their ground forces. Drawing upon large quantities of Soviet military equipment and military advisers the PLA commander in Korea, P'eng Teh-huai, began modernizing the PLA even while the war continued in a desultory but painful fashion on the bleak Korean terrain. During the next two years, while the truce talks dragged on, the PLA reorganized and reequipped its infantry battalions, regiments, and divisions. Artillery was increased; heavy weapons and heavy mortar battalions were added. UN forces found themselves opposed by tank, antiaircraft, armored car, and truck regiments. A deep defensive network of fortifications and tunnels was created along the front to thwart possible UN offensives. The PLA infantry divisions of late 1952 no longer resembled the light divisions that had crossed the Yalu in October and November 1950. With the help of Soviet advisers, PLA combat tactics were altered, improved, and tested.

During this period, Soviet assistance enabled the Chinese Communists to rapidly build up their air force. By the autumn of 1951 the Chinese air force was strong enough to engage in what the official

U.S. Air Force historian has described as "strenuous and not entirely ineffectual efforts to wrest air superiority over northwestern Korea away from the United Nations Command." Thereafter, the Chinese air force altered its objectives and utilized the continuation of the war for air combat training purposes in an effort to train a maximum number of pilots and to test equipment, tactics, and organization. By June 1952, the Chinese Communist Air Force had reached an estimated strength of about 1,800 aircraft, including 1,000 jet fighters, based mostly in Manchuria. Backed by the Soviet Far East air order of battle, the new Chinese Communist Air Force posed a formidable threat to the numerically inferior UN air force.[4] The increased combat power of the Chinese Communist forces was amply demonstrated to UN forces in many localized but costly engagements before an armistice was finally signed on July 27, 1953.

The PLA emerged from the Korean War, therefore, with a newly equipped army and an air force. With the close of hostilities Chinese leaders could turn their attention fully to the task of building a modern army and absorbing the lessons of the Korean experience. But, first, the swollen, conglomerate ranks of the PLA had to be thinned out. Several million regulars and "volunteers" were demobilized, and by 1955 measures were under way to rationalize and modernize the PLA along the lines of the Soviet Army. Extensive reforms in command, organization, and training were carried out under Soviet guidance. The traditional Chinese Communist practice of recruiting "volunteers," to serve for an indefinite period of time, through appeals to patriotism and self-interest or through social pressures, was replaced by conscription based on the principle of compulsory military service.

The shift to a regular army, based on conscripts drafted for a fixed period of duty, made it necessary to establish a permanent nucleus of professional officers to train the enlisted men and to assume responsibility for advancing the military profession. Thus, for the first time in the PLA, a professional officer corps was established in February 1955 by the decree "Regulations on the Service of Officers." These regulations introduced an explicit system of ranks, differences in uniforms and insignia, regular channels for entry into the officer corps, and professional criteria and regulations for advancement. Shortly thereafter, a differentiated pay scale system was introduced, and military honors and titles were conferred on army leaders.

The top leadership of Communist China was both aware of the need for these measures and somewhat apprehensive over their possible effect. Ellis Joffe has called attention to an editorial in *Jen-min Jih-pao* (*People's Daily*) of September 28, 1955 which stated that under conditions of revolutionary guerrilla warfare—when units were scattered, equipment was simple, and the men were volunteers—military ranks and distinctions had not been necessary. Discipline could be maintained through the close and prolonged association of military cadres and ordinary soldiers. The editorial noted, however, that the situation had changed. The introduction of conscription and the complexity of a modern army now required strict systems and regulations. The adoption of ranks was indispensable for efficient organization and discipline. Furthermore, the existence of ranks would ensure the high caliber of officers and provide an incentive for self-improvement, since promotion would depend on performance. At the same time the editorial offered the assurance that the introduction of a professional officer corps would not alter other fundamental features of the old revolutionary army model: namely, the comradeliness and unity between cadres and men, and the revolutionary soldierly model that had been held up to cadres and men alike.[5]

This assurance proved to be badly in error. What is remarkable is the extent to which central features of the older revolutionary military model described in Chapter 3 were abandoned or withered away. Modernization and professionalization of the army quickly contributed to a severe estrangement in its relations with both the Party and the civilian population. The rise of a young professional officer corps, recruited mostly from the new military academies, and the replacement of the demobilized veterans and "volunteers" with untrained conscripts, weakened traditional patterns of comradeship between cadres and ordinary soldiers.

By August 1, 1955 the rapidly growing gap between officers and men led Lo Jung-huan, then director of the General Political Department of the PLA, to comment apprehensively, if not with alarm, over the fact that the traditional PLA practices of comradely relations and patient persuasion were being weakened because some officers were refusing to reconcile them with the demands of the modernized Army. These officers, he said:

. . . put the rigid observance of discipline and the rigid control of the army as diametrically opposed to the practice of persuasion and education, and also put the measures to make the army more regular in character as diametrically opposed to the democracy that is necessary. They fail to understand the unity and unanimity of the two things. They have the mistaken notion that if the army is to be made more regular in character, we cannot talk of democracy, and if we talk of democracy the army cannot be made more regular in character. And so they exercise their powers indiscriminately, inflict punishment indiscriminately, and thereby seriously impair the glorious tradition of the unity between officers and men, between the upper and lower levels in our army . . . they do not mix freely with the men, show no more concern for the living conditions of the men, do not interfere when the food served the men is bad, and do not care for the ailments and individual difficulties of the men. The relationship between officers and men gradually becomes distant. If this situation is not corrected, there will be the danger that the internal unity of the army will be undermined.[6]

Despite efforts to correct this situation, the problem of officer-men relations grew worse in the next few years. The issues of the PLA's *Work Bulletin,* a secret internal journal published by the General Political Department of the PLA which came into the possession of the U.S. Government,[7] revealed a deep concern at the highest levels in the Party and in the armed forces over the extent to which the traditional ideal of comradely relations and the method of instructing via "patient persuasion" had fallen into disuse throughout the PLA.[8]

At the same time, professionalism quickly brought about a serious challenge to the political commissar system, particularly at the all-important company level that is regarded as the basic unit for combat and political work. The doctrinal prescription, "politics in command," was subjected to a surprisingly aggressive and successful attack. As we noted in Chapters 3 and 6, Chinese Communist leaders had assured supremacy of political control in the army by establishing a system of joint leadership by military commanders and political commissars under the overall direction and supervision of Party committees at each hierarchical level of army organization down to and including the company. It was precisely this central feature of the older "revolutionary" military model to which the young professional officers objected: They opposed the old system of party committees and political commissars on the ground that dual command was incompatible with the requirements of a modern army. In modern warfare, they contended, the command structure has to operate swiftly and smoothly, without interference by the cumbersome Party committee system. An editorial criticizing these views in 1958 noted that these officers "even openly advocate liquidation of Party committee leadership. . . ." [9]

Not only did these officers verbally assert the principle of "unity of command," which was alien to Mao Tse-tung's doctrine and Chinese Communist practice; they also put the new principle into effect, sometimes by aggressively pushing aside the political commissars.[10]

In this respect as in others, the young professional officers were moving rapidly to replace the Chinese Communist organizational model with the Soviet one in which, as we have noted, the political apparatus was not as thorough and played a more modest role.

Thus, in April 1961 the General Political Department of the PLA revealed in the *Work Bulletin* the startling fact that as of July 1960 about 7,000 companies in the army no longer had Party committees, and that in still others the Party committees were inactive.[11] As of October 1960, about one-third of all the companies in the PLA still had no Party committees.[12] At the same time, it was disclosed that the number of Party members in the companies had gradually declined; most of the platoons in the PLA lacked Party cells, and most of the squads had not even a single Party member. As Ralph Powell has noted, "this was a serious situation for a party that seeks 'absolute control' over the armed forces." [13] Thus, while the traditional practice of absorbing officers into the Party was maintained at higher levels, it is evident that a new generation of young officers and noncommissioned officers was emerging in the late fifties that was not being taken into the Party.

So widespread and fundamental an erosion of traditional norms and control mechanisms could hardly have taken place without the knowledge and acceptance, if not support, of high-level PLA authorities and, probably, some members of the Party leadership. In the April 1961 statement, the General Political Department explicitly charged that the leadership of the armed forces for several years had failed to pay sufficient attention to the organization of the all-important Party committees at company level. It is noteworthy that the remarkable weakness of Party organization in 1960 existed despite a series of Party campaigns in 1957 and 1958 that had attempted to combat "professionalism" and to tighten Party controls. Clearly these earlier rectification campaigns had been markedly unsuccessful. "It seems," one British specialist on the Chinese army concluded, "that the persistent interference by the Party in military matters had only served to increase opposition within the army to political control." [14] A likely explanation for the fact that the political apparatus had degenerated at the lower levels of the army into virtually a "paper organization," Joffe believed, is that top PLA leaders had "paid lip service to the political control system but failed to ensure its actual operation, perhaps because they agreed with many officers that the system was inimical to the combat efficiency of the army." [15]

Neglect of Party organization and controls within the armed forces was, in fact, but one of several policy issues over which controversy developed during these years between important elements of army leadership and the Party. As documented in official Chinese publications, several major disputes had arisen between professionally oriented officers, themselves Party members, and the dominant Party leaders, who supported the politically oriented military doctrines of Mao Tse-tung. These issues concerned the speed of technical modernization of the armed forces, the need for obtaining modern weapons abroad and for relying on foreign (particularly Soviet) military experience, the relative priority of economic development opposed to national defense construction, the appropriateness of using armed forces for economic tasks, the role and status of the militia, the primacy of "man over weapons." Western scholars also consider it likely that some Chinese military leaders, led by Marshal P'eng Teh-huai, who had commanded the Chinese forces during much of the Korean War and had since become Minister of Defense, and General Huang K'o-ch'eng, the PLA's Chief of Staff, were dismayed by the deterioration of relations between Peking and Moscow. Evidently P'eng and Huang opposed Chinese policies leading to the rupture and abrogation of Soviet defense assistance. While the circumstances are not entirely clear, these frictions came to a head in September 1959 when P'eng and Huang were removed from their positions. They were later accused, among other things, of "factionalism," advocating a "bourgeois military line," "military professionalism," "dogmatism," as well as with neglecting the Party organization in the PLA.

RESTORATION OF POLITICAL CONTROLS

Marshal Lin Piao was appointed as P'eng's replacement and, as the issues of *Work Bulletin* made clear, Lin's task was to reassert the Party's "absolute domination" over the armed forces, carry out a policy of military self-reliance, strengthen understanding and allegiance to Maoist doctrine, improve combat readiness and morale, and reinvigorate the traditional model of combat companies into which "professionalism" had made such serious inroads.

Following Lin Piao's appointment, concerted efforts were made to restore the ethos and practices of the old revolutionary army and to rebuild and reinvigorate the political apparatus within the PLA. Eighty-two percent of the total number of Party committees throughout the army were "adjusted." From Party organs at various other levels 78,000 cadres were assigned "to give concrete assistance to companies." Some 229,000 new Party members were recruited in the armed forces in 1960. By March 1961, all the companies that had lacked Party committees were reported to have established them once again. More than 80 percent of the platoons throughout the PLA were now said to have organized Party cells, and over half the squads reportedly had at least one Party member.[16]

Considerable attention was given to restoring the traditional methods of leadership and instruction described earlier in this study. Once again, these efforts focused on the companies. To this end, "Regulations Governing PLA Management and Educational Work at Company Level" were issued in mid-1961.[17] This was followed, a few months later, by "Four Sets of Regulations on Political Work in Company-Level Units of the PLA," which strengthened the hand of the political commissars in relation to military commanders and the Party committees.[18]

In 1961 a series of new military manuals were issued to the armed forces. These were in fact the first systematic codification of Chinese Communist military thinking and practice. Commissioned by Mao Tse-tung in 1958 and two years in preparation, the new manuals were considered to be an important instrument for combating "dogmatism" and the tendency to borrow "foreign" (Soviet) experience indiscriminately. The manuals embodied the military traditions and rich experience of the PLA which the older generation of Chinese Communist leaders wished to leave to the younger generation. That the manuals did not succeed in harmonizing Mao's military thinking, from which they took their guidance, with professional military views in the PLA was indirectly admitted by Marshal Yeh Chien-ying in his summing up to the Manuals Review Board. He conceded that the manuals were "not 100 percent perfect . . . but we can say that they are about 60 to 70 percent perfect." Admitting that "there are problems which remain to be solved," Marshal Yeh noted that a "minority" had expressed reservations to the content of the manuals on questions such as "concentration of a superior force," "the merger and identification of commandership principles with combat principles." [19]

Still another forceful attempt to reassert traditional Party principles and practices were the "Regulations Governing PLA Political Work," published in March 1963, which dealt once again with military doctrine, organization, political controls, and leadership methods.[20] The most striking feature of these regulations, as Joffe notes, is that "they contain nothing new. They bring together and formalize things that were said many times before." He concludes: "That it was considered necessary to do this not only underscores the leadership's constant concern with strengthening the political control system, but also suggests that as of early 1963 the system was still not fully operational." [21]

Nonetheless, judging from the tone as well as the content of public Chinese military writings, particularly in 1963 and 1964, Party leaders felt reasonably satisfied with the results of their efforts to correct the (to them) shocking internal situation of the armed forces revealed in 1959–1960. By early 1964 the political outlook of the PLA was regarded as sufficiently improved to hold up the armed forces as a model to other organized sectors within the country. A nationwide emulation campaign was launched, geared to the slogan: "Learn from the Experience of the People's Liberation Army in Political and Ideological Work." Moreover, Party leaders evidently believed that some of the political machinery and techniques of the PLA could be transferred to other sectors. Thus, "political departments," modeled on those within the PLA, were established in branches and units of the economic and industrial organization throughout the country. Even more important, former army officers and young men trained by the PLA were given positions of leadership in economic administration and management.[22]

THE RED VS. EXPERT PROBLEM

What overall assessment, then, can we make of the internal state of the PLA in recent years: its unity, cohesion, and morale? In attempting such an assessment, we sorely miss opportunities for direct observation of the present workings of the PLA system and its impact on cadres and ordinary soldiers. While the issues of the classified *Work Bulletin* for 1961 are extraordinarily revealing in many respects, they illuminate the state of affairs some six and seven years ago and much has happened since. Discussions in Chinese Communist mass media since then are less informative, though not without value to Western specialists skilled in "decoding" the jargonistic concepts and stylized phrases employed by the Chinese Communists. In any case, these public sources are hardly a substitute for interviews with Chinese soldiers and cadres who alone could give us, as did the prisoners we interviewed in 1951, direct access to the personal and psychological dimensions of these problems, and to the internal social processes of the PLA today.

It must be said, therefore, that we *know* extraordinarily little about the state of mind of the Chinese soldier today: how he reacts to norms and imperatives of the system of which he is a part, how well indoctrinated and assimilated he is within his unit, the character of small group relations in his unit, his likely reaction to indoctrination for war, the strength and character of his motivations for combat. On these and related questions, we can attempt only cautious judgments.

If the principle of political control has been reasserted and the organizational structure for it reestablished within all units throughout the PLA, important questions remain as to how well the principle works in practice. Similarly, if Party leaders have successfully cracked down on the aggressive, flagrant manifestations of military professionalism that occurred in the late fifties, the spirit and outlook of "professionalism" persists stubbornly though in muted form. Professionally-minded cadres and soldiers "adjust" to political indoctrination without fully assimilating it; they "accept" political controls often by attempting to redefine them in a formalistic fashion. Despite the progress made since 1960, the PLA evidently still has great difficulty in fusing professionalism with political controls. It may indeed be true, as Joffe holds, that in the PLA " 'Redness' and 'expertise' do not, in the final analysis, go together and some way out will eventually have to be found, perhaps by a new generation of more technically oriented leaders." [23]

This conflict between professional (expert) and political (red) elements is by no means confined to the PLA; it has emerged in all sectors of organized activity under the regime. In his recently published study of Chinese Communist organizational patterns and experience, Franz Schurmann concludes that the red and expert "contradiction" is the most important one in China today. Two different elites have emerged: a red cadre comprised of veterans of the Revolution or active, poor peasants whose skills are those of agitation, mobilizing the people, and fighting; and the experts, or professional intellectuals, who derive their position and status through education and who stress the need for rational management and hierarchy. Chinese Communist leaders want cadres who, as Mao Tse-tung said in 1938, should possess "both virtue and ability" i.e. ideally be both "red *and* expert." But the regime's effort to raise the "red cadres" to the same level as "good students" from bourgeois backgrounds has not fully succeeded; the ideal of uniting the values of "red" and "expert" within the same individual has not worked.[24]

The Soviet Army's experience with the red and expert problem does not provide a close parallel. As we noted earlier (p. 114), the Soviet and Chinese Communist armies emerged under rather different revolutionary-historical conditions which shaped the character of their organizational doctrine and practice along different lines. The Soviet Army was from the beginning a mixture of professional as well as revolutionary-egalitarian traditions. Nonetheless, despite the presence of both elements, "red" and "expert," from the start, the Soviet regime has experienced considerable difficulty over the years in achieving a stable blend or genuine synthesis of military professionalism with Party controls.[25] In contrast, the PLA started with and maintained for many years an exclusively revolutionary-egalitarian type of organization. Only later, when it became desirable to regularize and modernize their forces did Chinese Communist leaders attempt to graft "professionalism" on to the existing organizational model of the PLA. The effort to do this, quite understandably, was influenced directly by awareness of how the Soviets attempted to allow scope for military professionalism within a looser system of political controls than existed in the PLA.

At an earlier period, during the war with Japan, when the Chinese Communists and the Chinese Nationalists reached a *modus vivendi,* and when large numbers of students joined the communists for patriotic reasons, the Chinese Communist leaders found it expedient to relax somewhat the political controls in the army. At that time, it is reported, Party committees were maintained only at the division level.[26] However, relaxation of political controls under those circumstances—in the absence of a professional officer corps—was quite a different matter than in the mid-fifties. On the latter occasion, as we have seen, Chinese leaders found that "professionalism" was not neutral in its operational and political consequences, but that it profoundly threatened the requirements of political-ideological control within the PLA. The consequences of the experiment of moving in the direction of the Soviet model of looser political controls frightened the top Chinese leadership and led to the reimposition in 1960 of the stronger, more pervasive political apparatus that had been characteristic of the PLA in the late forties and at the time of its intervention in Korea.

Particularly since 1960 Chinese Party leaders have turned with missionary-like zeal to a revival within the PLA of doctrinal positions that had meaning in past years of revolutionary war. In the *Work Bulletin* leading Party officials recalled other near-fatal periods in the Party's history—1927–1929, 1934–1935, and 1941–1942—when adherence to the old Maoist revolutionary doctrine supposedly saved the day.[27] The desire to duplicate the doctrinal revival of earlier years has dominated the PLA's new approach, under Lin Piao, to finding politically acceptable safeguards for modernization of the armed forces. The operative goal has been to recapture as much as possible, under new conditions and with younger generations of soldiers, the halcyon days of revolutionary vigor, when the Army, Party, and People were united "like bone and flesh, like fish and water." [28]

Will the approach the Chinese leaders have chosen work sufficiently well or is it an anachronism that will inevitably give way, under unpredictable circumstances, to further experimentation with ways of dealing with the problem of red vs. expert? Lacking better information on the impact of this style of indoctrination on Chinese soldiers, it is difficult to offer confident judgments on these questions. But, certainly, there is no reason to doubt that PLA authorities are able, if they wish to, to recruit enough young soldiers into the Party to fill all the positions in the vast political organization throughout their army, as they claimed in fact to have done several years ago. The problem, as Chinese leaders know, is not one of numbers but of *quality:* That is, how does the indoctrination sit with the younger generation, how dedicated and willing are they to perform their functions in the desired manner? Not only the young conscripts but most of the junior cadres (and increasingly with the passage of time, the middle cadres as well) are being drawn from generations that have not shared in or only dimly remember the revolutionary experience of the thirties and forties.

A careful reading of the available issues of the *Work Bulletin* and of public Chinese Communist military publications since indicates that the regime finds it difficult to infuse younger soldiers and junior cadres with the kind of élan and dynamism that will enable them to "live" the old revolutionary ideology in the performance of their everyday duties. Critical in this respect, as our study has shown, are the company political officers and the junior cadres. PLA authorities are very much dependent upon them to create the kind of small group life in the basic units, the companies, that their organizational model calls for. As S. M. Chiu has noted: ". . . indifferent, incompetent, or ignorant commissars eventually may reduce the entire system to a mere façade." [29] Even if company commissars measure up to the ideal, their efforts can easily be frustrated by politically inferior junior cadres under them.* If other Party personnel and cadres in the com-

---

* As Hsiao Hua, director of the PLA General Political Department, put it: " 'Putting politics first' is not just the business of the few. In each company there should be organized a staunch contingent of political and ideological workers. . . . We should not rely on the political commissar alone. . . . If it is done only by the political commissar, it will be weak and ineffective." Hsiao Hua's report of January 24, 1966 to the PLA conference on political work, excerpts broadcast by Peking, January 24, 1966.

panies are not also imbued with the revolutionary élan of the older generation of communist fighters, they can hardly do their share in molding conscripts into soldiers that can participate effectively in the kind of politicized, egalitarian army Chinese leaders stubbornly insist must be maintained despite modernization.

There are the makings of a self-perpetuating deficiency. The dimensions of the problem facing PLA authorities in this respect have been formidable. Many of the revolutionary fighters and hard core communist cadres who survived the Korean War were in fact demobilized thereafter or moved upwards in the armed forces. Just when thousands of new, politically well-indoctrinated junior cadres were needed to take over and operate the system, professionalism was introduced; and, as we have seen, it made a shambles of political work in the companies. Although the political system was restored in 1960–1961, the fact that it had fallen into disuse and had not functioned effectively for perhaps five or more years must have severely weakened the ability of the diminishing number of genuine hard core Party cadres within the PLA to put the necessary verve into programs for its revival.

This is not to say that the effort has not been made. Since Lin Piao's appointment as Minister of Defense in 1959, repeated efforts have been made to get the cadres to carry out political work and educate the new conscript soldiers in the old style, to break down the social distance and barriers between cadres and conscripts, to establish comradely relations within the companies, to get cadres to rely upon persuasion and patient instruction rather than harsh methods. Persistent efforts have been made to evoke the glorious revolutionary traditions of the past. Meetings are held for the purpose of "recollection of past bitterness, contemplation of present sweetness." At these gatherings, older men recount the outrages committed before the Liberation by landlords, merchants, and imperialists before the younger men in order to whip up hatred and appreciation for the benefits of life under the People's Republic.

In some respects, to be sure, the task of indoctrination is easier than it was in the late forties and early fifties, when the PLA was forced to use large numbers of former Nationalist soldiers, many of whom were politically indigestible. Moreover, the repeated rectification and remolding campaigns have no doubt given authorities opportunities to locate and weed out "remnant bourgeois" elements. Then, too, the conscription process does offer the Party an opportunity to be more selective in recruitment than was possible earlier. To induct some 750,000 young men per year from among the approximately 6 million youths reaching the age of eighteen enables the PLA to conscript only those youngsters who are likely to be more reliable ideologically, and those whose family and occupational backgrounds the regime considers to be untainted. Even greater selectivity can be exercised in selecting soldiers for training as cadres.[30]

One can readily agree, therefore, with the conclusion General Griffith advanced in early 1965 that "it is not realistic to assume a crisis of morale in the PLA or to entertain the hope that the armed forces, or really significant elements of them, will prove disloyal to the party." When this is said, however, still another question remains: How deeply is the younger generation of cadres and soldiers capable of identifying with what, from its own perspective, must increasingly be seen as the revolutionary mythology of the older generation? That PLA authorities are able to secure the compliance of the younger soldiers and to get them to do their jobs is one thing; but whether they are also able to get them to internalize the revolutionary ethos offered them—that is, to genuinely mold them into the kind of communist soldier desired—is another matter. However skillful and persistent communist indoctrination may be, it is questionable whether it can make fanatics of younger people who have not themselves gone through the experiences from which genuine revolutionaries are created. On the other hand, what may be equally or more important is the strength of *nationalist* feelings among these youth, and whether PLA leaders are able to rouse them on these grounds if not by appeals to revolutionary idealism.

Our study of these matters in the PLA at the time of the Korean War of course cannot be extrapolated to the present situation, but it does suggest some relevant questions. To what extent are soldiers and cadres who have become Party members in the modern PLA "radishes" rather than "beets," as were so many of their predecessors some fifteen and more years ago—that is "red" outside but "white" inside? To what extent is their "redness" a necessary cloak for opportunism and career advancement? Another related question that is difficult to answer: To what extent are higher PLA authorities accepting the fact, as their predecessors often did in the late forties and early fifties, that many of the cadres and soldiers who seem to be well indoctrinated are really engaging in the practice of dissimulation, suppressing "bad thoughts" and behavior that may get them into trouble and simulating good morale and correct thoughts?

While firm answers to these questions are not possible, in 1965 Party leaders decided for reasons not altogether clear to reopen and press home their attack on the unsatisfactory ideological state of the PLA. After several years in which public criticism of the military had been virtually absent and, as we have noted, the army was praised and held up as a model for emulation, there was a partial renewal in 1965 of criticisms of deviationism and of "bourgeois" military thinking within the armed forces. These criticisms, though increasing in intensity, remained distinctly less strident in tone and less alarmist in content than those of the late fifties.

In still another effort to cope with important residues of "professionalism" in the attitudes and behavior of the cadres, the regime took the radical step in May 1965 of abolishing military ranks. Having introduced the system of ranks just ten years earlier, when a professional officer corps was created, the PLA now came full circle, returning to the revolutionary, egalitarian practice of no differentiation or distinction in mode of address, uniforms, or insignia. Everyone was ordered to wear the same kind of uniform with an identical red star cap insignia and a red collar badge. And, once again, everyone in the army from highest cadre to lowest soldier would be addressed as "comrade" by everyone else. References to rank would be replaced by job title: "company commander," "platoon leader," etc.

An editorial in *Chieh-fang-chün Pao,* May 25, 1965, explained that the system of ranks was being abolished to "further promote the revolutionization of our army." Ten years of experience with rank differentiation "has proved that it is not in conformity with our army's glorious tradition with the close relations between officers and men, between higher and lower levels, and between the army and the people." Its abolition, the editorial added, "will help eliminate certain objective factors contributing to breeding rank consciousness and ideas to gain fame and wealth."

Several months later, writing in early August on the occasion of the 38th anniversary of the founding of the PLA, Marshal Ho Lung,

Vice Chairman of the National Defense Council and a member of the Political Bureau of the Central Committee of the Chinese Communist Party, presented a point-by-point restatement of the traditional PLA military model prior to the experiment with professionalism in the mid-fifties. He coupled this with a detailed refutation of arguments within the PLA that the old egalitarian model and the associated military doctrine of "man over weapons" was no longer applicable under modern conditions. In the article, Ho Lung implicitly attacked P'eng Teh-huai and his followers who, "in the name of building a modern, regular army . . . advocated the abolition of the Party committee system in the army. . . ." and clearly implied that there were still remnants of this kind of "bourgeois thinking" within the army which had to be combated.[31] This ominous passage and, indeed, Ho Lung's article as a whole, suggested that there was important opposition, perhaps at a high level, within the PLA to the Party's recent intensification of measures against professionalism.

Several months later, in mid-November 1965, Lin Piao issued a new directive calling for renewed efforts for keeping "politics to the fore" within the PLA. In the following months increasing attention was given to various deficiencies in performance of political and educational work particularly at the company level. From these public criticisms it would seem that some Party committees were paying more attention to professional and technical work than to their political-ideological tasks; they failed in practice to put "politics in command" in a meaningful fashion. These public accounts indicated, moreover, that an undisclosed, but presumably small number of Party committees shirked their responsibility to struggle against erroneous "bourgeois military thinking" (i.e. professionalism) and failed to improve the understanding and application of Mao Tse-tung's thinking. Criticized, too, were tendencies to carry out political work in a routine, formalistic, and bureaucratic fashion.[32]

THE PLA AND THE GREAT CULTURAL REVOLUTION OF 1966

It was evidently about this time, in the fall of 1965, that Mao decided to undertake a purge of "intellectuals" in all walks of life and high Party functionaries who were considered guilty of "revisionist" and "bourgeois" tendencies and of opposition to the Party's goals and policies for building socialism at home and struggling against "imperialism" and "revisionism" abroad. The extent, significance, and outcome of this latest internal convulsion of the regime were not to become clear for many months. The purge proceeded slowly and, as its impact was felt and assessed, it may have taken directions not anticipated at its beginning. Indeed, Mao's effort to return China to revolutionary purity and to carry out a final great "cultural revolution" seemed to exacerbate, if not trigger, a major internal power struggle. Eventually, in July and August of 1966, charges of a conspiracy and plot to seize power and reverse the regime's policies were to be made. But revelations of "counterrevolutionary" activity emerged only belatedly and piecemeal, and at the present writing, they are difficult to assess. We shall focus in the remainder of this chapter on some further indications of the role of the PLA in the nationwide purge.

While the PLA was not the primary target of the purge, the nationwide campaign against "intellectuals" spilled over into the armed forces where it reinforced the recently intensified effort to cope with the evils of military professionalism. The application of the purge to the armed forces was apparently affected by a number of special considerations. Since 1959, it must be remembered the PLA had been the responsibility of Lin Piao, who was closely identified with and trusted by Mao. Whatever the explanation, the inadequacies of the PLA were criticized in 1965 and 1966 without allowing any implication of blame to fall on Lin Piao. In fact, Lin assumed an even more prominent position of trust during the course of the purge, being accorded a public position of importance second only to that of Mao himself, thus heightening speculation in the West that he was Mao's chosen successor. There was no suggestion in public Chinese accounts during the first half of 1966 that current deficiencies in political outlook and Party control within the PLA were in any way as severe as those in the late fifties. The possibility cannot be excluded, however, that an attempt was made to deliberately play down publicly for the time being unsettling developments that may have been taking place within the PLA at about this time.

Thus, in January 1966, hints of important conflicts within PLA leadership were included in the rationale for intensified struggle against professionalism and "bourgeois" thinking in the armed forces

General Lin Piao, perhaps the most successful leader the People's Liberation Army has ever had, November 5, 1950.

Lin Piao (left), heir apparent to Mao Tse-tung, conferring with Mao, in a picture monitored in Japan from a Peiping broadcast, September 16, 1966.

Yesterday and Today

that Hsiao Hua, director of the PLA's General Political Department, offered to a conference on political work. Alluding to the expanding purge of intellectuals and dissidents elsewhere in the nation, Hsiao Hua asserted that the class struggle in the country was "extremely complex" and sometimes "extremely sharp." In this connection, he recalled as having particular relevance for the present Mao's earlier historic warning that if the Chinese Communists did not continue the struggle against:

. . . landlords, rich peasants, counter-revolutionaries, bad elements and ogres of all kinds . . . then it would not take long, perhaps only several years or a decade, or several decades at most, before a counter-revolutionary restoration on a national scale inevitably occurred [and] the Marxist-Leninist party would undoubtedly become a revisionist party or a fascist party, and the whole of China would change its colour.*

Hsiao Hua implied that such a "dangerous situation" was at hand and that the role of the PLA was to serve in its traditional capacity as "the main instrument of the dictatorship of the proletariat."

Hsiao Hua then added an ominous but vague warning which would take on added interest and significance some months later: "The class enemy at home and abroad always regards our army as a sworn enemy and invariably seek ways and means to undermine and corrode us . . . the class struggle in society surely will, through all kinds of channels and forms, be adapted within the army." Having identified this threat, Hsiao Hua called upon the armed forces for renewed efforts to strengthen itself by keeping "politics to the fore" and by revolutionizing its ideology. Another reason for such efforts which Hsiao Hua gave, though without emphasizing its imminence, was the possibility of war. This made it incumbent on the PLA to strengthen its combat morale by strengthening its political consciousness:

As pointed out by Comrade Lin Piao, as far as our army is concerned, the best weapon is not the airplane, artillery, tank, or atom bomb but Mao Tse-tung's thinking. . . . In fighting, the most important factor is not whether one can shoot accurately with his gun, but rather whether or not

* Mao's warning, which Hsiao Hua paraphrased, is reproduced in part here. It appeared as a quotation (from a document dated May 9, 1963) in a Chinese Communist exchange with the Soviet Union: "Comment on the Open Letter of the Central Committee of the C.P.S.U. (9)," *Peking Review,* July 17, 1964, p. 26.

one fears death. . . . Victory is impossible if the theory that "weapons decide everything" is followed.*

Hsiao Hua's cryptic remark that the PLA was "the main instrument of the dictatorship of the proletariat" in the "dangerous situation" of class struggle that was unfolding could be interpreted, of course, as an indication that Lin Piao and the PLA were considered as especially trustworthy by Mao and, hence, were playing a special role in the purge that was under way. And, indeed, in the following months there were many signs that this was so. On May 13, 1966, for example, the PLA newspaper, *Chieh-fang-chün Pao,* attacked the Peking Municipal Party Committee secretary, Teng T'o, and by implication his boss, P'eng Chen, in the following terms:

You people called us a stick. That's right! We, the people's armed forces, are a stick. Furthermore, it is not an ordinary stick, but a heavy club of proletarian dictatorship, and it is used for the sole purpose of beating those harmful, antiparty and antisocialist people like you.

Given the fact that the purge now affected intellectuals *within* the Party, it was indeed remarkable that Mao and Lin should use the PLA newspaper to set the correct line. The incongruity of relying upon the army's journal to implement a purge of Party intellectuals could not but suggest that Mao lacked full trust in his Party apparatus and its organ, *Jen-min Jih-pao.*

For six months following Hsiao Hua's report, his cryptic allusion to the extension of the "class struggle" to the army was not fully clarified. However, the regime's demand that politics be given precedence in the armed forces over technical proficiency became more extreme in content and more strident in tone. Propaganda publications drove home the point that regardless of its military proficiency a PLA company was considered to fall below Mao's standards if it had not yet been thoroughly politicized in its outlook. Leaders of PLA units were severely criticized for placing mastery of techniques on a par with mastery of revolutionary ideology.[33] Distrust of experts and technicians was expressed in a rhetoric so extreme at times as to seem totally unreasonable, if not absurd. Thus, the Party took strong exception to the attitude, evidently widespread among cadres and sol-

* Excerpts of Hsiao Hua's report were broadcast on January 24, 1966 by Peking domestic service in Mandarin and in English. It is interesting that the paraphrase of Mao's warning was left out of the broadcast in English.

diers in the PLA, of concentrating on doing one's job well, which the soldiers apparently tried to justify on the grounds that this was after all a concrete way of demonstrating the soundness of one's political outlook. When challenged on this point, these cadres and soldiers took the position that "politics must be realized through other work. Otherwise it will be just 'empty politics.' " But they were admonished and warned that this was an unacceptable and dangerous attitude: "If one does not revolutionize one's ideas, but concentrates his efforts only on his job, it is possible one day one may find oneself destroyed by bourgeois ideas. It is very dangerous if one does not see this point." [34]

Published Chinese Communist accounts left unclear how the ultra-revolutionary rhetoric of indoctrination was being translated into concrete measures affecting schedules and activities within different units, personnel policies, and disciplinary measures of various kinds. Reading between the lines of such official statements, however, it was obvious that at least some, if not many cadres were appalled and shocked by the regime's fanatic insistence that revolutionizing ideology was more important than learning how to shoot accurately and mastering the more intricate techniques of modern warfare. One sensed that these cadres accepted the necessity of giving morale a firmer basis through political indoctrination but were irritated and alienated by the Party's unwillingness to comprehend and admit the necessity for a realistic position on the matter of learning military skills and getting the job done properly.

One could also infer from the developments described briefly here that the problem with the "experts" and professionally-minded cadres was perhaps even more severe than Party spokesmen cared to admit. Perhaps the rectification of these attitudes in the years since Lin Piao took charge of the PLA had in fact gone appreciably less well than the regime had believed, or publicly claimed, at that time. With the threat of war as a result of the growing involvement of the United States in the Vietnam war and its escalation to North Vietnam, was it possible that the "professionals" in the PLA—never really reformed, only silenced—had recently asserted themselves again and found new ears inside the Party who were listening? Or was it possible the regime's leaders feared such a development and exaggerated whatever indications of it that came to their attention?

Spring gave way to summer and there was still no announcement of a direct purge of PLA leadership. That action already had been or would be taken against one or more senior military leaders, however, could not be excluded. Such a possibility suggested itself, for example, when unnamed senior military officers were criticized for their alleged refusal to undergo ideological reform on the ground that their revolutionary past should exempt them from the necessity.[35] Moreover, the regime had announced a policy of pushing younger officers, considered by the Party as being politically reliable, into more responsible command positions. This policy was signaled in the Lin Piao directive of November 15, 1965 and was given further emphasis by Hsiao Hua in his report of January 24, 1966: "We must boldly break with accepted conventions and really promote commanders and fighters who are politically reliable, young, capable, and full of drive, and who have a good style of work." It was not clear from available materials, however, how radically this directive was being implemented.

On the other hand, with the passage of time the fact that Lo Jui-ch'ing, Chief of the General Staff, had not appeared publicly since November 1965 attracted increasing attention and Western analysts speculated that Lo may have been purged.[36] This interpretation received tacit confirmation when Lo did not appear on August 1 at the celebration of the thirty-ninth anniversary of the founding of the PLA and, instead, the major address was given by Yang Cheng-wu who was referred to as the "Acting Chief of the General Staff."

In an editorial on the occasion of the thirty-ninth anniversary, the PLA newspaper referred to the most recent of the "big struggles" within the armed forces without giving names or details; nonetheless, it made clear that several high-level military figures had been purged for opposing, together with some Party leaders, a number of the regime's policies:

Exposed in this struggle were representatives of the bourgeoisie who had got hold of important posts in the army and were important members of the counterrevolutionary antiparty, anti-socialist clique recently uncovered by our party. They had opposed the party's Central Committee and Mao Tse-tung's thought, had overtly agreed to but covertly opposed Comrade Lin Piao's directives on putting politics in the forefront . . . had talked about putting politics in command but in practice had given first consideration to military affairs, technique and specialized work. . . .[37]

Thus Lo Jui-ch'ing and others, who some years earlier had been given the job of bringing the PLA back to orthodoxy, ended by being ousted themselves for urging the military view on the Party leadership. What lay beneath the surface of this ironic course of events was not clear in detail. It is likely that Lo and other important figures in the PLA had felt that the measures adopted by the regime in 1965 to push the armed forces further into the mold of a revolutionary-egalitarian army were excessive and harmful. In addition, it is possible that, as P'eng Teh-huai evidently had in 1959, Lo too had taken issue with some of the regime's foreign policies and domestic programs insofar as they affected the interests of the armed forces.[38]

In the days following the thirty-ninth anniversary of the founding of the PLA, the regime finally lifted some of the mystery and uncertainty of the preceding six months regarding the implications of the purge for its internal policies. Mao Tse-tung now ordered greater integration between the armed forces and the Chinese people. The PLA was to serve as "a great school" for furthering the revolutionary thoughts of Mao. The whole country was called upon, once again, to learn from the PLA, to emulate it by turning factories, rural people's communes, schools, trading enterprises, service trades, Party and government organizations into "truly great revolutionary schools like the Liberation Army." This, Peking said, was Mao Tse-tung's "scientific answer to the question of how to prevent a restoration of capitalism, consolidate the dictatorship of the proletariat, and guarantee the transition to communism." [39] Thereupon, Peking published a number of policy decisions taken by the eleventh plenary session of the Central Committee during its meeting of August 1–12. It was made clear that the purge was to continue for some time. Special administrative measures were to be taken throughout the country to push forward the "great proletarian cultural revolution" and orders were given for a new "Great Leap Forward" in the economic sphere.

Hence, the regime had committed itself, if not to repeating in identical form the crudities of the "Great Leap Forward" of 1958, at least to making another scaled down, controlled effort to apply Mao's theory that China could make a dramatic breakthrough in capital development and economic growth by mobilizing the will and spirit of the Chinese masses.* Mao and his followers had never disowned the strategy of the "Great Leap Forward," even though it left the Chinese economy in a chaotic state and had to be abandoned. Rather, they implied that its failure was due to inadequacies of the cadres and organizations which were supposed to implement it. In this respect, however, Mao evidently believed by 1965–1966 that a more secure basis had been created thanks largely to the favorable development of the PLA under Lin Piao. Not only had the system of Party controls been rebuilt within the PLA, it had apparently recaptured some of the revolutionary spirit of the guerrilla army of Yenan days.

Moreover, if the developments of the sixties described in this chapter are viewed retrospectively, it appears that the regime's persistent efforts to revive the "guerrilla" spirit and to strengthen the Party's role in the PLA may have had the objective of laying the foundation for what, according to Chalmers Johnson, has become one of the PLA's major social functions: namely, the recruitment and training of new Party members not merely for the army but for the whole of Chinese society. "Under Lin Piao's regimen," Chalmers Johnson points out, "the army has unquestionably become the best training ground in the country for future political responsibility and leadership." During the past seven years large numbers of conscript soldiers were carefully screened and taken into the Party. After discharge from the PLA many of them have been sent to take their place as Party cadre in other organized sectors of society. Entrance of young soldiers into the Party while in the PLA, therefore, has become "an increasingly important first rung on the ladder for advancement in other fields in China. This elite-training function of the army," concludes Johnson, "may ultimately be much more important to the maintenance of the regime than any military preparedness." Moreover, since the "political departments," modeled on those within the PLA, were introduced into economic and industrial sectors of society in late 1963 (see p. 206), they have grown in importance to the point that "the PLA's influence is becoming ubiquitous. . . . At the present time, the PLA is serving as the chief model and organiza-

---

* This paragraph draws upon Chalmers Johnson, "Lin Piao's Army and Its Role in Chinese Society," in two parts, *Current Scene: Developments in Mainland China,* Vol. IV, Nos. 13 and 14, July 1 and 15, 1966.

tional instrument in an attempt to create an artificial civil war atmosphere in the Chinese economy." So far, however, the campaign has been pursued more cautiously than in the earlier "Great Leap Forward."

The problem of red vs. expert has been muted, not solved in the PLA and in Communist China as a whole. Present in some form in all revolutionary regimes undertaking modernization of their armies and of their societies, the conflict between redness and expertise has been peculiarly exacerbated in Communist China. For several years now, the older generation of Chinese Communist leaders has been acutely concerned over the revolutionary will of its heirs; its anxiety in this matter has been magnified by the imperatives of its ideological and political conflict with the Soviet Union. The struggle against "revisionism" abroad—the Soviet Union—has become inextricably linked in the eyes of the older Chinese Communist leaders with the struggle against "revisionism" at home. Such a linkage compounds the already difficult task of training successors who will be loyal to the "revolution" and at the same time also equipped to carry modernization forward. For the struggle against "revisionism" abroad inevitably creates excessive preoccupation with the danger of "revisionism" at home. It encourages harsh, inflexible approaches to the problem of "red" vs. "expert" that make it more difficult to move toward a better resolution of the conflict between the two.

Nonetheless, the prospects facing the regime in the course it has taken are by no means clear. It may very well be, as John Wilson Lewis suggested some time ago, that pursuit of the joint goal of "revolution and modernization" will prove to be infeasible, and that the Chinese Communists will eventually accept the fact that they cannot "produce modernity without the modern man." This point of view derives from the belief that what the Chinese Communists call "revisionism" has come to stay because it is the essence of the industrial society they and other communists elsewhere have sought to create.[40] Some adherents of this view, struck by the excesses of the current "purification" campaign in China, feel that it may eventually backfire, setting the stage for a more rapid "de-Maoization" at some point later than would otherwise occur.[41] Others, however, have offered a more cautious view of the future course of the regime: "Despite many predictions by outside observers that the second generation of Chinese leaders will abandon the guerrilla mentality, it is not yet clear whether the ascendancy of the PLA represents the last gasp of the old order or the choice of the future rulers." [42]

In conclusion, we can agree with Mao Tse-tung and others who hold that "the human element" is a vital factor in war. In this study we have indeed focused on the all-important human element, as conceived ideally in the Chinese Communist military model. We have considered in detail the policies and practices employed within the PLA to assure superior morale for its forces and, thereby, to bring to reality Mao's dictum that "man" can triumph over "weapons." We have considered what this means in terms of the norms and standards held up to cadres and soldiers, the kind of social organization and human relationships PLA leaders attempt to establish within their armed forces, the techniques and mechanisms of indoctrination and discipline they employ, and the system of pervasive political controls used within the armed forces in order to try to maintain high standards and to assure performance. We have considered both the strengths and weaknesses of the PLA military system when it was subjected to the stress of severe, prolonged combat outside its borders in Korea against a modern, professional army. And we have noted the major difficulties the regime experienced after the Korean War in modernizing its forces and installing for the first time a professional officer corps.

Even more so than its weapons and tactics, an army can prove its morale and combat motivation only in battle. Some units of the PLA took part in the border clash with India in 1962 in which, reportedly, the morale of Chinese soldiers remained high even though the fighting took place under difficult weather and terrain conditions. The fact remains, however, that the PLA has not fought on a large scale since the end of the Korean War. We can assume that its leaders are aware of some of the major uncertainties that would affect its performance in a new war of any magnitude.

The fighting qualities of the Chinese soldier are not in question. His toughness and battlefield courage were amply proven in Korea, and it would be imprudent to assume that the Chinese soldier today is not the equal of his forebears in these respects. In this connection it is interesting to find Mao Tse-tung's emphasis on "man-over-weapons" echoed in a sober injunction not to underestimate the Chinese soldier that appears in the U.S. *Marine Corps Gazette:*

The average Chinese soldier is still poorly armed by Western standards. We should not forget, however, that war is made by men, not weapons. . . . We must guard against overconfidence based on apparent U.S. weapons superiorities. . . . Chinese fighting qualities are unquestioned —stamina and fatalistic bravery will go far to make up for their weapons disadvantages. They have discipline that conquers the natural fear of death. . . .[43]

Discipline and bravery on the battlefield, however, depend on leadership and organization. An important key to the future effectiveness of the PLA is the quality of the leadership it can provide in small combat units. It is here that the pull and tug over "professionalism" since the end of the Korean War may have important consequences, though these are difficult to assess on the basis of available information. As we have seen, in the sixties PLA authorities largely abandoned the experiment of giving greater scope to military professionalism. They restored the principle of "politics in command" and tried to reintroduce politicized cadres into the organizational structure of the basic level companies. At the same time, PLA leaders attempted to recreate the kind of comradely relations, method of instruction, and discipline that prevailed in the earlier guerrilla type army. How well they have succeeded in these respects is uncertain. This particular way of providing combat units with effective leadership and with the kind of social cohesion needed for strong morale requires that the military cadre structure down to and below the squad level in each unit be staffed with Party soldiers or members of the Communist Youth branch who are well motivated and skilled in applying the human relations approach favored by the PLA. An inept company political officer or any substantial deficiency in numbers or quality of the cadres within the company weakens its cohesion and combat potential.

"Man-over-weapons," therefore, is not merely a matter of the fighting qualities of the individual Chinese soldier; it depends greatly on the ability of PLA leaders to meet the special personnel requirements of the military model they have chosen to rely upon.

Nor does the Party's present exhortation to believe in "man-over-weapons" come to grips with the fact that there are important limiting conditions beyond which superior morale can no longer compensate for the military advantages of a better-equipped foe. In Korea, the PLA used a type of offense and defense which minimized its disadvantages and turned to account its strengths. These tactics were largely an adaptation of Chinese Communist guerrilla warfare to larger-scale operations of a more orthodox character. At first, the application of these military tactics yielded important successes for the PLA in the winter of 1950–1951. But then the UN command succeeded in confronting the Chinese with a continuous, firm battle line across the Korean peninsula, and employed tactics of "rolling with the punch" of Chinese offensives and pushing ahead cautiously in its own offensive operations safeguarding its flanks and rear against the tactical maneuvers of the PLA. It became evident that the PLA had encountered novel conditions under which Mao's military doctrine could no longer be applied effectively. Chinese military morale declined sharply, requiring PLA leaders to place greater reliance for combat enforcement on coercive controls provided in each combat unit by the politicized cadres. With the cumulative physical and moral attrition of these cadres, the organizational controls they were supposed to provide over the rank and file weakened and finally collapsed under the pressure of the strong UN counteroffensive in late May 1951.

That reliance on "man-over-weapons" can be carried too far was plainly manifested in the spring of 1951. This aspect of the Korean experience is not likely to be forgotten or passed over lightly by professionally oriented military leaders in the PLA when assessing the capabilities of their armed forces in various future contingencies. The meaning of "man-over-weapons" and the limiting conditions under which it applies, however, are likely to be assessed more optimistically by some Chinese Communist leaders than by others.

As was stated in the Preface, this book has not attempted to answer the question of how well the PLA will fight in the future. It is doubtful that Chinese Communist leaders today are as united or as self-confident of their military doctrine and tactics as when they intervened in the Korean War. But it seems safe to say that against a strong opponent who can bring superior firepower and mobility to bear, the PLA will do better in relatively small-scale operations where its leaders can control the time, place, and duration of actual combat engagements rather than in protracted, large-scale fighting along fixed lines of battle.

Research Note

AS NOTED in Chapter 2, much of the information on which this study is based was obtained from eighty-four interviews with Chinese prisoners. This Research Note provides additional material on the interview procedures employed and the background characteristics of the eighty-four prisoners, and reproduces the text of the basic questionnaire that was used in making these interviews. (Questionnaires employed in making the other interviews referred to in Chapter 2 are not reproduced here.)

Of necessity, since I do not know the Chinese language, all of the interviews were conducted by Korean civilians who were fluent in Chinese. Prior to the time the services of these interviewers became available to me, they had been carefully selected, trained, and employed by representatives of an American survey research organization that was engaged in a study of prisoner attitudes for the U.S. Army. Despite the high caliber of these interviewers, my inability to interview the prisoners, except occasionally through an interpreter, and the need to have the respondents' replies translated by others imposed important constraints on the investigation. The interviewers were not allowed to rely on their own judgment in questioning prisoners. Rather, the interviews were structured by requiring interviewers to follow faithfully the general questions and more specific probes listed on the questionnaire. Similarly, the interviewers were required to write down as full a verbatim account as possible of the replies the respondent gave during the course of the interview.

Particular care was taken to establish and maintain good rapport with a prisoner who was being interviewed. Each interview took on the average of about one and a half to two hours. Interviewers generally reported good rapport and little difficulty in getting the information requested.*

The interviewers translated and recorded the Chinese respondents' replies into Korean during the interview. Later, a separate group of translators, more skilled in the English language, translated these interview protocols from Korean into English. The latter translation is the more difficult for Korean personnel since it involves translating from their own language into a foreign tongue. The rate of translation into English was approximately one interview a day per interviewer. These

* Difficulties which developed later with communist prisoners on the island of Koje were not current at the time of the present investigation.

translations, but not the originals from Chinese into Korean, were checked for accuracy.

The fact of a cumbersome translation of respondents' replies from Chinese to Korean and then from Korean to English, and the lack of immediate supervision over the first translation of course introduced constraints on the interpretation of the replies of the prisoners.

Under these circumstances I had to rely largely upon factual information provided by prisoners in analyzing the interviews; subtle interpretations of the prisoners' replies were excluded. In anticipation of this problem the questioning of prisoners was structured in ways likely to elicit information that would be useful for analysis despite the language and translation barriers.

The prisoners were selected for interview more or less fortuitously from among those available at the Processing Center of POW Camp No. 5. An effort to draw a truly representative sample of either the PLA as a whole or of the entire group of prisoners during any given time would have encountered practical difficulties. In any case it was felt that the nature of the study and the use of prisoners as informants rather than as members of a statistical sample did not require a controlled random sampling procedure. Accordingly, no effort was made to ensure a systematic sample. In any case, a randomly drawn sample of the prisoners as they came into the Processing Center, even were this a practical procedure under camp conditions, would not have been representative of the PLA as a whole. For, as survivors of the war who had fallen into our hands, the prisoners did not necessarily reflect the characteristics of those Chinese soldiers who had died, those who had deserted to the rear, those who were still members of the PLA. And as men recently in combat, the prisoners were not necessarily representative of units withdrawn for regrouping and recuperation, or of fresh units as yet uncommitted to battle.

The fortuitous selection of prisoners over a period of weeks did provide the broad representation of PLA units desired for this study. Practically all of the eighty-four men interviewed on our basic questionnaire had come from different units, most of them combat infantry units. Therefore, these prisoners provided data on approximately eighty different companies drawn from about thirty divisions, that is, somewhat less than 10 percent of all the combat companies in these thirty divisions. In almost all cases these soldiers came from units that had been part of the armies which comprised the initial intervention force of thirty divisions entering Korea in the late autumn of 1950. Therefore most of them had spent an extremely severe winter in Korea. Some of these eighty-four respondents had been part of the second major group of PLA armies entering Korea in March and early April, 1951.

Other background characteristics of the respondents on our basic questionnaire were as follows:

	Privates (61) [a]	Cadres (23) [a]
Method of entry into PLA		
Captured former CNA Personnel	54	11
Conscripts	6	4
Volunteers	1	7
Date of entry into PLA		
Pre-1947	0	4
1947–1948	10	10
Early 1949	17	1
Late 1949	19	1
Early 1950	6	3
Late 1950	9	2
Age		
Under 21	9	3
21–25	26	8
26–30	19	7
31–35	5	3
36 or over	1	2
Occupational background of prisoner		
Tenant farmer; farm laborer	14	5
Self-supporting farmer	12	2
Student	8	7
Regular army	8	2
Worker	9	3
Artisan	1	0
Shopkeeper, retailer	6	1
Government employee, professional	1	2
Absentee landowner	0	1
Education		
Nonliterate	16	5
Some elementary school	25	7
Completed elementary school	11	2
Some middle school	5	5
Completed middle school	3	4
Marital status		
Single	44	17
Married	15	4
Divorced	0	2
Widower	1	0

[a] Where the totals in each of the following tabulations do not add up to this figure, it means that information on that point was not obtained from certain respondents.

	Privates *(61)*	Cadres *(23)*
Religion		
None	54	17
Christian	2	4
Confucian	2	0
Buddhist	2	2

Following is the English text of the basic questionnaire employed in this study.

I. Attitude of Soldier Toward His Political Officers

    a. How long he knew him (or them)?

    b. Estimate of the *personal character* of political officers—what sort of person or man was he?

    c. Did you and the men in your unit have *respect* for political officers —in what sense did they respect him; for what?

    d. Did they *like* him? Did they have friendly feelings toward him? (How did such feelings show themselves in everyday life?)

    e. Did they *believe* what he told them—did they trust him, think he was honest and truthful (explain)?

    f. Did he ever *praise* them when they did their job well or fought well (explain)?

II. Taking Care of the Men

    a. In what way did the political officer take care of you?

    b. Do you think that political officers *or* military cadres were primarily responsible for, and interested in the *welfare* of the men—taking care of them, seeing they got enough food, a place to sleep, clothes, entertainment, and medical attention if they needed it?

    c. Did political officers do their best to get these things for the men? Did they make special efforts? Did the men appreciate what the political officers did for them? (How was such appreciation expressed?)

    d. Did the men ever take *any* of their problems to the political officers? What types of problems, how often was this done?

    e. Were there any problems that the men did not feel free to take to the political officers? Why?

    f. Were complaints against the military cadres ever taken to the political officer by any of the men?

III. War Indoctrination, Propaganda, and War News

    a. What did political officers tell men about the war in Korea? (Why they had to fight against U.S. and UN.) Did what the political officers say sound reasonable—did most men believe it?

    b. How often did political officers talk to the men about the war— while in Korea?

    c. Did they talk to the men while your unit was at the *frontline area?* How often and about what?

    d. Did political officers give the men news of the war developments —how often? What sort of news? Did they ever give news of unfavorable character?

    e. When things were not going so well, that is, when your unit or your armies were retreating or were having difficulties, what did the political officers say?

    f. What sorts of promises did political officers make to you? (explain details and circumstances)

IV. Role of Political Officers in Battle Motivation

    a. Before your unit started an offensive, did political officers ever speak to you or do special things for you? (explain)

    b. Before an important combat what did political officers do or say to make you fight better, to be more courageous? (explain)

    c. What did you and the men think about these special efforts made by the political officer before an offensive and before a combat? Did it help you to do better? (explain)

    d. When the men in your unit were tired of fighting or afraid of enemy weapons and death, what did your political officers do and say about it? (details)

    e. Was there any promise of benefits to you or your family?

    f. What kind of rewards (medals, promotion in status, special titles, etc.) were given for meritorious conduct or bravery? How did it affect you or the men in your unit?

V. Political Officers' Concern with Morale

    a. Were the political officers interested in the morale of the men?

    b. How did the political officers show their interest in morale? What did they do or say?

    c. How did political officers know whether morale was good or bad? How did they observe it and study it?

    d. What system was there for studying morale? How did the political leaders work together and with other people, such as squad leaders and military commanders, in order to study morale?

    e. Did the men know that political officers were observing their morale? What did they think about this?

    f. Were the men careful in any way not to show signs of bad morale? Why?

VI. Self-Criticism Meetings

    a. Do you know what a self-criticism or criticism meeting is? (explain)

    b. What was the purpose of such meetings?

    c. How often held? When and where? How many present? (details)

    d. What problems were brought up at self-criticism meetings?

    e. What happened at a typical self-criticism meeting? (details—how it started—who spoke, what followed, etc.)

  f. Were these self-criticism meetings useful? In what way? Did they have any effect upon the "guilty" person—and on the other men who were present?

  g. Was there anything about self-criticism meetings you and the men in your unit *liked?*

  h. Was there anything about such meetings that was *disliked* by the men?

  i. Were there special self-criticism meetings for cadres? (details)

VII. Relations Between Political Officers and Military Cadres

  a. Did the political officers and military cadres get along well with one another? Did they *ever* have any difficulties or conflicts with each other about *any* matter whatsoever?

  b. Were the political officers and military cadres good friends with each other? How would you describe their relationship?

  c. Did the military cadres *respect* the political officers? Did they ever show signs of *fearing* the political officers?

  d. Who had greater authority—the political officer or military cadre?

VIII. Political Defense Organization

  a. Did the *political* officers get along well with the political defense officer?

  b. Did the *military* cadres get along well with the political defense officer?

  c. How were the functions of these three authorities related, and how did they differ? How did these relationships work out?

  d. Whom did you fear most of these three authorities? Why?

  e. Did you notice that any special organization existed in your unit under the political defense officer and political officers? What kind of organization was it? How did it work out?

  f. What was the role of the Democratic Youth League Committee and the Party cell of your unit?

   What made you follow the army to the last, undergoing so many hardships in this war?

Notes

CHAPTER 1: THE CHINESE INTERVENTION IN KOREA

The quotation is from René Cutforth, *Korean Reporter* (London: Allan Wingate, 1955).

1. For an analysis of the Chinese Communist decision to enter the Korean War, see Allen Whiting, *China Crosses the Yalu* (New York: The Macmillan Co., 1960), and David Rees, *Korea: The Limited War* (New York: St. Martin's Press, 1964), pp. 104–14. On the miscalculation of the strength and intentions of Chinese forces in Korea, see Roy E. Appleman, *United States Army in the Korean War: South to the Naktong, North to the Yalu,* Chapter XXXIX, "The Big Question" (Washington, D.C.: Office of the Chief of Military History, Dept. of the Army, 1961).

2. Rees, *Korea,* p. 176.

3. L. Montross *et al., U.S. Marine Operations in Korea, 1950–1953, The East-Central Front* (Washington, D.C.: U.S. Government Printing Office, 1962), Vol. IV, 35.

4. Montross *et al., Marine Operations, The Chosin Reservoir Campaign,* 1957, Vol. III, 92.

5. Montross *et al., Marine Operations,* Vol. III, 93–94. The description of PLA tactics presented here by Montross is attributed partly to the study by S. L. A. Marshall, "CCF in the Attack" (EUSAK Staff Memorandum ORO-S-26, 5 January 1951). See also S. L. A. Marshall's fuller account of Chinese offensive operations in *The River and the Gauntlet* (New York: William Morrow & Co., 1953); and *Handbook on the Chinese Communist Army,* Department of the Army Pamphlet No. 30–51 (Washington, D.C.: Department of the Army, 1952).

6. Montross, Vol. III, 163–64, 166–68, 181, 184–85, 209–11, 225–26, 240–43.

7. In his official U.S. Army history of the Korean War, Roy Appleman also states that the 4th Field Army was the best field army of the PLA. In tracing its history, he notes that the 4th Field Army had played a prominent role in defeating the Nationalist armies and had fought from Manchuria to the capture of Hainan Island in the civil war without a major defeat. Appleman, *United States Army in the Korean War,* pp. 750–51. See also the historical notes on the 4th Field Army in Lt. Col. R. B. Rigg, *Red China's Fighting Hordes* (Harrisburg, Pa.: The Military Service Publishing Co., 1951), pp. 89–94.

8. The identification of the PLA armies sent initially into Korea is also given in Appleman, *United States Army,* pp. 766–69, and Rees, *Korea,* p.

136. Appleman adds that the 20th, 26th, and 27th Armies were each reinforced by a division taken from the 30th Army; and that this intervention force of 30 divisions was supported by several artillery divisions and truck regiments.

9. Partial identification of the new armies sent to Korea is given also by R. F. Futrell, *The United States Air Force in Korea 1950–1953* (New York: Duell, Sloan, and Pearce, 1961), p. 335.

10. Rees, *Korea,* pp. 194, 245–46.

11. Futrell, *The United States Air Force,* p. 336; Rees, *Korea,* pp. 245–46.

12. Futrell, *The United States Air Force,* p. 341. (Futrell's account is based on official Far East Command intelligence summaries.) See also Rees, *Korea,* pp. 255–58.

13. Montross, *Marine Operations,* Vol. IV, 127.

14. Harry S. Truman, *Memoirs, Years of Trial and Hope* (Garden City, New York: Doubleday & Co., 1956), Vol. II, 456.

15. Futrell, *The United States Air Force,* pp. 341–43; Montross, IV, 127–28; Rees, *Korea,* pp. 257–58.

16. For a balanced interpretation of this question, see Rees, *Korea,* pp. 258–59, 298–309.

17. Rees, *Korea,* p. 303. Additionally, Rees observes, it was the thirty-day *de facto* cease-fire on the ground in November and December 1951 which gave the communist forces a breathing space in which to construct "the vast fourteen-mile deep defensive network which protected the Communist armies for the remainder of the Korean War." (*Ibid.,* pp. 300–1.)

CHAPTER 2: THE INTERVIEWS

1. M. Janowitz (ed.), *The New Military: Changing Patterns of Organization* (New York: Russell Sage Foundation, 1964), p. 191. See also M. Janowitz and Lt. Col. Roger Little, *Sociology and the Military Establishment* (New York: Russell Sage Foundation, 1965), pp. 10–11; and M. Brewster Smith's earlier discussion of the ways in which the question, "Why do soldiers fight?" can be defined and dealt with in research; in S. A. Stouffer *et al., The American Soldier* (Princeton: Princeton University Press, 1949), Vol. II, 105–7.

2. Additional interviews were made in the following months by my colleague, Herbert Goldhamer, which I have not utilized and the results of which remain unpublished.

CHAPTER 3: THE CHINESE COMMUNIST MILITARY MODEL

The quotation from Mao Tse-tung is from *On Guerrilla Warfare,* Samuel B. Griffith, translator (New York: Praeger, 1961), pp. 90–91.

1. There are a number of historical examples of closely knit military-religious organizations, such as the Templars and Cromwell's Army. Hans Speier points out that one of the most closely knit military groups of this kind, the Janissaries, achieved their extraordinary cohesion by adhering to celibacy. Hans Speier, " 'The American Soldier' and the Sociology of Military Organization," in *Continuities in Social Research: Studies in the Scope and Method of "The American Soldier,"* Robert K. Merton and Paul F. Lazarsfeld (eds.) (New York: Free Press, 1950).

2. The major source for analysis of the bases for morale and combat motivation in the U.S. Army are the official surveys of soldiers' attitudes in World War II, reported in detail in the multi-volume study by Samuel A. Stouffer and associates, *The American Soldier* (Princeton: Princeton University Press, 1949). See also Janowitz and Little, *Sociology and the Military Establishment,* Chapter 4, "Primary Groups and Military Effectiveness" (New York: Russell Sage Foundation, 1965), and the important social-psychological study of a single combat unit in Korea by Roger W. Little, summarized in his "Buddy Relations and Combat Performance," in Morris Janowitz (ed.), *The New Military: Changing Patterns of Organization* (New York: Russell Sage Foundation, 1964), pp. 195–223.

3. On the taboo against talk of a flag-waving character among American combat soldiers in World War II, see *The American Soldier,* Vol. II, 150; also Roger Little, "Buddy Relations and Combat Performance."

4. For a detailed account, see the forthcoming study by Roman Kolkowicz, *The Soviet Army and the Communist Party: Institutions in Conflict,* especially Chapter III, "The Historical Perspective."

5. A detailed study of the bases of Soviet military morale reports that: Comradely solidarity in small, informal groups plays an important part and enters significantly into the motivations of the Soviet soldier in battle. . . . Under combat conditions the formalization of relationships among officers and men is greatly reduced. The genuinely personal qualities of the men become more apparent; the organization comes to rest more upon its informal bases, upon the spontaneously worked out human relations which have, in a sense, been held in check by the formal organization. . . . A change takes place in combat. The danger and the tremendous piling up of acute discomforts create a sort of community and solidarity among the men which hardly existed in the garrison. H. V. Dicks, E. A. Shils, and H. S. Dinerstein, *Service Conditions and Morale in the Soviet Armed Forces* (Santa Monica: The RAND Corporation, 1951), pp. 45–59, 234–40.

6. See, for example, *Mao Tse-tung on Guerrilla Warfare,* translated by S. B. Griffith. Secondary accounts based on Chinese Communist writings include S. M. Chiu, *A History of the Chinese Communist Army,* University of Southern California, unpublished Ph.D. dissertation, 1958; and the same author's "Political Control in the Chinese Communist Army," *Military Review,* Vol. 41, No. 8, August 1961; Ellis Joffe, "The Conflict between Old and New in the Chinese Army," *The China Quar-*

terly, No. 18, April–June 1964; and the same author's *Party and Army: Professionalism and Political Control in the Chinese Officer Corps, 1949– 1964* (Cambridge, Mass.: Harvard East Asian Monographs, No. 19; 1965). For a useful recent review of historical and analytic research on Chinese Communist military history and policy, see Scott A. Boorman and Howard L. Boorman, "Mao Tse-tung and the Art of War," *The Journal of Asian Studies,* Vol. XXIV, No. 1, November 1964, especially pp. 134–37.

7. Lieutenant Colonel Robert B. Rigg, *Red China's Fighting Hordes* (Harrisburg, Pa.: The Military Service Publishing Co., 1951); Jack Belden, *China Shakes the World* (New York: Harper & Bros., 1949); Evans Fordyce Carlson, *The Chinese Army: Its Organization and Military Efficiency* (New York: Institute of Pacific Relations, 1940). Brief accounts are to be found also in more recent publications, for example, L. Montross *et al., U.S. Marine Operations in Korea, 1950–1953* (Washington, D.C.: U.S. Government Printing Office, 1957), Vol. III, 85–91; Davis B. Bobrow, "The Good Officer: Definition and Training," *The China Quarterly,* No. 18, April–June 1964.

8. See, for example, Robert J. Lifton, *Thought Reform and the Psychology of Totalism* (New York: W. W. Norton & Co., 1961); Edgar H. Schein *et al., Coercive Persuasion* (New York: W. W. Norton & Co., 1961).

9. H. F. Schurmann, "Organizational Principles of the Chinese Communists," *The China Quarterly,* No. 2, April–June 1960. Schurmann adds, in his recently published book, that while "thought reform" attempts to produce motivation for commitment in individuals, "the ultimate aim of ideological indoctrination is to produce organizational solidarity. . . ." Schurmann, *Ideology and Organization in Communist China* (Berkeley and Los Angeles: University of California Press, 1966), pp. 50–51.

10. Schurmann, *Ideology and Organization,* pp. 34–35.

11. See, for example, Margaret Mead, *Soviet Attitudes Toward Authority* (New York: McGraw-Hill, 1951), pp. 26, 31, 67, 73; R. Kolkowicz, *The Soviet Army.*

12. Erik H. Erikson, *Young Man Luther* (New York: W. W. Norton & Co., 1958), p. 133. Erikson comments at length on the striking similarities between the procedures and underlying psychological processes of the Augustinian indoctrination and of modern Chinese "thought reform."

13. Schurmann, *Ideology and Organization,* p. 160.

14. On this point see Montross, *Marine Operations,* Vol. III, 88.

15. The development and workings of the political commissar system in the Soviet Army are described in Zbigniew Brzezinski, "Party Controls in the Soviet Army," *The Journal of Politics,* Vol. 14, No. 4, November 1952, pp. 565–91; and in Dicks, Shils, and Dinerstein, *Service Conditions and Morale.* For a more detailed discussion, see the forthcoming study by Roman Kolkowicz, *The Soviet Army and the Communist Party,*

which also contains a bibliography of Russian as well as English language materials on this topic.

16. A brief account of the nature of the Chinese Communist variant of the commissar system, as perceived in the late thirties and early forties, that relies in part on Japanese archival materials, is provided by Chalmers A. Johnson, *Peasant Nationalism and Communist Power* (Stanford: Stanford University Press, 1962), pp. 77–84. For fuller information on political work in the KMT, see F. F. Liu, *A Military History of Modern China, 1924–1949* (Princeton: Princeton University Press, 1956).

17. Rigg, *Red China's Fighting Hordes,* p. 72.

18. According to one political officer whom we interviewed, a member of the Company Party Committee served as Political Defense committeeman. According to another political officer, the Regimental Political Defense section placed two specially trained Party men in each company to observe the cadres and privates; this was supposed to be known only by the company political officer. Other accounts suggest that the Regimental Political Defense section periodically sent an inspector to the company who, with the aid of several company personnel, investigated the ideology of other company members. It is not unlikely that all these accounts are correct since they may describe the different types of contact which were maintained. Thus, the Political Defense committeeman in the Company Party Committee might have been the permanent liaison through which regular business between the regimental political defense subsection and the company was transacted. In addition, the regimental subsection might have designated one or two Party men within each company to serve as secret informants. Finally, special teams might have been organized at the instance of the regimental subsection to make thorough investigations of suspected individuals.

19. Dicks, Shils, and Dinerstein, *Service Conditions and Morale,* p. 284; see also Brzezinski, "Party Controls in the Soviet Army," p. 572.

20. Dicks, Shils, and Dinerstein, *Service Conditions and Morale,* pp. 313–14; Kolkowicz, *The Soviet Army and the Communist Party.*

21. General James Van Fleet, "The Truth About Korea," *Life* magazine, May 11, 1953, p. 134–35.

22. Brigadier General Samuel B. Griffith, USMC (Ret.), in a personal communication to the author, 1965.

23. Quoted in 2d Lt. L. M. Holmes, "Birth of the Fire Team," *Marine Corps Gazette,* Vol. 36, No. 11, November 1952. See also the classic, often-quoted study by S. L. A. Marshall, *Men Against Fire* (New York: William Morrow & Co., 1947).

24. General Samuel B. Griffith in a personal communication, 1965. [See also the biography of Col. Evans Carlson by Michael Blankfort, *The Big Yankee* (Boston: Little, Brown & Co., 1947), p. 15.] Griffith adds that, later, he participated on a board that considered the applicability of the Fire Team concept to the entire Marine Corps. A strong recommendation

to this effect was adopted by the Commandant in 1944. However, this was not a case of a simple transfer of organizational doctrine from the PLA to the U.S. Marines. Carlson's borrowing of the 3-by-3 organizational device from the PLA was only one of many antecedents, and not the first in point of time, leading to the Marine Corps' adoption of the Fire Team. Moreover, the theoretical concept of such an organization of the squad considerably predates Chinese Communist experience. On this point, see Lt. L. M. Holmes, "Birth of the Fire Team." I am indebted to General Wallace M. Greene, Jr., Commandant, United States Marine Corps, for calling to my attention Holmes' article and other materials which clarify the origins of the Fire Teams in the Marine Corps.

25. Jules Roy, *The Battle of Dienbienphu* (New York: Harper & Row, 1965), pp. 51–52, 71–73.

26. S. L. A. Marshall, in a dispatch from An Khe, South Vietnam. *Los Angeles Times,* August 7, 1966.

27. Edward A. Shils and Morris Janowitz, "Cohesion and Disintegration in the Wehrmacht," *Public Opinion Quarterly,* Vol. 12, No. 2, Summer 1948, pp. 286–87.

28. Shils and Janowitz, "Cohesion and Disintegration in the Wehrmacht," p. 299. This article also contains a brief discussion of the Nazi variant of the political commissar system, the *National Sozialistische Fuhrungsoffiziere* (N.S.F.O.), introduced in the winter of 1943 in order to strengthen indoctrination, security, and political control.

CHAPTER 4: THE ROLE AND PERFORMANCE OF COMPANY POLITICAL OFFICERS

The quotation from Mao Tse-tung is from *Selected Works* (New York: International Publishers, 1956–1962), Vol. I, 81.

1. On the U.S. Army in World War II, see Samuel A. Stouffer *et al., The American Soldier* (Princeton: Princeton University Press, 1949), Vol. 1, 365; Vol. 2, 98–104, 130–49. A perceptive commentary on this experience is provided in E. Shils, "Primary Groups in the American Army," in *Continuities in Social Research: Studies in the Scope and Method of "The American Soldier,"* Robert K. Merton and Paul F. Lazarsfeld (eds.) (New York: Free Press, 1950). For the Soviet Army in World War II, see Dicks, Shils, and Dinerstein, *Service Conditions and Morale in the Soviet Armed Forces* (Santa Monica: The RAND Corporation, 1951), pp. 45, 59, 234ff.

2. In these respects our materials are consistent with the general hypotheses advanced by Lucian Pye in his discussion of the role of personal friendships among Malayan Communists. Pye, *Guerrilla Communism in Malaya* (Princeton: Princeton University Press, 1956), p. 149.

3. Direct questions on this point were not asked; relevant material was

volunteered by respondents on questions relating to the personal character of the political officer and to like or dislike of him on the part of the men. There is probably some justification for assuming that those who volunteered information on this point had enjoyed either very comradely or very unfriendly relations with their political officer, and that those who did not volunteer information did not have either extremely friendly or extremely unfriendly relations with him.

4. See Robert B. Rigg, *Red China's Fighting Hordes* (Harrisburg, Pa.: The Military Service Publishing Co., 1951), pp. 109–10; Jack Belden, *China Shakes the World* (New York: Harper & Bros., 1949), p. 342.

5. Of course, a political officer did not always take this line. Frequently he attempted to encourage the men by telling them that the sooner they finished the war in Korea, the sooner they could all go home, etc.

6. There were also indications that cowardly action by the leader, gross errors in conduct of military affairs, illegal requisitioning, or unfair distribution of food and clothing, etc., could also be made the subject of complaints.

7. Respondents were not asked directly whether they identified with the in-group or the out-group, or whether indeed the unit was divided in this fashion. In answering questions about attitudes toward the political officer, however, most of them made it clear that they considered the unit to be divided in this way and revealed their own identification by the terms of reference employed. In practically all cases the inference made in the text as to a private's identification with in-group or out-group was supported by the respondent's answers to a variety of questions throughout the interview. There were hardly any cases where inconsistent cues were provided within the interview on the matter of the private's identification. In the case of one of the privates in our sample, insufficient material was obtained during the interview to enable a judgment as to whether he belonged to either the in-group or out-group within his unit.

8. There is considerable documentation for this in our interviews, though the estimated proportion of former CNA personnel differed in some of our respondents' estimates.

CHAPTER 5: CRITICISM MEETINGS AND THE MORALE INFORMANTS SYSTEM

1. R. J. Lifton, *Thought Reform and the Psychology of Totalism* (New York: W. W. Norton & Co., 1961). See especially Chapter 5, "Psychological Steps."

2. There are a number of detailed accounts of Chinese Communist techniques of group indoctrination, propaganda, and social control. See, for example, A. Doak Barnett's succinct discussion of the method of "study" (*hsueh hsi*), in his *Communist China: The Early Years, 1949–55* (New York: Praeger, 1964), Chapter 8, "Group Indoctrination." Both Barnett's

study and Franz Schurmann's broader sociological treatment of the subject in his *Ideology and Organization in Communist China* (Berkeley and Los Angeles: University of California Press, 1966), pp. 30–33, 45–53, emphasize the critical role of the group in creating and maintaining correct thought in the individual. Their findings regarding the approach to indoctrination employed in Chinese civil society and its effectiveness parallel the present discussion of its workings in the PLA. See also Franklin W. Houn, *To Change A Nation: Propaganda and Indoctrination in Communist China* (New York: Free Press, 1961), and Theodore H. E. Chen, *Thought Reform of the Chinese Intellectuals* (Hong Kong: Hong Kong University Press, 1960).

3. Robert B. Rigg, *Red China's Fighting Hordes* (Harrisburg, Pa.: The Military Service Publishing Co., 1951), p.171.

4. A useful summary of these views, drawing upon the work of Hsien-chin Hu, Francis L. K. Hsu, Zing-yang Kuo, Weston LaBarre, John K. Fairbank, Martin Yang, Lucian Pye, and Harold D. Lasswell, is presented by Paul Hiniker, "Chinese Attitudinal Reactions to Forced Compliance: A Cross-cultural Experiment in the Theory of Cognitive Dissonance," Center for International Studies, M.I.T., Cambridge, Massachusetts, May 1965, pp. 9–19.

5. *Ibid.,* pp. 58–59.

6. Schurmann, *Ideology and Organization,* pp. 49–51. A somewhat more cautious estimate of the effectiveness of Chinese Communist indoctrination was provided earlier by A. Doak Barnett, *Communist China: The Early Years,* pp. 97, 102–3.

7. Pye reports that 80 percent of the former members of the Malayan Communist Party he interviewed had adjusted to self-criticism meetings by ritualizing all of their "confessions" and that their political commissars, for reasons of their own, tolerated this. "Thus, for all concerned, it was desirable to treat the problem of self-criticism as an elaborate game. . . ." Lucian Pye, *Guerrilla Communism in Malaya* (Princeton: Princeton University Press, 1956), pp. 258–59.

8. Pye reports that almost all of his respondents had undergone trying experiences in criticism meetings, experiencing a keen sense of shame and social isolation, prior to hitting upon a successful way of ritualizing their "confessions." *Guerrilla Communism in Malaya,* p. 257.

9. Lucian Pye has suggested some possible psychocultural explanations for the effectiveness of shaming and other group pressures upon Malayan Communists (of Chinese racial stock), which may apply also to members of the Chinese Communist Army. See *Guerrilla Communism in Malaya,* pp. 253, 257.

10. See H. V. Dicks, "Observations on Contemporary Russian Behaviour," *Human Relations,* Vol. 5, No. 2, 1952.

CHAPTER 6: LEADERSHIP IN COMBAT UNITS

The quotation from Mao Tse-tung is from *Selected Works* (New York: International Publishers, 1956–1962), Vol. I, 106.

1. Robert B. Rigg, *Red China's Fighting Hordes* (Harrisburg, Pa.: The Military Service Publishing Co., 1951), pp. 23–24, 66–70. See also Ellis Joffe, "The Conflict between Old and New in the Chinese Army," *The China Quarterly*, No. 18, April–June 1964, pp. 128–30; Ralph L. Powell, "The Military Affairs Committee and Party Control of the Military in China," *Asian Survey*, Vol. III, No. 7, July 1963, p. 347; Donald W. Klein, "The Next Generation of Chinese Communist Leaders," *The China Quarterly*, No. 12, October–December 1962.

2. On this difference between the Soviet and Chinese Communist variants of the political commissar system see also Chalmers A. Johnson, *Peasant Nationalism and Communist Power* (Stanford: Stanford University Press, 1962), pp. 79–80. For a more general comparative treatment of historical experience in creating revolutionary armies out of existing remnants of the preceding regime's armed forces, see Katharine Chorley, *Armies and the Art of Revolution* (London: Faber & Faber, 1943).

3. Information on this point was supplied by Herbert Dinerstein in a personal communication to the author. For a fuller account of relations between political officers and military commanders in the Soviet Army, see H. V. Dicks, E. A. Shils, and H. S. Dinerstein, *Service Conditions and Morale in the Soviet Armed Forces* (Santa Monica: The RAND Corporation, 1951), pp. 285–86, 290–91, 295–301.

4. Rigg, *Red China's Fighting Hordes*, pp. 13, 76, 108, 131, 283; Jack Belden, *China Shakes the World* (New York: Harper & Bros., 1949), p. 480.

5. This account is based on materials obtained from our interviews with prisoners who had been military cadres in the PLA, some of whom had been formerly with the Nationalist Army. See also Rigg, *Red China's Fighting Hordes*, pp. 81, 88, 90–91, 95, 108, 124, 131, 237–38, 272–78.

CHAPTER 7: MOTIVATION AND CONTROL OF COMBAT PERSONNEL

1. Robert B. Rigg, *Red China's Fighting Hordes* (Harrisburg, Pa.: The Military Service Publishing Co., 1951), p. 177.

2. This practice was followed also during the civil war; see Jack Belden, *China Shakes the World* (New York: Harper & Bros., 1949), p. 344.

3. See also the account of PLA pre-battle preparations by a leading Chinese Nationalist General, Sun Li-jen, quoted by Rigg: " 'In this way the

soldiers not only got more acquainted with the mission before them but had . . . a feeling of self-importance.' " *Red China's Fighting Hordes,* p. 317.

4. Roy E. Appleman, *United States Army in the Korean War: South to the Naktong, North to the Yalu* (Washington, D.C.: Office of the Chief of Military History, Dept. of the Army, 1961), pp. 751, 752, 756, 763, 765, 770, 778; Malcolm W. Cagle and Frank A. Manson, *The Sea War in Korea* (Annapolis: United States Naval Institute, 1957), p. 168; S.L.A. Marshall, *The River and the Gauntlet* (New York: William Morrow & Co., 1953), pp. 7–9; Allen Whiting, *China Crosses the Yalu* (New York: The Macmillan Co., 1960), pp. 193–94; Rigg, *Red China's Fighting Hordes,* p. 177.

5. L. Montross *et al., U.S. Marine Operations in Korea, 1950–1953,* Vol. IV, *The East-Central Front* (Washington, D.C.: U.S. Government Printing Office, 1962), pp. 22, 100–1. Montross adds that it mattered little that Chinese prisoners gave such information since air reconnaissance kept the Eighth Army well informed on the enemy buildup in the spring of 1951.

6. See H. V. Dicks, "Observations on Contemporary Russian Behaviour," *Human Relations,* Vol. 5, No. 2, 1952, p. 160.

CHAPTER 8: WAR INDOCTRINATION

The quotation from Mao Tse-tung is from *On Guerrilla Warfare,* Samuel B. Griffith, translator (New York: Praeger, 1961), pp. 88–89.

1. The relevant materials in Samuel A. Stouffer *et al., The American Soldier* (Princeton: Princeton University Press, 1949), are to be found largely in Vol. I, Chapter 9, "The Orientation of Soldiers Toward the War"; Vol. II, Chapter 2, "General Characteristics of Ground Combat," esp. pp. 97–104; and Chapter 3, "Combat Motivations Among Ground Troops," esp. pp. 149–67.

2. *The American Soldier,* Vol. I, 484–85; Vol. II, 107, 149–51, 167, 191.

3. E. A. Shils, "Primary Groups in the American Army," and Hans Speier, " 'The American Soldier' and the Sociology of Military Organization," both in *Continuities in Social Research: Studies in the Scope and Method of "The American Soldier,"* Robert K. Merton and Paul F. Lazarsfeld (eds.) (New York: Free Press, 1950).

4. *Ibid.,* pp. 22–24.

5. On the difficulty of sorting out the importance of variables affecting combat motivation see also the remarks by Shirley A. Star and M. Brewster Smith, two of the authors of *The American Soldier* in Vol. I, 461, 465–67; and Vol. II, 155–56, respectively. Also relevant to this point is the explanatory model of the conditions under which disintegra-

tion of primary group ties in the small combat unit takes place, which Shils and Janowitz presented in "Cohesion and Disintegration in the Wehrmacht." A brief but useful restatement of this theory was provided recently by Morris Janowitz in *The New Military* (New York: Russell Sage Foundation, 1964), pp. 191–93; and by Janowitz and Little, *Sociology and the Military Establishment* (New York: Russell Sage Foundation, 1965), p. 94.

6. Robert B. Rigg, *Red China's Fighting Hordes* (Harrisburg, Pa.: The Military Service Publishing Co., 1951), p. 250. There are many other firsthand accounts of the value which Chinese Communist leaders placed upon political indoctrination in the evolution of their army. See also, for example, Edgar Snow, *Red Star in China* (New York: Random House, 1938).

CHAPTER 9: THE EROSION OF MORALE

1. A brief account of the changes which General Ridgway introduced and of the subsequent course of the war is given by him in his book, *Soldier* (New York: Harper & Bros., 1956), pp. 204–7, and in David Rees, *Korea: The Limited War* (New York: St. Martins Press, 1964); see particularly Chapter 10, "The War of Containment."

2. Our interviews provided data on these points for cadres up to and including company level. Our interviews yielded less information on attitudes at battalion levels and almost none at all for regimental and higher levels. Other intelligence sources, however, reported that General Lin Piao, Commander of the Chinese Communist forces in Korea, attributed the failure of his "Third Phase" offensive in January 1951 to lack of air and tank support. See R. F. Futrell, *The United States Air Force in Korea 1950–1953* (New York: Duell, Sloan, & Pearce, 1961), pp. 263–64.

3. Lynn Montross *et al., U.S. Marine Operations in Korea, 1950–1953, The Chosin Reservoir Campaign* (Washington, D.C.: U.S. Government Printing Office, 1957), Vol. III, 352–56.

4. In addition, according to a captured Chinese staff cadre, in February 1951 each regiment of the Fourth Field Army sent cadres to attend a special air-ground training conference in Mukden to learn how to identify their units by use of panels to communist aircraft overhead. Futrell, *The United States Air Force,* p. 265.

5. Detailed questions on this point were asked of the eighteen hard core veterans interviewed with a special questionnaire. In addition, references to Russia were volunteered by some prisoners interviewed with the basic questionnaire employed for this study.

6. It is likely that many PLA units which had entered Korea in late autumn 1950 with their old-fashioned weapons were also eventually issued the more modern Russian infantry weapons.

7. For an account of Soviet assistance in the reequipment and buildup of Chinese Communist forces in Korea, see the forthcoming study of the Chinese army by General S. B. Griffith.

8. Implicitly at variance with the account presented here is David Rees' view that the two massive Chinese spring offensives of April and May 1951 had as their objective the military conquest of South Korea. See his *Korea: The Limited War,* p. 244. However, Rees does not base his interpretation on what was being said to the Chinese troops but, rather, on announcements by Radios Pyongyang and Peking.

CHAPTER 10: THE EROSION OF ORGANIZATIONAL CONTROLS

1. L. Montross *et al., U.S. Marine Operations in Korea, 1950–1953, The East-Central Front* (Washington, D.C.: U.S. Government Printing Office, 1962), Vol. IV, 127; see Chapter 1, above, p. 9.

CHAPTER 11: DEVELOPMENTS IN THE PLA SINCE THE KOREAN WAR

The quotation from John Wilson Lewis is from "Revolutionary Struggle and the Second Generation in Communist China," *The China Quarterly,* No. 21, January–March 1965, p. 146.

The quotation from Franz Schurmann is from *Ideology and Organization In Communist China* (Berkeley and Los Angeles: University of California Press, 1966), pp. 171–72.

In preparing this chapter I have drawn upon a number of studies published by professional students of Chinese military affairs and have supplemented them with my own reading of documents and source materials such as the twenty-nine issues of the secret PLA publication, the *Work Bulletin.* The best and most comprehensive treatment known to me of developments in the character of the PLA in the years after the Korean War is Ellis Joffe's monograph, *Party and Army: Professionalism and Political Control in the Chinese Officer Corps, 1949–1964* (Cambridge, Mass.: Harvard East Asian Monographs, No. 19; 1965). Also of considerable value have been several articles in the special issue of *The China Quarterly,* No. 18, April–June 1964, on recent developments in the PLA: John Wilson Lewis, "China's Secret Military Papers: 'Continuities' and 'Revelations' "; Alice Langley Hsieh, "China's Secret Military Papers: Military Doctrine and Strategy"; John Gittings, "China's Militia"; Ellis Joffe, "The Conflict between Old and New in the Chinese Army"; Davis B. Bobrow, "The Good Officer: Definition and Training"; John Gittings, "The 'Learn from the Army' Campaign"; Harold P. Ford, "Modern Weapons and the Sino-Soviet Estrangement." An earlier, still useful analysis of the classified PLA *Work Bulletin,* prepared by Ralph

L. Powell for the U.S. Department of State, is his "Politico-Military Relationships in Communist China," October 1963. Useful materials and insights are present in Hanson W. Baldwin, "China As A Military Power," *Foreign Affairs*, Vol. 30, No. 1, October 1951; John Gittings' older article: "Political Control of the Chinese Army," *The World Today*, August 1963; J. Chester Cheng, "Problems of Chinese Communist Leadership As Seen in the Secret Military Papers," *Asian Survey*, Vol. 4, June 1964; S. M. Chiu, "Political Control in the Chinese Communist Army," *Military Review*, Vol. 41, August 1961; Alice Langley Hsieh, *Communist China's Strategy in the Nuclear Era* (Englewood Cliffs: Prentice-Hall, 1962), and the same author's "The Sino-Soviet Nuclear Dialogue: 1963," *The Journal of Conflict Resolution*, Vol. VIII, No. 2, June 1964; David A. Charles, "The Dismissal of Marshal P'eng Teh-huai," *The China Quarterly*, No. 8, October–December 1961. I have also benefited from General Samuel B. Griffith's "Communist China's Capacity to Make War," *Foreign Affairs*, Vol. 43, No. 2, January 1965, and part of the manuscript of his forthcoming book on the Communist Chinese Army. Finally, Franz Schurmann's recently published study of *Ideology and Organization in Communist China* (Berkeley and Los Angeles: University of California Press, 1966), has enabled me to see some of the developments in the PLA in a broader perspective.

1. Ellis Joffe, *Party and Army: Professionalism and Political Control in the Chinese Officer Corps, 1949–1964* (Cambridge, Mass.: Harvard East Asian Monographs, No. 19; 1965), p. 12.

2. Franz Schurmann, *Ideology and Organization in Communist China* (Berkeley and Los Angeles: University of California Press, 1966), pp. 40, xlii.

3. For a vivid discussion see Admiral Turner Joy, *How Communists Negotiate* (New York: The Macmillan Co., 1955).

4. R. F. Futrell, *The United States Air Force in Korea 1950–1953* (New York: Duell, Sloan, and Pearce, 1961), pp. 230–33, 370–99, 471.

5. The *Jen-min Jih-pao* editorial is quoted and paraphrased by Joffe, "Party and Army: Professionalism and Political Control in the Chinese Officer Corps, 1949–1964," pp. 37–38.

6. Quoted from *Jen-min Jih-pao*, by Joffe, "Professionalism and Political Control in the Chinese Officer Corps," pp. 74–75.

7. Twenty-nine issues of the secret military journal, *Kung-tso T'ung hsün* (the title of which is translated by western scholars variously as *Work Bulletin, Work Report, Bulletin of Activities, Military Papers*), covering the period January 1, 1961, when the first issue appeared, through August 26, 1961, were released by the Department of State to scholars on August 5, 1963. In 1966 a complete translation of these issues of the journal was published by the Hoover Institution on War, Revolution and Peace, Stanford University, under the title, *The Politics of the Chinese Red Army*, edited by J. Chester Cheng. In referring to the *Work Bulletin* I

will give both the issue of the journal and the page on which it is to be found in the volume edited by Cheng.

8. The issues of the *Work Bulletin* also reveal serious deficiencies in the PLA's training and morale occasioned by food shortages, lack of spare parts and fuel, and the impact of family hardships on the soldiers' attitudes.

9. *Chieh-fang-chün Pao* (*Liberation Army News*) of July 1, 1958, quoted by Joffe, "Professionalism and Political Control in the Chinese Officer Corps," p. 61.

10. *Ibid.,* pp. 62–63.

11. *Work Bulletin,* No. 23, June 13, 1961; in Cheng (ed.), p. 595.

12. *Work Bulletin,* No. 3, January 7, 1961; in Cheng (ed.), p. 81.

13. Powell, "Politico-Military Relationships in Communist China," p. 8.

14. John Gittings, "Political Control of the Chinese Army," p. 331.

15. Joffe, "Professionalism and Political Control in the Chinese Officer Corps," pp. 137–38.

16. *Work Bulletin,* No. 23, June 13, 1961; in Cheng (ed.), pp. 593, 595. In addition to increasing the Party's strength, the Military Affairs Committee (the principal political-military organ of the Chinese Communist regime) directed that about 65 percent of all young soldiers should be recruited into the Communist Youth League. *Work Bulletin,* No. 1, January 1, 1961; in Cheng (ed.), p. 5.

17. New China News Agency (NCNA), Peking, July 5, 1961; in *Survey of China Mainland Press* (*SCMP*), No. 2540, July 19, 1961.

18. NCNA, November 21, 1961; in *SCMP,* No. 2630, December 1, 1961.

19. *Work Bulletin,* No. 26, July 13, 1961, and No. 29, August 1, 1961; in Cheng (ed.), pp. 651–57, 727–35.

20. These Regulations have evidently not been published fully; a summary appeared in *Chieh-fang-chün Pao,* May 8, 1963; in *SCMP,* No. 2984, May 22, 1963.

21. Joffe, "Professionalism and Political Control in the Chinese Officer Corps," pp. 142–43; see also Gittings, "Political Control of the Chinese Army," pp. 333–35.

22. John Gittings, "The 'Learn from the Army' Campaign," *The China Quarterly,* No. 18, April–June 1964; Ralph L. Powell, "Commissars in the Economy: 'Learn from the PLA' Movement in China," *Asian Survey,* Vol. V, No. 3, March 1965; F. Schurmann, *Ideology and Organization in Communist China,* pp. 12, 150, 187, 303–5.

23. Joffe, "The Conflict between Old and New in the Chinese Army," pp. 139–40.

24. Franz Schurmann, *Ideology and Organization,* pp. 8, 51–52, 163–64, 170–72. See also John Wilson Lewis, "Revolutionary Struggle and the Second Generation in Communist China," *The China Quarterly,* No. 21, January–March, 1965.

25. See the forthcoming study by Roman Kolkowicz, *The Soviet Army and the Communist Party: Institutions in Conflict.* The Israeli Army provides still another interesting case in which, in an entirely different kind of historical context, "revolutionary"-egalitarian and professional elements were eventually successfully merged. See Amitai Etzioni, "The Israeli Army: The Human Factor," in three parts, *Jewish Frontier,* Vols. 26 and 27, November 1959, January and February 1960.

26. S. M. Chiu, *A History of the Chinese Communist Army,* University of Southern California, unpublished Ph.D. dissertation, 1958, pp. 180–81.

27. John Wilson Lewis, "China's Secret Military Papers: 'Continuities' and 'Revelations,'" *The China Quarterly,* April–June 1964, p. 77.

28. Gittings, "Political Control of the Chinese Army," p. 327.

29. S. M. Chiu, "Political Control in the Chinese Communist Army," pp. 34–35.

30. Samuel B. Griffith, II, "Communist China's Capacity To Make War," *Foreign Affairs,* Vol. 43, No. 2, January 1965, pp. 229–32. See also Peking NCNA Domestic Service broadcast on the selection and training of young cadres, January 16, 1966.

31. An English text of Ho Lung's widely published article, "Democratic Tradition of the Chinese People's Liberation Army," appeared in *Peking Review,* No. 32, August 6, 1965.

32. See, for example, the seventh in a series of editorials on placing politics to the fore, entitled "The Key Lies in the Leadership of the Party Committee," in *Chieh-fang-chün Pao,* April 5, 1966.

33. Article entitled "Acquiring 'Advanced' Techniques Ruins the Foundation," in *Jen-min Jih-pao,* May 21, 1966; *SCMP,* No. 3708.

34. Report of a forum sponsored by the PLA Air Force for discussion of the relationship between politics and one's job, in *Chieh-fang-chün Pao,* May 17, 1966, broadcast by Peking radio, May 17, 1966.

35. *Jen-min Jih-pao,* February 6, 1966; quoted in *New York Times,* February 8, 1966.

36. See, for example, *New York Times,* July 10, 1966, and *Wall Street Journal,* July 15, 1966.

37. *Chieh-fang-chün Pao,* August 1, 1966, as broadcast by Peking NCNA in English.

38. This thesis is argued by Victor Zorza, a communist-affairs analyst for the *Manchester Guardian,* in an article for *Look* magazine, August 23, 1966. Zorza finds indications in public statements which Lo Jui-ch'ing made in the summer of 1965 that the Chief of the General Staff of the PLA disagreed with the regime not only on purely military issues having to do with its emphasis on "man-over-weapons" but that Lo linked this criticism with a broader questioning of the regime's hard policy toward the United States and Russia. See also the account of an interview with Chen Yi, Chinese Communist Minister of Foreign Affairs and Deputy Prime Minister, obtained in Peking in December 1965 by a leftist Mexican magazine.

In this interview Chen Yi noted that the fact that his government was pursuing a hard line against both the Soviet Union and the United States was being criticized as ill-advised by "revisionist" and "bourgeois" elements in China. Renato Leduc, "We can live without rubles and without dollars says Chen Yi to Siempre," *Siempre,* December 22, 1965, pp. 12–13. (I am indebted to Herbert Dinerstein for calling this article to my attention.)

39. NCNA International Service in English, August 1, 1966.

40. Lewis, "Revolutionary Struggle and the Second Generation in Communist China," p. 146.

41. *Wall Street Journal,* July 15, 1966.

42. Johnson, "Lin Piao's Army and Its Role in Chinese Society," Part II, *Current Scene,* Vol. IV, No. 14, July 15, 1966, p. 10.

43. Joc Weiler, "CHICOM Small Arms and Tactics," *Marine Corps Gazette,* Vol. 46, No. 12, December 1962, pp. 41, 45.

Index